1857
Revisited

1857 REVISITED

Based on Persian and Urdu Documents

Prof. S.M. Azizuddin Husain

KANISHKA PUBLISHERS, DISTRIBUTORS
NEW DELHI-110 002

KANISHKA PUBLISHERS, DISTRIBUTORS
4697/5-21A, Ansari Road, Daryaganj
New Delhi-110 002
Phones : 2327 0497, 2328 8285
Fax : 011-2328 8285
e-mail: kanishka_publishing@yahoo.co.in

First Published 2007

ISBN 978-81-7391-973-2

PRINTED IN INDIA

Published by Madan Sachdeva for Kanishka Publishers, Distributors, 4697/5-21A, Ansari Road, Daryaganj, New Delhi-110 002; Typeset by Sunshine Graphics, Delhi, and Printed at Nice Printing Press, Delhi.

To

Anil

From

Aziz

Acknowledgments

First of all I would like to thank my father Late Prof. S.M. Kamaluddin Husain (dt. 21.2.2006) who told me the history of our family from my childhood that resulted in my interest in history. I am grateful to my brother Mr. Anil Nauriya, who suggested me that I work on these Persian and Urdu documents relating to 1857 and this work is the result of his suggestion in 2000. I thank my colleague Prof. Gyan Prakash Sharma, Coordinator, DRS, in History for giving me the grant to work on this project and then a publication grant for its publication.

I would like to again repeat what I said in the acknowledgement of my book—Structure of politics under Aurangzeb published in 2002, "In my academic career two Hasans have played a major role—the first was my esteemed teacher Professor Saiyid Nurul Hasan and the second, Professor Mushirul Hasan. These two Hasans have added 'HUSN' (beauty) to my life and career.

I am highly grateful to my colleagues, Dr. Farhat Nasreen, Ms. Snigdha Roy and Mr. Mohammad Musab for extending help in the completion of this work. I thank my friends Prof. Narayani Gupta, Prof. Sunita Zaidi, Prof. Seema Alavi, Dr. Rizwan Qaiser, Dr. M.S. Ranawat, Mr. Mukul Kesavan, Mr. M.S. Shakeb, Mr. M.H. Mozaffari, Dr. Mehdi Khwajae Peeri, Dr. Meena Gaur, Prof. B.L. Bhadani, Dr. Pramod Mehra, Dr. Muhammed Tazim, Ms. Taiyaba Munawer, Mr. Muhammed Ali and Mr. S.A. Kazim for their kind support.

I thank the staff of National Archives of India, New Delhi and Bhopal, U.P. State Archives, Lucknow and Allahabad, Khuda Bakhsh Library, Patna, Azad Library and Research Library, Department of History, Aligarh Muslim University, Aligarh, Natnagar Shodh Sansthan, Sitamau, Rajasthan State Archives, Bikaner, Zakir Husain Library, Jamia Millia Islamia, New Delhi and Reza Library, Rampur, for their kind help and cooperation.

I am grateful to Mr. Mohammad Rashid and Mr. Mohammad Shahid for typing Persian and Urdu Text of Mutiny papers. The present book would hardly have been possible without the friendly, prompting and personal interest of Mr. Madan Sachdeva, Chairman, Kanishka Publishers, Distributors, New Delhi. It is significant that this book is published from Shahjahanabad, which was the centre of revolt in 1857.

Finally, I am happy to acknowledge the kind support of my wife Prof. Talat Aziz. My daughters Dr. Atiya and Zeba, have always given me the feeling of fulfillment so necessary for any creative step in life.

29th March, 2007

S.M. Azizuddin Husain

Department of History and Culture
Jamia Millia Islamia, New Delhi-110025

Contents

Preface

Basically I am a student of medieval Indian history and 1857 belongs to modern Indian history. But my brother Anil Nauriya, advocate, Supreme Court of India, who is also interested in history and writes on modern Indian history, suggested to me on 26th January, 2000 that I work on Persian and Urdu documents on 1857 available in National Archives of India, New Delhi. I welcomed the idea because no work has been done on these documents. I am highly grateful to Anil for his timely advice. I have selected 150 documents to mark the 150th anniversary of 1857. As is now pointed out by William Dalrymple, "A collection as astonishingly rich and as beautifully catalogued as the Mutiny papers, and one located so centrally in the National Archives of the capital city, within sight of the Rashtrapati Bhawan, have been so little consulted. After all, the contents—some 20,000 Urdu and Persian documents—describe in fabulous detail as to what happened in Delhi. It is a collection which uniquely preserves the actions and thoughts of courtiers, the soldiers of the different repay regiments, and both the elite and the ordinary people of Delhi." But the task was difficult because these documents are in *shikasta* script. As Prof. Irfan Habib rightly pointed out that, "There may be found in Persian/Urdu written in the cursive hand (*Shikasta*), four possible variants, and one has to know by context what word represents the form at a particular place. Unfortunately, there are very few people left who can read Urdu and Persian, particularly the *Shikasta* script...... If Dalrymple is able to do so, he belongs to a very small number of people who are competent in this; and their number is steadily declining." Dalrymple writes in acknowledgement: "This book would have been quite impossible without the scholarship and industry of my colleague Mahmud Farooqi...notably the remarkable translations from the sometimes almost indecipherable *shikastah* of the Urdu files in the Mutiny papers—is the product of his dedication, persistence and skill." It indicates that the reading of the script was done by Mahmud Farooqi and not by Dalrymple.

These documents were not much consulted because medieval Indian historians who know Persian considered the 1857 period beyond the realm of their specialization and post-1947, historians of modern Indian history have little or no knowledge of Persian. These Historians also worked on 1857 but few were equipped to understand the Persian and Urdu documents dealing with 1857. This is a limitation in our historiography. When Akbar (1556-1605) assigned the task of writing *Akbar Nama* to Abul Fazl, he placed all documents at the disposal of Abul Fazl so that he could write the history of his age based on contemporary documents. Akbar converted the *diwan-i-am* of Fathpur into Mughal archives. Medievalists think that the period of 1857 does not fall within their area of specialization and modern Indian historians do not generally consult the documents which are in Persian and Urdu. A hundred and fifty years have passed since the uprising of 1857 but these documents are still waiting for the kind attention of historians. As Ghalib rightly said—

زاہد تنگ نظر نے مجھے کافر جانا

اور کافر یہ سمجھتا ہے کہ مسلمان ہوں میں

1857 is an important aspect of Indian history. Scholars, both Indian and British, look at the events of 1857 with various views. Some call it mutiny, some say it was revolt, a *Ghadar* or *baghawat* against the tyrannical rule of the British regime and still a few others call it a war of independence. The British called it a 'sepoy mutiny'. Work has been done on 1857 but yet there is lot to be done. Since the 13th century to 1891, Persian was official language in most of the parts of India whether governed by Muslims, Hindus or Christians. Therefore on 1857, a lot of source material is available in Persian and Urdu language. These documents are available in the following places:

1. National Archives of India, New Delhi and Bhopal,
2. U.P. State Archives, Lucknow and Allahabad,
3. Bihar State Archives, Patna,

4. Madhya Pradesh State Archives, Bhopal,
5. Punjab State Archives, Patiala,
6. Haryana State Archives, Chandigarh,
7. Rajasthan State Archives, Bikaner,
8. National Library, Kolkata,
9. Zakir Husain Library, Delhi,
10. Azad Library, Aligarh,
11. Natnagar Shodh Sansthan, Sitamau,
12. Salar Jang Museum, Hyderabad,
13. Delhi State Archives, Delhi,
14. Commissioner's Office, Mehrauli, Delhi,
15. Khwaja Hasan Nizami Collection, Delhi,
16. *Mal Khanas* of District Headquarters, such as Aligarh, Etawah, Agra, Bijnor, Fathpur, Muradabad, Meerut, Lucknow, Bulandshahr, Etah, Mathura, Barabanki, Sultanpur, Azamgarh, Badaun, Bareilly, Farrukhabad, Ghazipur, Jhansi, Jonpur, Lalitpur, Mirzapur, Muzaffarnagar, Saharanpur, Patna, Calcutta, Allahabad, Panipat, Mewat, Sonipat, Rohtak, Faridabad, etc.
17. *Roznamchas, Tazkiras* and *Diwans* of contemporary Persian and Urdu poets.

Outside India, records are available in British Library, London, National Library, *Majlis* library and *Astana-i-Quds* Library, Iran. There is also a possibility of some records in the National Archives of France.

W. Taylor wrote—Patna Crisis in 1858. Sir Saiyid Ahmed Khan was the first Muslim scholar who wrote two books on 1857—*Sarkashi-i-Zila Bijnor* (1858) and *Asbab-i-Baghawat-i-Hind* (1859) in Urdu. Zakaullah also wrote a book—*Tarikh-i-Urooj-i-Engleshia*. Saiyid Muhammed Ali Musavi wrote—*Marghoob-i-Dil*, in 1867. The other scholar who wrote on 1857 was Rajanikanta Gupta in 1890. In 1907, we celebrated the fiftieth anniversary of 1857. Lala Hardayal launched a news paper—*Gadar*, on this occasion. V.D. Savarkar wrote a book on 1857 in Marathi—*The Indian War of Independence*, in 1908.

I partly agree with H.K. Patel when he opines, "1857 left no significant literary heritage either for Hindi or Urdu." He can be correct for his assessment of Hindi but for Urdu he seems to be in darkness. Urdu scholars and poets wrote much on 1857 during 1857 itself like Mushafi, Ghalib, Sir Saiyid, Zakaullah, Saiyid

Muhammed Ali and others. In towns like Aligarh, Muradabad, Bijnor, Amroha, etc., contemporary Persian and Urdu poets wrote verses on 1857. Some are published and some are still lying in the manuscript forms. Marx also wrote on 1857.

In 1957, that is, after independence we commemorated the 100th anniversary of 1857 but no project was planned or proposed on 1857. We are having thousands of documents in Persian and Urdu dealing with 1857. National Archives of India, New Delhi has 20,000 documents, National Archives of India, Bhopal, has 600 Persian and 8157 Urdu documents, U.P. State Archives, Lucknow and Allahabad, has thousands of documents and files dealing with the towns like Muradabad, Aligarh, Bulandshahr etc., who took part in mutiny.

There are two custodians of Muslim culture in India, Aligarh Muslim University, Aligarh and Jamia Millia Islamia, New Delhi which were the result of some movements and not a result of an act of Parliament. Both Universities have departments of history, Islamic Studies, Urdu and Persian. When we were celebrating the 100th anniversary of 1857, in 1957, one wonders why no project was launched on Persian and Urdu documents dealing with 1857. Prof. Irfan Habib, while reviewing the book of William Dalrymple—The last Mughal, The fall of a Dynasty, Delhi 1857, opines, "The difficulties in dealing with documents in Persian and Urdu, especially when written in cursive hand, are always to be kept in mind. It is generally expected that a historian, whether British or Indian, or any other, must combine the work of decipherment, transcription and comprehension with his own work. In serious historiography none of these tasks can be framed out." We see that Imperial Record Department published the—Press list of Mutiny Papers of 1857. Being a collection of the correspondence of the mutineers at Delhi, reports of spies of English officials and other miscellaneous papers were published from Calcutta in 1921. It was also done by the British. There are some mistakes also. But it appears that no Indian historian since 1947 has ever reviewed this press list which is in English and not in Persian or Urdu. In July, 1920, Khan Sahab Saiyid Abu Muhammed was placed by Government on special duty in the office of Board of Revenue to sort and index the old Oudh Records of 1858-1890. It shows that the colonial regime was doing all this work systematically. But we see that even the historical sources written in *naskh* and *nastaliq* like Babur Nama, *Akbar Nama, Ain-*

i-Akbari, Tuzuk-i-Jahangiri etc., were also edited and translated by British scholars. These sources were not written in *shikast*. Only a few Indian scholars like J.N. Sarkar, Saiyid Hasan Askari, Shaikh Abdur Rasheed, Najeeb Ashraf Nadvi, Satish Chandra, Z.A. Desai, I.H. Siddiqi, Moinul Haq, Johari, Muzaffar Alam, Azra Nizami, Tasnim Ahmed, Azizuddin and others edited or translated some Persian manuscripts dealing with history. In the Andhra Pradesh Archives, Hyderabad, lacs of documents on Mughal history are simply lying there. No press list and no calendar of these documents published. In National Archives of India, New Delhi, 1,37,000 documents dealing with Aurangzeb and Muhammed Shah's reign are available. No index or calendar of these documents has been published till this day. All these projects of indexing, calendaring and translations of Persian documents and texts were done by the British since 1920 with the help of Indian scholars. Yet, till 2002 when Dalrymple took help of Mehmud Farooqi, Indian historians themselves failed to take the help of Indian scholars to work on such projects? It indicates something of a lapse. It appears that we historians prefer simply to review the works of Bailey, Richards and Dalrymple. If British scholars had not translated the major Persian sources of medieval Indian history like *Babur Nama* or *Ain-i-Akbari*, the pace and scope of research on medieval Indian history going on in the AMU, Aligarh, Jamia Millia Islamia, Delhi University, Jawaharlal Nehru University, Patna University, Allahabad University, Calcutta University, Lucknow University, Hyderabad University and other regional Universities and Colleges would have been still more limited.

I agree with Prof. Irfan Habib when he opines, "There may be found in Persian/Urdu written in the cursive hand (*shikasta*) four possible variants, and one has to know by context what word represents the form at a particular place. If one wants to write a history of the French Revolution, one not only needs to know French but should also be able to read cursively written documents in the French of the time. Unfortunately, there are very few people left who can read Urdu and Persian, particularly the *shikasta* script which was once taught in schools but is no longer being taught since independence. If Dalrymple is able to do so, he belongs to a very small number of people who are competent in this; and their number is steadily declining. That is one major reason why archival material is not being used as widely as it should be, and not because historians are lazy. When Urdu was killed through a conscious policy, a large part of our past was naturally locked up for us." In this significant comment Irfan Habib raised some important issues which have to be answered and should be taken serious note of: (*a*) Reading a *shikasta* is difficult; (*b*) Very few people are left who can read *shikasta* and their number is declining; (*c*) During the British Raj *shikasta* script was taught but after independence it is not being taught and (*d*) Urdu was killed by a conscious policy. These are some of the major factors responsible for not using the archival material available in Persian and Urdu.

But if we knew all that, why did we not make efforts to solve these problems? If the members of education commissions dropped the training of Persian and Urdu *shikasta* from the curriculum of schools after Independence that is highly deplorable but AMU, Aligarh and Jamia Millia Islamia are not like Delhi University or Jawaharlal Nehru University who do not have their own Senior Secondary Schools. Aligarh and Jamia have education from Nursery to Ph.D. Aligarh and Jamia are free to frame their own curriculum for schools and are not bound to follow the national curriculum framed by NCERT, so why did scholars at Aligarh and Jamia did not make any effort for including the teaching of Persian and Urdu *shikasta* script in curriculum of their own schools which was already there during British Raj. Nobody could have stopped them from teaching Persian and Urdu *shikasta* script at Aligarh and Jamia. If these languages were being taught at the school level, then they could have been introduced at the graduate level at Aligarh and Jamia. Students attending Honours or subsidiary in Persian and Urdu should also have a paper for *Shikasta* reading and its transcription. But no such effort has been made. Secondly, no encouragement was given to the students to pursue these languages because we thought that the privilege of reading of *shikasta* should remain confine to ourselves only. Ghalib's pupils also said in *Rekhta* and the tradition continued after Ghalib but Alas! We do not have historians of medieval Indian history who could read Persian and Urdu. As Ghalib rightly said-

ریختہ کے تم ہی استاد نہیں ہو غالبؔ
کہتے ہیں اگلے زمانے میں کوئی میرؔ بھی تھا

In the Andhra Pradesh Archives, Hyderabad, lakhs of documents on Mughal history are lying there. No press list and no calendar of these documents published. In National Archives of India, New Delhi, 1,37,000 documents dealing with Aurangzeb and Muhammed Shah's reign are available. No calendar of these documents has been published till this day. If British scholars had not translated the major Persian sources of medieval Indian history like *Babur Nama* or *Ain-i-Akbari,* the pace of researches on medieval Indian history going on in the AMU, Aligarh, Jamia Millia Islamia, Delhi University, Jawaharlal Nehru University, Calcutta University, Patna University, Allahabad University, Hydrabad University and other regional Universities and Colleges would have been very negligent.

We do not have historians of medieval Indian history who can read Urdu and Persian written in *Naskh* or *Nastaliq*. What to say of people who can read Persian *shikasta* but can't read printed Persian historical texts. I agree with Irfan Habib when he opines,"Urdu was killed by a conscious policy." The Government of India did not promote Persian or Urdu after Independence but nobody could have dared to stop us at Aligarh and Jamia to select in our departments of History, Persian and Urdu knowing scholars. So we can conclude that not just the Government and others but we too are equally responsible for the present worsening situation in our researches.

Prof. Irfan Habib writes, "This is one major reason why archival material is not being used as widely as it should be, and not because historians are lazy." The factors identified by him show that not only are we lazy but also that we are myopic. Why did we not train our students to be experts of Persian and Urdu *shikast* so that they could have consulted the archival material? It is not a question of 1857alone. How much documentary evidence of Inayat Jang Collection of documents in National Archives of India and A.P. State Archives, Hyderabad dealing with Mughal history has been utilized by historians of medieval Indian history? Our researches are based on *Ain-i-Akbari* and *Mirat-i-Ahmedi.* Lakhs of revenue documents in Persian *shikasta* are available in various archives of India, how much of those are consulted by us? Prof. Mushirul Hasan opines, "In short, we need to view the 1857 Rebellion not always from the point of view of victors or the vanquished like the unexplored Mutiny Papers at the National Archives of India, there are other voices that are waiting to be heard. I suspect our lazy historians would continue to rely on conventional wisdom and not heed those voices." Our former Vice Chancellor, Prof. Muhammed Mujeeb used to say that monuments have their own language and they talk to those who know their language. The same can be applied to documents specially those that are in *shikasta* script as is explained by Irfan Habib, "the cursive hand (*shikasta*) has four possible variants, and one has to know by context what word represents the form at a particular place." As pointed out by Mushirul Hasan, "When we do not know the language how will those other voices be heard"? If we have cassettes of Lata Mangeshkar but we do not have a player we can't listen to her songs. So is the case with these documents. As one poet rightly said, "We have systematically through our policy of recruitment of young scholars of medieval Indian history destroyed that capability."

جلاتھا جسم جہاں دل بھی جل گیا ہوگا

کرید تے ہو جواب راکھ جستجو کیا ہے

We created historians of medieval Indian history working on Sultans of Delhi, Bengal, Gujarat, Kashmir, Deccan, Jaunpur and Mughal emperors, who have little knowledge of sources. I agree with Prof. Irfan Habib when he writes, "I cannot say how far the stack of 20,000 documents in Persian and Urdu in the National Archives has stood 'virtually unused'. Whether for the first time—it is hard to tell, especially if they haven't been catalogued and are therefore inaccessible to ordinary historians." Dalrymple himself accepts: (*a*) that he is not the first person to write history of 1857 from Urdu and Persian sources; (*b*) That he did not discover the collection and (*c*) That the Mutiny papers in National Archives are uncatalogued. I have also consulted these documents with the help of an index. Out of 8000 documents, around 200 documents have the endorsement of the date of its issue to historians which suggests that some documents were consulted by historians. Dalrymple has used the collection of the Mutiny papers in Persian and Urdu to the maximum possible extent which is reflected in his writings. Then why did we create a class of "ordinary historians?" Just like Mughal *mansabdars* were divided into three categories, in the same manner we find that there are two categories of historians as defined by Irfan Habib: (*a*) Historians who are able to access to their sources and (*b*) Historians for whom access to sources is not possible. He kept them in the category of ordinary historians. I fully agree with Prof. Irfan Habib, especially in regard to historians of medieval Indian history working on Sultans of Delhi, Bengal, Gujarat, Kashmir, Deccan and Jaunpur and Mughal emperors; for most of them Persian sources are inaccessible and their researches are based on English translations of Persian texts and secondary works. This is not only the position of the historians of medieval Indian history working in regional colleges, Universities but also to Central Universities like Delhi University, Jawaharlal Nehru University, Central University Hyderabad, Jamia Millia Islamia and Aligarh Muslim University. I fully agree with Prof. Irfan Habib when he opines, "Unfortunately, there are few people left who can read Urdu and Persian, particularly the *Shikasta* script."

On the basis of the prevailing situation Prof. Mushirul Hasan's apprehension is correct when he says, "I suspect our lazy historians would continue to rely on conventional wisdom and not heed those voices." Because for listening to those voices one has to learn Persian and then *shikasta* script and then one had to go to National Archives India, New Delhi, Bhopal, U.P. State Archives, Lucknow and Allahabad, Bihar State Archives, Patna, Rajasthan State Archives, Bikaner. Documents at the National Archives of India are neat and clean but the documents at regional archives are mostly full of dust because no body touches these documents, so it is easy "to rely on conventional wisdom" as is supported by Prof. Mushirul Hasan. That is why, Dalrymple is forced to write, "I am little surprised that a collection as astonishingly rich and as beautifully catalogued as the Mutiny Papers, and one located so centrally in National Archives of the capital city, within the sight of the Rashtrapati Bhawan, have been so little consulted." Here I would like to add one thing that National Archives of India, is not more than 20 kms from three Central Universities, that is, University of Delhi, Jawaharlal Nehru University and Jamia Millia Islamia and all the three Universities have specialists of both medieval and modern Indian history. So these voices are waiting to be heard since 1857. Earlier these voices were kept in Calcutta Jail and now in Delhi Jail.

The Indian Council of Historical Research, was established in 1973, by the then Minister of Education, Professor Saiyid Nurul Hasan, for the compilation of history and other related works of history. ICHR also did not pay any attention to the preparation of the Index or the Calendar of documents related to the Persian and Urdu documents of 1857. In 1990, ICHR should have taken this decision so that by now we could be have had some work on Persian and Urdu documents relating to 1857. In 1990, some scholars like late Dr. Z.A. Desai and late Prof. S.A.I. Trimizi were alive and they were the experts of *shikasta*. If this project would have been assigned to them they would have done it with great interest and pleasure but now experts of reading *shikasta* are very very scanty. In 1957, we commemorated 100th anniversary of 1857 but we did not make any plan in 1957. Leading Indian historians are the members of ICHR. Now in 2006, ICHR has formed a committee to work on Persian and Urdu documents relating to 1857 and in 2007, we are going to commemorate 150th anniversary of 1857, so this work even can't take off, what is the question of bringing any work in 2007. But there is a saying in Persian—

دیر آید درست آید

Even the delayed work is also good. The project which ICHR has started in 2006 will hopefully be completed and published before 2057, when our next generation will commemorate the 200th anniversary of 1857, as a Urdu poet rightly said—

کون جیتا ہے تیری زلف کے سر ہونے تک

Who will remain alive to see you in full bloom? This is not a new thing in history. It is recorded by Abul Fazl Mamuri a historian of Aurangzeb's reign that one day a noble brought his child to the court of Aurangzeb and requested Aurangzeb to assign him a *mansab* (rank) Aurangzeb replied that a *mansab* could not be assigned to a child. Noble submitted that you assign him a *mansab* today, he will receive *jagir* when he will be a bearded man. The same is the case of ICHR, it has formed a committee to work on Persian and Urdu documents in 2006 because in 2007, we are going to commemorate 150th anniversary of 1857, so if it will not possible in 2007, so by 2057, it will be completed. So working of ICHR in

2006, is not very different from the position of Mughal empire in the first half of 18th century. Let us learn lessons from the west. William Dalrymple's work based on Persian and Urdu documents relating to 1857, published in 2006 and we are only planning.

First of all we did not work on these documents and the other threat to these documents is their preservation. After a period of 150 years these documents have become brittle because they were kept in varying temperature of 2° to 42°. Only in National Archives of India, the stack area is air conditioned but in State Archives of Lucknow, Allahabad, Patna, Bikaner, Bhopal etc., they have been kept facing 150 summers and winters as it is. Dalrymple only faced few summers to work on these documents but these documents are facing both winter and summer without any air conditioning. First of all we do not have their readers and secondly after sometime these documents will be perished. Paper has become brittle and is difficult to touch and read those documents and at the same time these documents not only mishandled but manhandled because we are not aware of their importance. All the government of the states will celebrate the 150th anniversary of 1857 without paying any attention for the preservation of documents relating to 1857.

After crushing the revolt of 1857, British army not only killed Indians but also demolished monuments and the houses in the localities of Shahjahanabad, Muradabad and Aligarh etc. Sir Saiyid Ahmed did a most commendable work that he listed all the monuments of Delhi and published a book *Asarus Sanadid* in 1846. In 1852, British Government demolished one bastion of Red Fort, mosque built by Aurangabadi Begum, wife of Shahjahan and the tomb of Zebun Nisa to clear the passage of railway line. After 1857, they demolished Kashmiri *Darwaza,* Kabuli *Darwaza,* Calcutta *Darwaza,* Kailaghat *Darwaza,* Nigambod *Darwaza* and the fortified wall at several places so that Shahjahanbad remain approachable, without any hurdle. Inside the *Qila-i-Mubarak,* they demolished some of the monuments, destroyed the gardens and built barracks for the British army. I don't agree with William Dalrymple when he suggests, "the barracks should of course have been torn down years ago." No, these barracks should be given full protection so that we and our coming generations could see how the British army officers defaced a beautiful monument? The magnificent Lahore *Darwaza* was renamed the Victoria Gate. Pavilions of Bagh-i-Hayat Bakhsh were turned into urinals for

British army officials. Mosque built by Akbari Begum, wife of Shahjahan in front of *Jama Masjid* was also demolished. Sir Saiyid saved the inscription of that mosque and when he built *Jama Masjid* at Aligarh, he placed those inscriptions in the central arch of University's Jama mosque. Shahjahan had assigned a big piece of land between *Jama Masjid* and *Qila-i-Mubarak* to the builders of Taj Mahal and Shahjahanabad to build houses, so after 1857 whole area of *Kocha* Bulaqi Begum and Khanam Bazar were demolished. Ghalib wrote that from *Jama Masjid* to Raj Ghat the whole area was demolished and bricks were lying there. W. Taylor, Commissioner of Patna writes in his book—*Patna Crisis* that, "I (Taylor) have ordered him (Pir Ali Khan) alongwith all those connected with him (Pir Ali) to be killed and, their houses to be razed to the ground." Houses of those Indians, who took part in the revolt of 1857, were also demolished in Aligarh, Muradabad, Najibabad. The court yard of *Jama Masjid* of Najibabad was auctioned and today private houses are located within the four walls of the mosque and dirty drains are flowing in the court yard of the *Jama Masjid*. In Independent India no attention was paid for the preservation of Red Fort and most of the work was left incomplete. Broken stones of the railings etc., are lying here and there and there is no one to repair the same. It shows our attitude towards our cultural heritage.

But Zakaullah gives another view in his work—*Tarikh-i-Urooj-i-Engleshia*, that *Wahabi maulvis* of Delhi hated Bahadur Shah and wherever the *imam* of the mosques was appointed by him they did not pray in those mosques because they declared Bahadur Shah as *bidati*. Zakaullah writes that the *wahabi* people of Delhi had a belief that even if one brick of the fort was used in any house, to stay in that house was abominable. In relation to the celebration of *Id al-Azha*, Zakaullah writes that king used to go to *Id Gah* to pray and to do sacrifice of camel but if today he would have gone there people would have sacrificed him. Then he makes a comment that since then British were ousted from Delhi and the Delhi was taken over by the revolters, there was not a single crime which a person could do was left un-committed. These wahabi *ulema* declared Bahadur Shah as *bidati* because now Bahadur Shah had nothing to give them. Which Mughal emperor was not a *bidati*? Today Saudi Kings are following hereditary monarchy, which is also a *bidat*. Can any *wahabi* maulvi dare to declare Saudi monarchs as *bidati*? Also, the whole Shahjahanbad was built with the support of Mughal emperor, Shah Jahan, so why *wahabi maulvis* were living in Shahjahanabad? They should have built a hut on the banks of river Yamuna, why they were living in *havelis* of Shahjahanabad? Since Muawiyah, all hereditary monarchies of the whole Muslim world were un-Islamic in nature and character including the present Saudi monarchy. But today no *wahabi maulvi* can dare to declare Saudi hereditary monarchy as un-Islamic because Mughal kingship was at its fag end so they declared it as un-Islamic. Had any *alim* declared Aurangzeb's authority as un-Islamic? The glory of the Mughal government was over and now everything was out of their control and specially in this period of crisis criminals had taken full advantage of it. Even in Mutiny papers we come across such incidents and when it was reported to Bahadur Shah, he took a serious note of it but he was totally helpless. As far as Zakaullah's comment that Mughal Emperor would have been sacrificed. Though Zakaullah does not provide any reason for it, it seems that his order for banning the sacrifice of cow must have played a negative role among Muslims and Muslims must be having anger against Bahadur Shah. Zakaullah's tilt is towards British Raj because he desired a good administration but he was not aware of the price that Indians had to pay for this administration in due course of time.

Shah Abdul Aziz declared India as *Darul Harb*, Maulana Saeed Ahmed Mujaddadi declared *Jihad* against British from *Jama Masjid* of Shahjahanbad, Maulvi Pir Ali Khan took lead in Patna, *Maulvi* Liyaqat Ali in Allahabad, Shabbir Ali in Amroha and Maulvi Abdul Jalil declared *Jihad* against British from the *Jama Masjid* of Aligarh. In the newspapers published from Delhi, the verses of the *Qasida* composed by Saiyid Naimatullah Vali (d. 570/1174) that Shah of the *darwaish* will strike his sword and will kill the Christians but the last verses is having the year which is 1274 AH which comes to 1853 and not 1857. I think nobody had taken note of it and just got encouragement to fight against the British. These verses gave energy and strength to its readers. In the case of Shabbir Ali, Robert D. Philip wrote in the judgement dated 18th November, 1858 that "in small towns there was also no town except of Amroha where British forces faced so much resistance from the people of Amroha where there was no big leader guiding them." Ghazi Muhammed Amin Amrohvi wrote a *masnavi* on 1857 so his descendents kept the pages of his *masnavi* not in one house but they distributed pages of this *masnavi* among their relative so that if one gets hold of few pages so he could not come out with any idea about its theme. Though most of the rulers of Punjab and Rajasthan supported the British but the people of Punjab and Rajasthan opposed the British and gave asylum to those Indians who fled from Delhi after the failure of 1857. Main centres of revolt were Delhi, Meerut, Lucknow, Allahabad, Bengal, Jhansi, Ballabhgarh, Kanpur, Aligarh, Bulandshahr, Muzaffarnagar, Rohailkhand, Chandpur, Bareilly, Mandawar, Kiratpur, Najibabad, Amroha, Dadri, Khair, etc. But in Bijnor and at few other places it had taken the communal turn. In Delhi people were having great hate for British. We see that even when Bahadur Shah left the Red Fort and British became successful in demolishing Kashmiri Gate, so Jiwan Lal, an eye witness to the events writes in his *Roznamcha* that "a distance of six *farlang* from Kashmiri Gate to Red Fort was covered by the British forces after a gap of five days." This shows the resistance of Indians against British. Recently we have seen that after the fall of Saddam Husain in Iraq, American and British forces entered in Baghdad without facing any resistance.

Historians who have worked on 1857 had discussed in detail the causes of the revolt of 1857 but I can quote one example of my own family. Shujaud Daula had performed the *azadari* of Muharram at Jalali Distt. Aligarh, in 1774 and got impressed form one of my ancestor Saiyid Shah Khairat Ali, a sufi of *Kubravi* order. Later on Asifud Daula had given a *maafi* of five villages for the *imambara* of Saiyid Shah Khairat Ali in 1787. In 1804 all the five villages were confiscated by the British government. It reflects the high handedness of British authorities. While I was working on 1857 and looking at the documents available in U.P. State Archives, Lucknow, so luckily I got this file on 2nd August, 2006 at 12.15 p.m. It was a great experience of my life. It was a happy occasion as well as saddening. Happy because I got this file but sad that I came to know about this file after the death of my father Prof. S.M. Kamaluddin Husain, who wrote the history of our family as well as the genealogical account. If I would have discovered it during his life time it would be a great happy occasion for me and him as well. I had taken the Xerox copies of some of the important folios of this file and made a file of it. When I went to Jalali, my home town, I kept it on the grave of my father. There will be thousands of such cases where British government had done injustice with Indians. All this led Indians to get up and fight against the tyrant British regime in India in 1857. In 1857, wherever, they saw British killed them and sacrificed their own life.

Bahadur Shah had desired to be buried in India, his homeland but during his last days when he was in Rangoon, he became sure that this wish of his would not be granted. Realising this, he said:

کتنا ہے بد نصیب ظفر دفن کے لئے
دو گز زمیں بھی مل نہ سکی کوئے یار میں

Ultimately he was buried in Rangoon. People used to talk about this verse and Bahadur Shah's attachment to his homeland. Babur who founded the Mughal Empire, left his last will to be buried in Kabul but Aurangzeb praised India that it was a beautiful country. But Bahadur Shah II, the last Mughal emperor wished to be buried in India and he described India as *'Koi Yar'* or friends land. But now when we are celebrating the 150th anniversary of 1857, the prices of land in Delhi have gone up considerably. An Urdu poet has commented on this wish of Bahadur Shah to be buried in Delhi:

دہلی میں آکے رہنے کی خواہش کریں نہ اب
رنگون میں پڑے رہیں اپنے مزار میں
کہدو ظفر سے دلی کے اس کوے یار میں
دو گز زمین ملتی ہے ستر ہزار میں

(Tell Zafar to remain buried in his own grave in Rangoon because in Delhi, the prices of land have gone up and is seventy thousand rupees for two meters). This is the contrast between 1857 and 2007.

1857 in itself was a year of contrasts. On one hand, we find a revolt against the British and the result was a great British repression. But on the other hand, on the basis of Dispatch of 1854 prepared by Charles Wood, President of Board of Control sought to create a properly articulated scheme covering all stages of educational development. With the result, three Universities were established at the Presidency towns of Calcutta, Bombay and Madras in 1857, on the pattern of London University. Some of the Indian graduates of these Universities started National Movement for freedom.

1

Introduction

The Foundation of Turkish rule in India was laid by Turks in 1206. These Turks got settled in India and started assimilating in Indian society and culture. Then in 1526, Babur, the Mughal emperor, laid the foundation of the Mughal Empire in India. Akbar, by following the policy of *Sulh-i-Kul* (Peace with all), tried his best to do away with differences among Indians. Mughal government provided a common platform for both Hindus and Muslims. Since the 12th century AD, Sufis also played an important role in the direction of conflict resolution and peace in India. Persian poetry right from the foundation of Delhi Sultanat down to 18th century made a significant contribution for assimilation and peace in Indian society and culture. This process culminated, in the verse of Khusrau:

من تو شدم تو من شدی، من تن شدی تو جاں شدی

تا کس نگوید بعد ازیں، من دیگرم تو دیگری

I have become you and you have become me, I have become the body and you have become soul. So that nobody could say that I am different from you and you are from me.

But Aurangzeb's re-imposition of pilgrimage tax in 1670 and *jizya* in 1679, did damage that rhythm which was created by Akbar by abolishing both the taxes in 1563 and 1564. It was finally abolished by Farrukh Siyar. The Hindus felt hurt and discriminated. This ultimately passed the way for the disintegration of Mughal Empire. Sir Saiyid Ahmed Khan was the first Muslim historian who opined that Aurangzeb's policy of re-imposition of *jizya* played a damaging role and divided Hindus and Muslims. Feeling of hurt is obvious from the writings of modern historians like J.N. Sarkar, S.R. Sharma, A.L. Srivastava and others. British historians had taken full advantage from this policy of Aurangzeb and highlighted Aurangzeb's decision to collect *jizya* from Hindus. Both Hindu and British historian declared this tax as an open discrimination against Hindus. Not only these eminent historians but other educated Hindus also raise the point of discrimination. Though *jizya* was abolished at a later stage but a scar was left.

The East India Company had started its career as a trader in India. During the reign of Mughal Emperor Jahangir (1605-1627), East India Company had established factories at Surat, Bharoch, Ahmadabad, Agra and Masulipatam by 1623 AD. However, from the very beginning, East India Company tried to combine trade with politics. They had far reaching designs and were planning things accordingly. Conditions in the southern part of India were more favourable to the British as they did not have to face a strong Indian rulers there like Mughal Emperors of the north. The British opened their first factory in the south at Masulipatam in 1611, but they soon shifted the center of their activities to Madras (Chennai), the lease of which was granted by the local ruler in 1639. They constructed a small fort called Fort St. George.

Bombay (Mumbai) was acquired by the East India Company from Portugal in 1668 and was immediately fortified, but due to the danger of the rising Maratha power, they made Surat as the headquarters of the East India Company on the west coast. In 1857 documents and urdu newspapers published during 1857, it is recorded as 'Mumbai' and not Bombay. It shows that British named it as Bombay. The East India Company had opened its first factory in Orissa in 1633.

During Shahjahan's reign (1627-58) they were given permission to trade at Hugli in Bengal. It soon opened factories at Patna, Balasore and Dhakka. Then East India Company dreamt of capturing political power in India. Hostilities between the Mughal Emperor Aurangzeb (1658-1707) and the British broke out in 1686, after British had sacked Hugli and declared war against the Mughals. The war ended disastrously for the British. They were defeated and driven out of Bengal. Their factories at Surat, Masulipatam and Vishakhapatam were seized and their fort at Bombay besieged. The British submitted to Aurangzeb that the ill crimes they have committed may be pardoned. Aurangzeb pardoned the British, but Aurangzeb was not aware that these British traders would one-day arrest his great grandson Bahadur

Shah II and shoot his sons at *Khooni Darwaza* in Shahjahanabad Pardoning the British was a great blunder of Aurangzeb. It led to the foundation of British rule in India. In 1717, the East India Company secured a *farman* (order of the Mughal Emperor) from Mughal Emperor, Farrukh Siyar, confirming the privileges granted in 1691 and extending them to Gujarat and Deccan.

During the first half of the 18th century Bengal was ruled by the *Nawabs*. Nawab Ali Wardi Khan exercised strict control over the British traders and prevented them from misusing their privileges. In 1750, Clive attacked and occupied Arcot. In 1756, Sirajud Daula become the Nawab of Bengal and demanded of the British that they should follow the conditions for trade laid down by Murshid Quli Khan. The British refused to follow as they felt strong after their victory over the French. The breaking point came when without taking Sirajud Daula's permission, the East India Company began to fortified Calcutta (Kolkata). Sirajud Daula considered this action of the British as an encroachment upon his authority. Sirajud Daula ordered both the British and the French to demolish their forts at Calcutta and Chandernagar. French followed the order, but British refused to do so because now they considered themselves in a position to defy the order of Sirajud Daula. They further demanded the absolute right to trade freely in Bengal. This was a direct challenge to *Nawab's* authority. Sirajud Daula asserted his position and seized the British factory at Qasimbazar and occupied Fort William on 20th June, 1756. British entered into an alliance with Mir Jafar, Manik Chand, Amirchand, Jagat Seth and Khadim Khan. With the result a battle was fought at Plassey in 1757, in which Sirajud Daula was defeated and killed by British forces. British crowned a puppet *Nawab*—Mir Jafar. Persian and Urdu poet Iqbal said—

جعفر از بنگال و صادق از دکن
ننگ دنیا، ننگ دیں، ننگ وطن

(Jafar of Bengal and Sadiq from Deccan, Stigma of the world, the faith and the nation).

The battle of Plassey paved the way for foundation of British rule in India. When Mir Jafar could not fulfill their demands then they appointed Mir Qasim as the *Nawab* of Bengal. However, Mir Qasim in a short duration of time got disillusioned from the attitude of British and started distancing from them. Mir Qasim was defeated in a series of battles in 1763 and fled to Awadh where he formed an alliance with Nawab Shujaud Daula, of Awadh and Mughal Emperor, Shah Alam II. The three fought with the British army at Buxer in 1764 and were defeated. This was one of the decisive battles of India, like the battle of Tarain and the first battle of Panipat in 1526. It established the British as masters of Bengal, Bihar and Orissa and placed Awadh at their mercy.

In 1766, British aligned themselves with the Nizam of Hyderabad in dethroning Hyder Ali from Mysore, but they could not succeed in their project. Then in 1775, the British clashed with the Marathas which continued upto 1782, but in 1782, British signed Salbai treaty which saved them from combined opposition of Indian rulers. Then again they exerted pressure on Mysore because Marathas promised to help them against Hyder Ali. But Hyder Ali defeated the British. Warren Hastings developed friendship with the Nizam and the Marathas and concentrated on his struggle against Mysore. In 1781, British defeated Hyder Ali. British signed peace treaty with Tipu Sultan in 1784, but a war again began in 1789 and ended in Tipu's defeat in 1792, in which he was killed while fighting against British.

The next large-scale expansion of British rule began under Wellesley (1789-1805). Wellesley followed the policy of Subsidiary alliance. Marathas were defeated at Assaye in 1803. The second Anglo-Maratha war had shattered the power of Maratha chiefs. The Rajputana states had been controlled for a long time by Sindhia and Holkar. Now Rajputs lacked the energy to reassert their independence and readily accepted British authority, Spirit of Haldi Ghati was over by this time. Thus, by 1818, the entire Indian sub-continent excepting the few regional powers had been brought under British authority. What happened to India is being summed up by an Urdu poet in the following verse.

اس گھر کو آگ لگ گئی گھر کے چراغ سے

(This house is burnt from the flame of its own lamp.)

Dalhousie was appointed as Governor-General of India in 1848. He thought that Indian allies had already served the purpose of facilitating British conquest of India and could now be got rid of profitably. On the other hand, he thought that British exports were suffering because of the mal administration of these states by their Indian rulers. So he followed the policy of 'Doctrine of Lapse'. Many states were annexed by applying this doctrine. Dalhousie also took away the cotton—producing province of Berar from the Nizam in 1853. Dalhousie was also keen on annexing Awadh. The French press also unanimously denounced the methods of British colonialists. The Pruduct Reveu des Deux Mondes wrote: "The Company is little concerned with easing yoke. During the last ten years particularly, it has practiced on the large scale, a system of annexations, of dispossessions, of confiscations." What to say for Rajas and the Nawabs, even one *maafi* for the *Imambara* of Saiyid Shah Khairat Ali at Jalali, Distt. Aligarh assigned in 1787 AD by Nawab Asifud Daula, was also confiscated in 1804 by the British government. But the task was a little bit difficult. Awadh had been obedient to the British over the years. But Nawab Wajid Ali Shah was accused of having misgoverned his state. So Awadh was also annexed in 1856.

The Industrial Revolution in England completely transformed England's economy and its economic relations with India. It led to rapid economic growth. They needed raw material. There was abundant raw material in India. Main objective of British was to transform India into a consumer of British manufactures and a supplier of raw material and a consumer of British products.

The 'Economic Drain' was peculiar to British rule. Mushafi, an Urdu poet had said about drain of wealth in 1824.

ہندوستان کی دولت وحشمت جو کچھ کہ تھی کافر فرنگیوں نے بہ تدبیر کھینچ لی۔

(These British snatched all wealth of India.)

The British, consequently, spent large part of the taxes and income they derived from the Indian people not in India, but in England, their own country.

British also declared Indian institutions corrupt and decadent, and Indian thought narrow and unscientific. They also declared Indian system of medicine, Ayurveda and Unani as unscientific and introduced their own systems of medicine; in India. They were highly critical of Indian society and culture. Indian civilization was looked down upon with contempt.

The British paid attention to the introduction of modern education in India. But British wanted to use modern education to strengthen the foundation of their own empire in India. They opened schools for both male and female Indians to create a class which would serve as their spokes persons. To some extent they also became successful in this policy.

Now it is clear that the discontent which arose in 1857 was much more than a mere product of sepoy discontent. It was the result of the policies followed by British when they became successful in defeating Sirajud Daula in 1757 and wining the battle of Buxer in 1764. The period of the growth of discontent among the Indian rulers and the people coincided with certain important decision taken by the British government from 1757 to 1857. Thus wide spread and intense dislike and hatred of British rule prevailed among large numbers of Indian masses and soldiers. The process of building up the British Empire in India between 1757 and 1857 resulted in unrest, suspicion and discontent amongst various sectors of Indian people.

From 1763 to 1856 there were large numbers of rebellions. William Dalrymple sums up, "For by the early 1850, many British officials were nursing plans finally to abolish the Mughal court, and to impose not just British laws and technology on India, but also Christianity. The reaction to this steady crescendo of insensivity came in 1857 with Great Mutiny...... Delhi was the principal centre of uprising." It was also accepted by the Italian democratic press. La Ragiene wrote on 5th September, 1857. "India which was once well governed by the Musalmans, is now horribly ruled by Christians."

All the rebels recognized Bahadur Shah II, as their Badshah. Bengal, Awadh, Rohailkhand, Bundelkhand, Bihar, and the East Punjab all shunned off British authority. Centres of revolt were at Delhi, Kanpur, Lucknow, Bareilly, Jhansi, Muradabad, Aligarh, Amroha, Ballabhgarh and Arah. Bahadur Shah, Nana Sahab, Azimullah, Begum Hazrat Mahal, Rani Laxmi Bai, Tanteya Tope, Kuwar Singh, Nahar Singh, Maulavi Ahmadulah, Maulvi Liyaqat Ali, Maulvi Abdul Jalil, Maulvi Nasimullah were outstanding leaders of the revolt. Hindu-Muslim unity played a significant role. But there are some instances where it had taken a communal turn. In Bijnor Hindu Jats looted and burnt the houses of Muslims and here Sir Saiyid's house was also looted and burnt. Some instances of communal tension also reported from Delhi. British also financed some Indians to create commercial hatred among Hindus and Muslims.

The Sindhia of Gawalior, the Holkar of Indore, the Nizam of Hyderabad, the Raja of Jodhpur and Mewar, Nawab of Bhopal, Nawab of Tonk, Raja of Patiala, Raja of Nabha, Nawab of Rampur, Raja of Jind and other Sikh chieftains of Punjab, the Maharaja of Kashmir, and many other Hindu and Muslim taluqdars and zamindars not only did not support Indians but gave active support to British to suppress Indians. But we find that the people of Rajasthan, Punjab, Malwa, Bhopal, Rampur, Aligarh and Jammu were also opposing the British. They did not agree with the opinion of their rulers who were supporting the British. Bengal, Western Punjab, Bombay, Madras and whole of south remained undisturbed. The money-lenders were hostile to the rebels. Big merchants of Delhi, Bombay, Calcutta and Madras supported the British. The modern educated Indians did not support the rebels. They believed that British would modernize various aspects of Indian society and culture. Only with the passage of time they learnt that British had no such desire at all.Their design was something else. Those who opposed British in 1857, had a better understanding of the evils of British rule on India.

Persian and Urdu poetry played a significant role in the revolt of 1857. Verses of contemporary Persian and Urdu poets and their letters are an important contemporary source to study various aspects of 1857. Historians of modern Indian history who worked on 1857 did not use this source of information available in Persian and Urdu language because of the lack of knowledge of source language, so their researches only cover opinion based on English and Hindi sources relating to 1857. The other opinion is missing from their writings. In the light of Persian and Urdu sources we have to re-write the history of 1857.

We get some information from the *kulliyat* of Ghalib (collection of verses), *Ghalib ka Roznamcha* (Diary of Ghalib) and *khutut-i-Ghalib* (letters of Ghalib) Sir Saiyid Ahmed Khan wrote—*Tarikh-i-Sarkashi-i-Bijnor* (The history of rebellion at Bijnor) and *Asbab-i-Baghawat-i-Hind* (Causes of Indian revolt) Zakaullah wrote—*Tarikh-i-Hind* (History of India), Zahiruddin Dehlavi wrote—*Dastan-i-Ghadar* (The story of mutiny) *Fughan-i-Dehli* (The lament of Delhi). It is a collection of poems of some forty Urdu poets on the ruin and plunder of Delhi. They describe the events very vaguely indicate that the Muslims have been the chief victims. Muhammed Husian Azad composed a '*Nazm*' (poem) on the victories of armies of the East over the British.

It was published in his father, Maulana Muhammed Baqar's paper—*Dehli Urdu Akhbar* of 24th May, 1857. Saiyid Muhammed Ali wrote *Marghoob-i-Dil* in 1870 dealing with the history of Shahjahanabad. There are long poems and verses on the sack of Lucknow by Barq Luckhnawi, Munir Shikohabadi. We get one book in Persian written by Behari Lal Brahmin Qannauji: *Oza-i-Siyasi Dar Hind, 1857* (Political condition of India during 1857). He is critical of Indians and supportive of British. There are about 20,000 documents in Persian and Urdu in National Archives of India, New Delhi, U.P. State Archives, Lucknow. Rajasthan State Archives, Bikaner and Jaipur, Bihar State Archives, Patna, Azad Library, Aligarh Muslim University, Aligarh we have immense material on 1857 in Persian and Urdu, which has not been utilized by historians. Lot of material on 1857 is also available in regional languages also.

When Turks conquered Delhi, they named it as *Hazrat-i-Dehli.*

حضرت دہلی

Ziauddin Barani, author of *Tarikh-i-Firoz Shahi*, declared Dehli as رشک بغداد (an envy of Baghdad). Amir Khussrau praised Delhi in his superb way.

حضرت دہلی کنف دیں و داد
جنت عدن است کہ آباد باد

Khushhal Khan Khatak a Pushtu poet and a noble of Aurangzeb's reign (1658-1707) praised Delhi in his poetry.

شہر دہلی تھا جنتوں کا شہر
اونچی اونچی عمارتوں کا شہر
خوبصورت وہ کوچہ و بازار
گوناں گوں پیاری نعمتوں کا شہر
دہر میں ہے اگر کوئی جنت
تو اسے سمجھ جنتوں کا شہر

Bernier a French traveller visited Delhi in 17th century. He holds the opinion, "Delhi also may possess beauties adapted to a warm climate...Here is held a bazaar or market for an endless variety of things; which like the Pout-neuf at Paris. The capital of Hindustan is not destitute of handsome buildings. You may judge from what I have said, whether a lover of good cheer ought to quit Paris for the sake of visiting Delhi."

Mirza Sangin Beg wrote a book—*Sairul Manazil* in 1827, dealing with Shahjahanabad's monuments etc. He had given a long list of the buildings of *Qila-i-Mubarak* which does not exist today. It shows that those buildings were demolished by the British because now we find some buildings inside the Red Fort which were constructed by British. Manuscript copy of this source is also preserved in the museum of Red Fort itself.

In 1827, Mirza Sangin Beg, the author of *Sairul Manazil* observes about Chandni Chowk.

یہ دلچسپ بازار ہے چوک کا
کہ ٹھہرے وہیں، بس جہاں دل لگا

Sail Chand in his work *Tafrihul Imarat* which he wrote in 1825 writes about the beauty of Delhi.

گرچہ دہلی بر و نق از نہری است
اکبر آباد ما عجب شہری است

(Though there is life in Delhi but Akbarabad (Agra) is a different city altogether).

Sir Saiyid was having a great reverence for eastern culture. Sir Saiyid knew that by 1818, the entire sub-continent had been brought under British authority and our cultural heritage will be neglected and harmed. So he wrote—*Asarus Sanadid* in 1846. It is an important documents our monuments of Delhi. Sir Saiyid writes—

از نقش و نگار درودیوار شکستہ
آثار ید است صنادید عجم را

(From the broken walls and the mehrabs, reflects the beauty of their makers from Iran). And again says about the memories relating to these monuments.

بیاد نقش عمارات شهر یاراں ہیں

کہ این سپہر جفا پیشہ چوں بہ بست وشکست

Sir Saiyid was having right apprehension that in 1852 one bastion of Red Fort, Aurangabadi mosque and the tomb of Zebun Nisa was demolished to connect Delhi with railway track. With the result *Shiatus Sefa* mosque was dilinked from Shahjahanabad.

Hali praises about Delhi in his own way though he was the resident of Panipat but he considered Delhi as the centre of excellence and all the eminent scholars used to live there in Delhi.

تیرا معمورہ تھا اک عالم میں مرجع اور مآب

آن کرلیتے تھے یاں ٹھیکی جہاں کے انتخاب

بستے تھے اطراف سے آ آ کے تجھ میں شیخ وشباب

کر دیا تھا تیری آبادی نے ملکوں کو خراب

جھمکتا تھا تجھ میں ترک وفرس روم و زنگ کا

دستہ تھا گویا تو گلہائے رنگا رنگ کا

That is why, British destroyed the city of Delhi. What happened to Delhi after 1857 is explained by Mushafi, a Persian and Urdu poet

ہے صاف تو یہ گلشن دہلی میں خزاں ہے

It is clear that Delhi is passing through autumn.

or

دلی ہوئی ہے ویراں، سونے کھنڈر پڑے ہیں

ویراں ہیں محلے ،سنسان گھر پڑے ہیں

Delhi is ruined, broken structures are left. Mohallas are ruined, houses are without life.

Ghalib wrote about Chandni Chowk.

چوک جسکو کہیں وہ مقتل ہے
گھر نمو نہ بنا ہے زنداں کا
شہر دہلی کا ذرہ ذرۂ خاک
تشنۂ خوں ہے ہر مسلماں کا

(The chowk has become a slaughter place,
And the home has become the replica of a prison,
Every particle of the earth of Delhi,
Has become thirsty of the blood of Muslims)
Mirza Ghalib writes—

مسجد جامع سے راج گھاٹ دروازے تک بے مبالغہ ایک صحرائے لق ودق ہے۔
اینٹوں کے جو ڈھیر پڑے ہیں وہ اگر اٹھ جائیں تو ھوکا مکان ہو جائے۔

(From Jama Masjid to Rajghat there are mounds of bricks and if those are cleared it will look like a desert.)

Mir Mehdi Majruh wrote a Ghazal and sent to Ghalib for his review, its last verse was

میاں یہ اہل دلی کی زبان ہے

Ghalib reacted very sharply and said 'O! Mir Mehdi don't you feel ashamed by saying that this is the language of the people of Delhi. Now people of Delhi are Hindus, workers, Punjabis or Christians, whom you are praising. There is no Urdu Bazar. Where is Urdu? Where is Delhi? It is not a city, now it is a camp and the cantonment. No fort, no city, no bazaar and no canal.' Ghalib writes to Nawab Alauddin Khan

میری جان یہ وہ دلی نہیں جس میں تم پیدا ہوئے۔۔۔ ایک کیمپ ہے۔ مسلمان

اہل حرفہ یا حکام کے شاگرد پیشہ، باقی سراسر ہنود

(My dear, this is not that Delhi, where you were born, now it is a camp.)

Ghalib writes, in one of his letter

اپنے مکان میں بیٹھا ہوں۔ دروازے سے باہر نکل نہیں سکتا۔ سوار ہونا اور کہیں

جانا تو بڑی بات ہے۔ رہا یہ کہ کوئی میرے پاس آوے شہر میں ہے کون جو آوے۔

"I am sitting in my house and can't go out of my house. Who will come to meet me? There is no one left in the city."

Ghalib says:

قصہ کوتاہ قلعہ اور جھجھر اور بہادر گڑھ اور بلب گڑھ اور فرخ نگر کم و بیش تیس لاکھ

روپے کی ریاستیں تھیں۔ شہر کی عمارتیں خاک میں مل گئیں۔

Let us be brief Forts, of Jhajhar, Bahadurgarh, Ballabhgarh and Farrukh Nagar all were demolished. Buildings of the city were all ruined.

Ghalib says:

''جو مسلمان شہر میں آباد ہونا چاہے وہ ٹکٹ خریدے اور اپنی حیثیت کے مطابق

جرمانہ دے۔''

Muslims who wanted to re-settle in the city, they should purchase a ticket and pay a penalty according to their status.

Ghalib says:

کل سے یہ حکم نکلا ہے کہ یہ لوگ (مسلمان) شہر سے باہر مکان، دکان کیوں

بناتے ہیں۔ جو مکان بن چکے ہیں انھیں گرادو۔ آئندہ کے لئے ممانعت کا حکم

سنادو۔ آج تک یہ صورت ہے۔

Since yesterday this order is circulated that why these (Muslims) built houses and shops outside the city. Those have already been constructed be demolished and for next time they should be warned.

Sir Saiyid Ahmed Khan provides a searching analysis of the events. He places the blame on the British whose policy had denied Indians the good will of the population. "It was for the government to try and win the friendship of its subjects, not the subjects to try and win that of government." He added, "Now the English has been in existence upward a century, and upto the present hour it has not secured the affection of the people." Sir Saiyid's book is a political document on 1857 and no student of Indian history can ignore it.

Altaf Husain Hali's motto throughout was: "We must change with the time." The Quran being read in northern India for about seven hundred years but no one had quoted it for promoting Muslims to accept and accelerate the pace of change. Now Hali quoted from the Quran, "God does not change the condition of people who do not care to change their own condition."

If we study the writings of Sir Saiyid, Azad, Hali, Nazir, Shibli and Sharar in the light of prevailing conditions we shall see that they had awakened to the needs of the people and wanted to infuse them with hope.

Delhi and other towns such as Muradabad, Faizabad, Lucknow, Amroha, Kol were important centers of culture, were also ruined. These towns produced Persian and Urdu poets. Apart from other themes they also wrote verses against the high handedness of British rulers. When British officials received reports that some poets also encouraged Indians through their poetry to revolt against British government, those poets were also arrested and hanged. The martyred poets of 1857 were: (1) Mirza Ahmed Beg Dehlavi (2) Mirza Ghulam Mohiuddin Dehlavi, Ashki (3) Shahzadah Mirza Rahimuddin, Ejad. (4) Abdul Hakim Dehlavi, Bismil (5) Mirza Ashoor Beg, Sanai (6) Maulvi Kifayat Ali Muradabadi and others. When Kifayat Ali was being taken for hanging so he was reciting the following verses:

کوئی گل باقی رہے گا نے چمن رہ جائے گا
پر رسول اللہ کا دین حسن رہ جائے گا
نام شاہان جہاں مٹ جائیں گے لیکن
حشر تک نام و نشان پنج تن رہ جائے گا

No flower will be left, no garden will remain,
But the religion of Prophet of God will survive.
The names of the Emperors of the world will be erased, but upto the day of resurrection five names will remain. (Muhammed, Ali, Fatima, Hasan and Husain)

وہی صہبائی جو تھے صاحب قول فیصل
ایک ہی ساتھ قتل ہوئے پدر اور پسر

Maulana Sehbai was killed by Britishers alongwith his son.
Maulana Sadruddin Azurda said—

کیونکر آزردہ نکل جائے نہ سودائی ہوکر
قتل اس طرح بے جرم جو صہبائی ہو

Why Azurda should not go out stray when Sehbai is executed without committing any crime.

نو جوانوں کو ہوئیں پھانسیاں بے جرم و قصور
ماردی گولیاں پایا جسے کچھ زورآور

Young people were hanged without having committed any crime. Whosoever was found guilty was gunned down.

Moinuddin wrote his *Roznamcha* but if we read it then it appears that he wrote in a condition of fear and harassment. He had told his family members and friends that it should not be published during his life time. Jeewan Lal also wrote his

Roznamcha, which also sheds light on the condition of Delhi prevailing in 1857. Ghazi Muhammed Amin Amrohvi wrote *Masnavi* relating to 1857 and about the atrocities of British army on Indians. So his descendents kept the pages of his *masnavi* in the custody of different family members so that even if one gets hold of its pages so they could not make any point out of those stray pages. This shows the situation of fear after the suppression of revolt of 1857. Abdul Latif wrote *Tazkira-i-Fatehan-i-Hind,* in which he had described that how Bazar Khanam was looted by British army.

European, Russian and British press also played an important role on the question of the revolt of 1857.

On 5th September, 1857, the 'Morning Post' declared that, "Every Briton with the heart of a man in his bosom feels pledged to his country that the British Empire in India shall endure if for no other reason then for the purpose of exterminating and rooting out from the face of the earth the Mohammedan and Brahminised demons who have committed crimes on British women and maidens too horrible to name."

The 'Radical New castle' Chronicle dated 17th July, 7th August and 23rd October, 1857, reflecting the growing imperialist fervor of its proprietor, Joseph Crown, spoke of "this magnificent dependency of the British Crown" and criticized Caning's "clemency", saying: "It is no time for mercy now; our vengeance should be sharp and bloody, and of such a nature as to make our Indian subjects tremble in future at the name of Delhi...(they should be) exterminated as if they were so many wild beasts."

The Non-Confirmist, reflecting "Little England" views, on Ist July, 1857, felt that, "this mutiny perhaps is part of the penalty.... (for having allowed ourselves) to be dragged into Chinese hostilities and (having) allowed an English Minister...to prosecute war with Persia."

Reynold's Newspaper, representing a non-socialist working class stand point, at once expressed sympathy with the rebels. On July 5, 1857, it wrote of "the commencement of that tremendous retribution, which, if there be justice in the world, the gigantic and East India Company are certain to evoke...." It declared that "While deploring the excesses in which the revolted regiments have indulged, our sympathies as they always have been are with the weak against the strong—with the oppressed struggling with their tyrants—with the tortured, plundered, enslaved and insulted natives of India, in striving to free themselves of the iron yoke of their cruel, remorseless, rapacious and lugpo critical masters.... Our sympathies are with the mutinous scoundrels whom The Times and its colleagues wish to make an example of, by shooting, hanging and gibbeting."

When the "atrocities" were blazoned abroad, the paper remarked: "We at home only hear one side of the question.... The provocation has been great." (Renold's Newspaper dated 26th July, 1857).

"Sepoys were rebels not patriots because they had voluntarily surrendered their liberties into the keeping of the English! Yes! They surrendered their liberties into the keeping of the English! Yes! They surrendered their liberties in the same fashion as a traveller does his purse with the highwayman's pistol levelled at him." (Reynold's Newspaper dated 11th October, 1857).

Ernest Jones had long been interested in India. He had written a series of newspaper articles in 1853, and while in prison on 1857 had composed a long poem "The Revolt of Hindostan" or "The New World", which was re-issued when the revolt occurred. In its preface Jones makes his celebrated amendment to the Imperial slogan: "The British Empire on which the sun never sets." "On its colonies," he wrote, *the sun never sets, but the blood never dries*.

On Ist August, 1857, Jones wrote that, "The revolt turns out to be, as we assumed our readers from the commencement, not a military mutiny but a national insurrection of one thing we are certain—that whether this insurrection be suppressed or not, it is the procurer to our loss of India...our advice is ...recognize the independence of the Indian race...one hundred years (ago)...a foreign tribe, the peelers of the earth, the merchant-robbers of Headen hall street, stole on a false pretence into the heart of this mighty galaxy of empires and robbed it of its jewel...independence...within that reign of 100 years a millennium of guilt has been committed by the rebels, but emphasized the provocation and called British military slaughters during the Peninsular war."

He declared that, "The Hindu cause is just—the Hindu cause is noble...God save the Hindu cause." He emphasized that English working people should have, "sympathy...for their Hindu brethren. Their cause is yours—their success indirectly yours as well."

The French press also did devote a great deal of attention to the 1857 revolt.

L'Estaffette, a republican paper, indignantly declared on 29th August, 1857: "If the English persist in their cruel oppressive policy, the Great Powers, and France above all, will have to intervene to see that the Indians are not slaughtered as though they were a vile herd."

The French press also unanimously denounced the misdeeds of the East India Company and the methods of British colonialists, which they felt were mainly responsible for revolt.

L'Estaffette wrote much more strongly: "Does India remain a colony under the detestable English domination? No, the English have made it an immense prison, strewn with gallows and gibbets. They are beginning to understand in England that the imprudence of the missionaries has contributed greatly to the present explosion."

Jonguiere Antouelle, in the Revue de Paris enlarged on the picture: "British influence is diminishing in Constantinople, she is threatened in Suez. In Persia she is involved in an armed peace which threatens war. She is found odious in China. In India she is crumbling and from that time, the whole of Turkey has been rejoining. The entire East disgraces England."

Le Pays wrote in September, 1857 "The end of the British Empire in India would signify the triumph of barbarism over civilization."

Prevost Para dol wrote on 9th November, 1857, in the Journal Des Debats: "England is our ally. We must not, therefore, profit by her difficulties at the risk of breaking the alliance."

The legitimist Catholic press had no sympathy for the Indians, but saw in 1857 revolt a blow against Protestant England.

The French democrats denounced with more fervor than the moderate or reactionary papers the crimes of the British before the revolt and during its suppression.

Revue de Paris dated 3rd October, 1857 observed: "It is confirmed that the religious question was no more than a pretext. The real cause is general resurgence of nationalism."

Journal des Debats wrote, "The question is not to find out whether all Indians are more or less civilized, more or less united, but to establish whether the last insurrection had been provoked by the excesses of the agents of the company or whether this revolt is truly national."

Criticizing Le Siede which was affirming that after the departure of the English, the Indians would start fighting each other, L' Estaffette retorted: "It is the business of the Indians. In any case, it is surprising that a democratic journal should want the virtues of foreign domination."

But the letters from readers demanded much more. One reader wrote, "Intervene in favour of the Indians, launch all our squadrons on the seas, join our efforts with those of Russia, make an appeal to all the people of Asia, arm them, send them against British India, chase out the oppressors, re-establish the empire of the great Mughal—such is the only policy truly worthy of the glorious traditions of France."

Another person saluted the freedom movement of Asia: "Who knows whether all the people of India will not rise to chase out the English. If these eventualities are reached, France would have a great role to play on the banks of Ganges, in making herself the protector of a vast confecteralia of Indian nations."

L' Estaffette, wrote on 11th September, 1857, "We have said so before and we repeat: Our sympathies are with Indians because love of mother land, of national independence are things sacred for us."

It was in 1857 that the Italian democrats made an effort to seize power. Italian press also shared its opinion on the nature and character of the revolt of 1857. Joseph Massari, wrote in Rivista Contemporanea (Contemporary Review) of Turin in July, 1857, "Confusing races and geography, will imagine that the Indian rebellion is a bid for independence and an indication of the aspiration to form an Indian nation. But those who can think and are familiar with the real state of affairs will not fall into such gross blunder. The sepoy rebellion is purely an act of military sedition, kindled by the religious fanaticism of the Brahmins, the desire for independence and liberty has got nothing to do with it."

It is interesting to note that in the Catholic camp the Indian rising was used as an instrument to polemise against England. The 'Civilita Cattolica (Catholic Polity) the principal organ of the Jesuits, used British repression in India to argue that if it was right for the British to crush by force a national upsurge in a territory under their control, it would be a right for the Italian government to suppress the people under its own rule."

The Italian democratic press openly expressed its sympathy and admiration for the Indians opposing British. Italia del Popolo (People's Italy) of Genoa. In its issue of 8th July, 1857 wrote, "England seems to have no other thought than that of India, so much has she been touched to the quickly rebellion. 'Her system of liberty at home and slavery abroad' led to the loss of her best provinces in America in the last century, and now, let us see, what happens in India. She will probably be able to pacify and quench in blood this first great attempt at emancipation by that unfortunate people. But the blow has been struck, the fire kindled, and in any case, we apprehend, this may not be the end of it. What will become of England without India?"

Later on, in an editorial on 17th August, 1857, journal came out with a severe verdict on England's work in India, "It is said, even according to the testimony of her own statesmen, that England herself makes use of such repressive methods in India of which, out of brazen hypocrisy, she reproached Ferdinand Bourbon in Europe. Through treachery, fraud and violence she occupied the states of the king and the princes who are her friends and allies. She extends loans in order to violate contracts. To occupy unjustly the territory of others, she does not refrain from fomenting cruel enmities between brother and brother, between father and son, between son and mother. In short, she has brought upon her head the curses of 150 million people whose voice, though that of barbarians and non-Christians will ascend to the throne of God to demand vengeance and receive it."

La Ragiene wrote on 5th September, 1857, "India which was once well governed by the Musalmans, is now horribly ruled by Christians."

The first report of the Indian revolt of 1857 reached Russia on 27th June, 1857. Ignatieu wrote: "The uprising in India is not a chance mutiny of several native regiments against the company; it is rather an expression of the desire of the region to free itself from a hateful foreign yoke."

The second opium war was launched by Britain and France against China in 1856-60. Bowring, British Minister to China, had appealed to Canning for help; now it was the turn of the later to ask Elgin for help. While on the way to China, Elgin received on 3rd June, 1857, a dispatch from Canning which gave an account of the widespread rising in India and asked for help. Elgin was impatient to fulfill his mission in China, he had to satisfy Caning's request. Thus was the British expeditionary force to China stopped half-way by the heroic Indian people. Although the Indian people's uprising was cruelly suppressed by the British colonialists, and the second opium war ended in defeat for China, the struggle for national liberation of these two countries continued unabated.

Towards the end of the mutiny, Lord Canning, the Governor General, wrote to Queen Victoria about the rabid and indiscriminate vindictiveness of Europeans in India, "Not one man in ten seems to think that the hangings and shooting of 40,000 or 50,000 men can be otherwise than practicable and right, he reported in amazement, for his own hatred of such violence earned him the nickname of 'clemency' Canning. Queen Victoria agreed with him."

Robert Montgomery, the Lieutenant Governor of the Punjab, wrote to Major Hudson: "All honour to you for catching the king and slaying his sons." William Russell, the correspondent for the Times, noted in his diary how British forces had burned Indian villages with all their inhabitants, in revenge for earlier Indian atrocities. "As a more refined torture, Mohammedans—who abhor the pig-, were even sewn up in pig-skin and daubed with pork lark before they were killed". The Red Fort—An account of the siege of Delhi in 1857, London, 1956.

Mutiny papers preserved in different archives are having valuable information regarding various aspects of the revolt of 1857.

Bahadur Shah issued an order dated 18th April, 1857, banning the music during the days of Muharram. Sufis laid the foundation of *azadari* of Muharram in India during 13th century and made it a part of Indian society and Culture. Mughal Emperors were having a great regard for *ahl-i-bait* (family members) of Prophet Muhammed. Bahadur Shah's order for banning the use of music during the days of Muharram shows his respect to Imam Husain. Bahadur Shah directed the *Kotwal* of Shahjahanabad to sent the copies of this order to all the *thanedars* of Shahjahanabad.

Document dated 20th May, 1857, shows that one *Imambara* was built by Ishrat Ali and the land for the construction of this *imambara* was assigned by Mughal emperor Akbar II. But Hyder Ali, illegally occupied this *imambara*. *Mutawalli* of this *imambara* submitted a representation to Bahadur Shah for the removal of Hyder Ali from his occupation of *imambara*. It reflects the situation of lawlessness that developed in Delhi, after the break of mutiny.

Document dated 21st May, 1857 shows that some women and children were arrested on the suspicion of being Christians but later on it was discovered that they were not Christians. But it is quite amazing that during 19th century it became difficult to make a distinction among Christian, Hindu and Muslim women.

An application dated 27th May, 1857 was submitted by the Hindu and Muslim residents of Dargah of Hazrat Nizamuddin Aulia, *Katra* Iradatmand Khan, Arab Sarai and Nizampur that the Gojars of the area are involved in loot and plunder of the area in the night and it has become difficult for us to sleep at night. It shows that Gojars had taken full advantage of the prevailing situation and instead of assisting Indians they were creating problems for them. Today only the Basti Nizamuddin and Arab Sarai exist while *Katra* Iradatmand and Nizampur have lost existence. Now this area is designated as Nizamuddin East and West. Let us revive the old names of this locality and Delhi government should trace *Katra* Iradatmand and Nizampur wherever it were located during 1857.

A letter dated 10th June, 1857, addressed to some honourable person of Shahjahanabad but his name is not mentioned. Text of the letter is related to a marriage proposal of Asghar Ali, son of Saiyid Zaheer Ali. The person is asking details about the boy and specially his genealogical account and the property he has under his possession. It reflects the priorities in matrimonial alliances during 19th century.

Hafiz Abdur Rehman submitted an application dated 10th July, 1857, to Bahadur Shah saying that due to non-availability of any job in Shahjahanabad, I started selling *kabub* to earn livelihood for my family. Some *Qasais* were arrested for slaughtering a cow. When they were taking these *Qasais* to the *thana,* I was preparing meat for *kababs,* Policemen considering me a *Qasai* also arrested me and put me in jail. He requested Bahadur Shah that he may be released. Bahadur Shah ordered for his release. This application sheds light on three aspects: (*a*) People of Shahjahanabad were facing financial crisis due to non-availability of jobs. And a *Hafiz* of Quran, had to start the work of selling *kababs* to earn his livelihood. (*b*) Order for banning cow slaughter in 1857 was strictly followed in Shahjahanabad and people involved in that were punished. (*c*) It also reflects the inefficiency of the police department during 1857, that an innocent person who was not involved in cow slaughter was also arrested and put in the jail and only after the intervention of Mughal Emperor, Bahadur Shah, Hafiz Abdur Rehman was freed.

Shaikh Ghulam Nabi a resident of Amroha submitted an application dated 12th July, 1857 to Bahadur Shah that he was serving in British army at Banaras but he left the service and wanted to serve him. Similar application dated 19th July, 1857 was also submitted by Ghulam Abbas resident of Muzaffar Nagar and there is a document dated 12th Zilhijja, is having a list of thirty-eight Muslim residents of Amroha, who joined the service of Bahadur Shah. It reflects the involvement of people with Bahadur Shah that they resigned from their positions in British army and joined Mughal army where the payment of salary was not expected.

There is an order of Bahadur Shah dated 4th August, 1857, in which Emperor had directed the officials of *Thana* Mehrauli to forbid the peasants from cultivation which they had started under Qutub Minar, as it would harm the monument. Bahadur Shah was so careful about these monuments. But in Independent India a road was taken out after breaking the wall of the Fort of Rai Pithora just at a distance of 20 meters from *Quwwatul Islam Masjid* on which buses are plying. Though it is against the law passed by Parliament but who cares for it.

Bahadur Shah issued a circular dated 27th July, 1857 that he is addressed by people as *Hazrat Jahan Panaḥ* but I have decided not to use this title and in future people should address me *Gharib Parwar Salamat*. It shows the drift from the Mughal theory of kingship followed by Mughal Emperors.

Bahadur Shah issued an order dated 29th July, 1857 for banning the sacrifice of cow. He directed the *Kotwal* and the *thanedars* of Shahjahanabad that on the occasion of *Id-al-Azha* no Muslim should be allowed the sacrifice of cow. Just to take care of the sentiments of Hindus, Bahadur Shah must have issued this order.

There is a letter of Raja Nahar Singh of Ballabgharh dated 31st July, 1857, addressed to Bahadur Shah saying that he had built one *Jama Masjid* in Ballabhgarh and one mosque inside the fort for Muslims. He is fully faithful to the Emperor. Some people were misguiding Bahadur Shah that he is supporting British but it all becomes un-true because Nahar Singh fought against British and was hanged by them in Chandni Chowk. Bahadur Shah was of the view that the *Nawab* of Jhajjar will support him but when time came he refused to provide any support to the Emperor but we find that *Nawab* of Jhajjar was also killed by the British.

Bahadur Shah wrote a letter to *Nawab* of Jhajjar saying that he was fed up with the developments taking place in Delhi. "You provide me some camels and some soldiers to accompany me. First of all, I shall go to the *dargah* of Qutubuddin Bakhtiyar Kaki and from there to Mecca and shall spend the rest of my life there." This letter was found by some British army officer inside the palace of the Red Fort. Army officer wrote on the back side of the letter that "We were not aware of this plan of the king."

Letter dated 30th August, 1857, is addressed to the Emperor saying that we are facing starvation and nobody is helping us because we see that most of the people of Delhi are supporting British.

There is order of the British dated 26th July, 1857 in which an inquiry is being made that whether the fort of Jahangirabad has been completely demolished or not. In reply it is said that due to heavy rains it is difficult to take up the work.

We also get information relating to towns like Aligarh, Amroha etc. in U.P. State Archives. On 4th July, 1857 a meeting was held in the *Kotwali* of Aligarh to discuss the issue of 1857, in which Lala Chhote Lal, Nand Kishor, Jani Aga Shankar, Lala Tulsi Prasad, Hakim Tafazzul Husain, Shaikh Ziauddin and Khwaja Najaf Ali were appointed as Panch. In the Friday prayer, Abdul Jalil, delivered a *Khutba* to declare *jihad* against the British. Nasimullah recruited soldiers from Akbarabad, Bhikanpur, Dataoli, Atrauli and Chandpur. Maulvi Nasimullah was killed while fighting against British. On 19th October, 1857, Aligarh was re-conquered by the British forces. Not only the participants were hanged by the British but their house located in Mohalla Bani Israelan and Chah Garmaya were razed to the ground.

One opinion developed that Indian unrest between 1857 and 1859 was a fruit of the conspiracy of the Muslims only or as exclusively a Muslim revolt. In a large part of the North Western provinces, in the districts where Muslims are numerous and the influence of the Mughal Emperor was strongly felt, the revolt took a Muslim colour and assumed to some extent the character of *jihad* against infidels. But mutiny did not, however, find favour with the entire Muslim community. A section of Muslims from diverse parts of the country were also reported to have openly sympathized with British government. Muslims of Calcutta reposed their faith in the policy of British government. Maulavi Imdad Ali passed a resolution, expressing their loyalty to British government and promising their entire support to the suppression of the mutiny. The attitude of the Nizam of Hyderabad Nawab of Bhopal, Nawab of Tonk and Nawab of Rampur towards British government was quite friendly. Statement made by Bahadur Shah, in the court in self-defence indicates that he was a prisoner in the hands of the mutineers and that he had no genuine sympathy with them. His letter addressed to Nawab of Jhajjar, clearly shows that he wanted to migrate from Delhi to Mecca. Personal physician of Bahadur Shah, Hakim Ahsanullah Khan was having links with British. It is proved from the letters of Col. Keith Young. He was one of the trusted advisers of Bahadur Shah. When Hakim Ahsanullah's entry into the Red Fort was banned so Bahadur Shah protested against this move. But sepoy mutiny thrived on the disaffection of both the Hindus and Muslims. Majority of the revolted sepoys were supplied by the Hindus but most of the leaders came from among Muslims. Muslim *ulema* passed *fatwa* of *jihad* against *Firangis* and delivered sermons on Fridays to arouse feelings of Muslims against British government. That is why, we find the Muslims were punished very badly because British thought that basically Muslims played a dynamic role in arousing the feelings against them with their *fatwas* and Friday sermons. Maulana Saeed Ahmed Mujaddidi declared *jihad* against British government from Jama Mosque of Delhi. *Ulema* from Allahabad, Muradabad and Aligarh etc., declared *jihad* against British government from their respective *Jama Mosques* of those well established old towns. Sir Saiyid Ahmed Khan was observing all these developments and he was forced to write—*Tarikh-i-Sarkashi-i-Bijnor* and *Asbab-i-Baghawat-i-Hind*, to show that only Muslims were not responsible for this revolt.

The revolt of 1857 was no sudden occurrence. For nearly a century there had been fierce popular resistance to British domination all over India. From 1757 to 1856 there were many rebellions against British authority. Not only then but even in 1930 S.M. Edwards wrote a book—The Mughal rule in India, he opines, "The alliance of Mewar and Marwar against Aurangzeb as an indicator of a national uprising by the Rajput clans in defence of their country and religion." To promote this view Robert Hallissy quoted this opinion in his book entitled—The Rajput rebellion against Aurangzeb (1977). But they call 1857 as revolt, mutiny etc., and not a national uprising or an alliance of Hindus and Muslims against British in defence of their country and religion. How they apply different parameters for the same problem? No doubt British became successful in suppressing this revolt, but it left the "Echo of Freedom", which later on converted into a 'National Movement' under the leadership of Mahatma Gandhi. William Dalrymple sums up, "The same year that Ghalib died in Delhi, 1869, there was born in Porbandar in Gujarat a boy called Mohandas Karamchand Gandhi. It would be with the political movements headed by Gandhi, rather than those represented by Zafar, or in deed by Lord Canning, that the future of India would lie." But even at the fag end of the story, British instead of handing over a united India to Indians but became successful in the partition of the country.

My grandfather Ustad Qamar Jalalvi who migrated to Pakistan in 1947 had said referring nostalgically to the home he had left behind.

نہ کرتا رہا چاہے صیاد لیکن
تسلی تو تھی باغ میں آشیاں ہے

Even if the tyrant would not have freed us, at least we were content that our house is in the garden.

2

Calendar of 150 Mutiny Papers

1
National Archives of India
Document No. B-139, F. 1
Dated 16th April, 1857

Yad Dasht (Recorded Statement)

Rs. 400 half of which is Rs. 200 is taken on loan from Lala Shiv Raj through Muzaffarud Daula. When he will receive his salary he will return the money.

****

2
National Archives of India
Document No. 130-185
Dated 18th April, 1857

General Taley Yar Khan visited the *Kotwali* and directed that an order should be issued to all the *Thanedars* of the city that during the month of *Muharram* prohibit the playing of music. Send this order to all to follow the direction.

Order is signed by Sad Bakhsh Khan, *Naib Kotwal* and Bunyad Singh, *Naib Kotwal*, dated 18th April, 1857. Bears the seals and the signatures of the following persons:

1. Sajdia Singh, *Thanedar*, Dariba; 2. Badal Khan, *Thanedar*, Rajghat; 3. Muhammed Nizamuddin, *Thanedar*, Faiz Bazar; 4. Muhammed Mirza, *Kotwal* of the city; 5. Muhammed Razaullah

Khan, *Thanedar*, Turkman; 6. Mir Bakhsh, *Thanedar* Chandni Chowk; 7. Ali Jan, *Thanedar*, Badarpur; 8. Ghulam Husain, *Thanedar* (Not readable); 9. Mir Amanat Ali Khan, *Thanedar*, Goralabad; 10. Muhammed Ikramullah Khan, *Thanedar*, Kashmiri *Darwaza*; 11. Muhammed Amir Ali, *Thanedar*, Nigambod.

****

3
National Archives of India
Document No. 6
Dated 29th Ramazan, 21 Julus, Dated 18th April, 1857

Document dated 14th April, 1857 bearing seal of Mir Muhamed Sultan Zahiruddin *Sipah Salar* 1273.

Hukm Nama (Order) *Hawaldar* Major Moosisus Daula Mirza Fazil Beg Bahadur is directed to provide protection to Bhawani Debi, his house and all his property.

****

4
National Archives of India
Document No. B-193, F. 1,
Dated 16th May, 1857

Akhbar-i-Durhi-i-Khassa-i-Darbar-i-Mualla dated Ist *Ramazan* 21 Julus/16th May, 1857.

Reporting that forty-nine Britishers were arrested and army was called in to kill all of them.

Abstract from the court diary regarding slaughter of European prisoners.

****

5
National Archives of India,
Document No. 73, F. 1
Dated 20th May, 1857

Addressed to the Emperor,

Relating to *Imam Bara* located in *Kucha* Bulaqi Begum belonged to Husaini Begum wife of Sadiq Ali. Land for the construction of this *Imambara* was assigned by Muhammed Akbar Shah Badshah II in his 6th regnal year to Ishrat Ali Khan. It was constructed under the supervision of Saiyid Abdur Rahim Shah. Then Anjuman Nisa appointed Saiyid Abdur Rahim Shah as the *mutawalli* of the *Imambara*. *Majalis* of *Muharram* were organized in this *Imambara* upto 1845 A.D. On the day when Abdur Rahim Shah died, so Hyder Ali alongwith other royal soldiers occupied the soldiers occupied the *Imambara*. Then on 26th January, 1846, Hyder Ali alongwith other soldiers were expelled from the *Imambara* on Court's orders. This land of the *Imambara* is a *waqf* property and can't be divided among the descendents.

1. It is quite surprising at Mirza Sangin Beg, Sir Saiyid and Bashiruddin Ahmed has not mentioned about this *Imambara* in Kucha Bulaqi Begum.
2. Ishrat Ali Khan had built one *Majlis Khana* in the campus of *Dargah-i-Shah-i-Mardan* during the reign of Mughal emperor, Muhammed Akbar Shah II. It bears his inscription.

****

6
National Archives of India,
Document No. 73, F. 1
Dated 20th May, 1857

Representation submitted by Haider Husain that Mir Azizuddin servant of Hyder Husain resident of *Qila-i-Mubarak* that the *Imambara* was built by *Nawab* Ishrat Ali Khan, *Khwaja Sara* of the Emperor. For a period of fifty years he had given it to his sister

Anjumanun Nisa and her husband Abdur Rahim. Since they were issueless, the possession of this *Imambara* was passed on to their adopted son Sadiq Ali. Then Sadiq Ali's son Sarfaraz Ali became the *Mutawalli* of this *Imambara*. When he was suffering from some mental problem, Hyder Husain was appointed as its *mutawalli*. Sarfaraz Ali got married to the sister of Sahab-i-Alam Bahadur. Now Sahab-i-Alam Bahadur and the mother of Sarfaraz Ali are living in that *Imambara*. It is ordered that Bhao Singh should go to Kucha Muhammadi Begum and ask Sahab-i-Alam Mirza Raja Bakht Bahadur to vacate it. But he refused to vacate the *Imambara*.

Representation was submitted by Nooruddin, Khwaja Ghulam Ali, Muhammed Bakhsh *Maimar*, Saiyid Hyder Husain. Report of action taken submitted by Bhao Singh.

1. It seems that Mirza Jahangir had converted that *Imambara* located in *Kucha* Bulaqi Begum into his house built by Ishrat Ali Khan. It is ordered that Mirza should vacate that *Imambara* Mirza Sangin Beg does not mention about this *Imambara* but he mentioned about *Feel Khana* of Mirza Jahangir in the same locality, p. 39.

****

7
National Archives of India
Document No. B-109, F. 1
Dated 21st May, 1857

Addressed to the Emperor

As per your order Amir Begum and Badshah Begum along with their children were arrested because they were identified as Christians and were kept in the *Kotwali*. But some people submitted that they are Muslims. We can free them. We are waiting for your orders.

Qazi Faizullah, *Kotwal* of the city of Dehli

Dated 26th *Ramazanul Mubarak*, 1273 A.H.

Bearing seal of Abul Muzaffar Sirajuddin, Muhammed Bahadur Shah Badshah Ghazi.

****

8
National Archives of India
Document No. B-100, F. 12
Dated 25th May, 1857

Bearing seal of—Sultan Mirza Muhammed Khizr Bahadur seal of the office of colonal, 1273.

Thanedars and *Kotwals* of the city should know that men named Khuda Bakhsh second, and Agha Mirza and Abdullah were arrested because they were identified as Christians. In the course of enquiry it was established that they are not, so it is ordered that they should be freed.

Recorded on Ist *Shawwal*, 1273.

****

9
National Archives of India
Document No. B-100, F. 11, 12
Dated 25th May, 1856

Bearing seal of Colonal Sultan Mirza Muhammed Khizr Bahadur 1273.

It is to inform the *Thanedars* and *Kotwals* of the city that Mrs. Muhammadi Khanam, Waziran, Sakina Khanam, Munni, Noorbi, Abran, Rahimi, Bakhshi Khanam, Husaini Khanam alongwith children Husain Mirza son of Muhammadi Khanam, Mustafa Beg son of Fizza Khanam, Karim Bakhsh son of Rahiman, Alijan, son of Munni, Bahadur second son of Munni, Ali Bakhsh son of Munni, Qadir Mohsin, son of Munni, Ghulam Rehman son of Waziran, Peer Bakhsh son of Rahiman, they were 18 in total, who were considered as Christians and were arrested. After getting the proof that they are Muslims, it is being ordered that they should be released. It is ordered that immediate action should be taken.

Recorded on Ist *Shawwal*, 1273/25th May, 1856.

****

10
National Archives of India
Document No. B-68, F. 5
Dated 27th May, 1857

We the Muslim and the Hindu residents of the *Dargah* of Hazrat Nizamuddin Aulia, state that since the officials of *Thana* Badarpur have been posted at Arab Sarai, we are living in peace.

Now the residents of *Katra*, Arab Sarai and the *Dargah* of Hazrat Nizamuddin Aulia can sleep at night. Loot and plunder of the area is stopped completely. The *Thanedar* has taken the *muchelkas* (bonds) of the *Gujars* of the area. We have recorded this *mehzar* (Decree) so that it can be useful at any moment of the time.

Dated 3rd *Shawwal*, 21 Julus 27th May, 1857. Signatories with their seals.

1. Mir Khurshed Ali, resident of the *Dargah*.
2. Singh Ram *Numberdar*, resident of Katra Iradatmand.
3. Tika Ram, resident of Katra Iradatmand.
4. Thakurji, *zamindar*, resident of Katra Iradatmand.
5. Saiyid Qamaruddin, resident of the *Dargah*.
6. Saiyid Sharfuddin, resident of the *Dargah*.
7. Saiyid Zahorul Hasan, resident of the *Dargah*.
8. Saiyid Badiuddin, resident of the *Dargah*.
9. Mir Ali, resident of the *Dargah*.
10. Gorimal *Zamindar*, Nizampur.
11. Gulab Singh, resident of the *Dargah*.
12. Bhagwandas, resident of the *Dargah*.
13. Jagannath, resident of the *Dargah*.
14. Ram Prasad Brahman, resident of the Arab Sarai.

****

11
National Archives of India
Document No. B-110, F. 171
Dated 6th June, 1857

Addressed to *Kotwal* of the city that Mohabbat Ali got wounded.

Addressed to *Thanedar*.
Dated 13th *Shawwal,* 21 regnal year.
Seal is not readable.

****

12
National Archives of India
Document No. B-192, F. 2
Dated 10th June, 1857

Letter addressed to some elderly honourable person.

Received your letter alongwith the letter of Khadim Husain. I agree with your decision but as far as the maternal grandfather of the person concerned, he was a Saiyid. But I have no knowledge whether the boy is a Saiyid, Mughal or a Pathan. In the end of his name Khan is written but before his name Saiyid, Mir or Mirza is not mentioned. So we do not know whether he is a Saiyid or simply a Muslim. From the side of his mother he has a noble lineage. Whether he lives with his brothers or not? What is his age? He lives in which *Mohalla,* is also not known. He owns a *haveli* or lives in a rented house. Whether he has acquired some education or not, He is having some property in his possession like houses and shops or not. Whether he is having fair colour or wheatish? He is having beard or not. I need answers to all these questions. For me everything is acceptable but I want to know something about him like, is he an educated person? What about his religion that he should not be a follower of other sect? I do not mean that he should be a very handsome person but I want that atleast his personality should be acceptable. When I shall answer to all these quarries, only then shall we be able to decide the matter and can perform the ceremony of engagement.

With regards.

Names of addressee and addressed person are not mentioned. During the second half of 19th century people were very much conscious about their genealogical background. It shows that among Muslims inter sect marriages were not liked.

****

13
National Archives of India
Document No. B-192, F. 1/4
Dated 10th June, 1857

Addressed to some honourable person

After regards I state that I received your letter through Rahim Bakhsh. Name of the person you have mentioned belongs to a low caste. His ancestors were basically barber by caste but during the reign of Shah Alam, one of them was appointed as *darogha*. You can see that one of his sister is married to Musahibud Daula's brother Anisud Daula and the other sister slipped with one of his friend. His elder brother got married with the daughter of Mian Kanjan who is the brother in law of Sahab Ram. Those who are having such background you can imagine about their genealogy. In future when you appoint someone, try to verify about them. Mirza Sadiq is my friend and knows the people of Delhi very well and is aware of their genealogical records. If some intiative is taken by Bakhshi ji in this case, you please ask Mir Ashoor Ali to inform me. Please accept my regards.

Some names appeared in his letter but this letter was written by whom or to whom his address is not known. It reflects the position of society during the second half of 19th century.

****

14
National Archives of India
Document No. B-192, F. 03
Dated 10th June, 1857

Letter addressed to Mohib Ali Khan

Relating to the inquiry about the genealogy of Mir Ashoor Ali maternal nephew of Mir Kabir Ali. He is the resident of *mauza* Faridpur which is at a distance of one *Karoh* (Two kilometers) from here. People of Faridpur endorsed that his genealogy is perfect and he is a perfect Saiyid. These Saiyids have been living there for a period of around six hundred sixty years. This *mauza* is inhabited by Saiyids only. They are basically the part of *Sadat-i-Bareha*. Some Saiyids live in Pindoli. The ancestors of these Saiyids were same. They are perfectly alright as far as their genealogy is concerned.

Submitted by Asghar Ali, son of Saiyid Zahir Ali. Bearing seals of—Saiyid Mehfooz Ali, Saiyid Asad Ali, Imdad Ali, Ali Husain, Mir Sajid Ali.

Bears five seals but not readable.

Bears endorsement of Saiyid Ashoor Ali, teacher, Madrasa-i-Lucknow.

Bears seal of Saiyid Nisar Husain Husaini.

****

15
National Archives of India
Document No. B-192, F. 1
Dated 10th June, 1857

Addressed to some elderly person

Wali Husain writes about the illness of the person concerned that he prays for his recovery through the blessings of the patient of Karbala, Ali Ibnul Husain *Alehis Salam*. Letter is related to some marriage proposal through Mir Abdullah. He is anxious to know his genealogical records. What he is doing? Even if he earns four *Paisas*. He also wants to visit Lahore in this connection but conveyance is not available. Writes that Mir Ashoor Ali is well.

Letter sent through the custodianship of *Hazrat Imam Zamin Alehis Salam*.

Hakim Husain Ali Khan
Dated 10th *Shawwal*, 10th June, 1857.

****

16
National Archives of India
Document No. B-60, F. 64
Dated 18th June, 1857

Roznamcha of Chandni Chowk, in the area of *Kotwali*. Persons serving in the artillery. Hafiz Aminuddin, *Thanedar*, Mir Shamsher Ali, *Jamadar*, Muhammed Khan, Barq Andaz, Raziuddin, *Barq Andaz*, Hyder Ali, *Barq Andaz*, Sub Khan, *Barq Andaz*; Ghulam Husain, Abdur Rahim, Shaikh Sarai, Rahim Jat, *Barq Andaz*.

Timings of their duties are mentioned.

****

17
National Archives of India
Document No. B-111, F. 20
Dated 3rd July, 1857

Kotwal Sahab, the most affectionate, God may increase your status.

From Faizullah, *Subehdar*, with Salam and respects. Regarding the repair of Lahori Gate. Due to some fault it can't be used. Nusrat Khan did not send the carpenters to repair it. It is the order of the king that Lahori Gate should be opened from tomorrow morning.

On second page estimate was submitted *Nails, Etak, Labour.*
Dated 13th *Ziqad*.

****

18
National Archives of India
Document No. B-111 b, F. 20
Dated 3rd July, 1857

Bearing seal of Muhammed Khan *Sipah Salar-i-Afwaj* 1253.

Kotwal of the city of Dehli,

We are sending the carpenter employed by the state.
Dated 10th *Ziqad*, 73.

****

19
National Archives of India
Document No. B-199, F. 121
Dated 8th July, 1857

Letter addressed to Mirza Zahiruddin, complaining about the position of the treasury and low income. Due to paucity of resources we are not in a position to pay salaries of the persons serving. We are trying to take one lac twenty thousand rupees on loan.

Dated 15the *Ziqad* 21 *Julus*. 8th July, 1857.

****

20
National Archives of India
Document No. B-101, F. 132
Dated 10th July, 1857

Application of Hafiz Abdur Rehman addressed to Mughal Emperor saying that he used to sell meat but he is not a *Qasai* (butcher) by caste. Due to some problem all the professions are closed in Shahjahanabad. Due to this problem I was not in a position to earn for my meal. I have started selling *Kababs*. Yesterday, some butchers were arrested by army men for killing cows. When they were passing through my shop, I was preparing meat for making *kababs*, they thought that I am also a butcher so they also arrested me and put me in jail alongwith other *Qasais*. Your people can enquire about it from my neighbours in the *mohalla* that I am not a *Qasai*. I humbly request you to order for my release from the jail. Vide order No. 483, it was ordered that applicant be released.

Order was issued that since applicant is not a *Qasai,* so issue a *parwana* to *Kotwal* of the city that the applicant be sent in the office to record his statement. You also write that who are the people under arrest, write their names and addresses, dated 17th *Ziqad,* 21 *Julus*. (10th July, 1857). This order was received in the office on 22 *Ziqad,* 21 *Julus* (16th July, 1857).

****

21
National Archives of India
Document No. B-99, F. 1
Dated 12th July, 1857

Second page
Petition from Ghulam Nabi, a *sawar* of the 13th Inrq on leave a resident of Amroha.

Signature

Bismillah Hirrehman Nir Rahim,

Hazrat Parwar Salamat Hazrat Zille Subhani Khalifatur Rehmani Khuld Allaho Mulkaho.

Janab Ali, *Khanazad* has surrendered. I have taken leave and came from Adilpur, near Banaras. I stayed for two or three days at my residence in Amroha and now I am here at your service. I am the only person of my regiment who has joined you. I am submitting it for your information.

Applicant
Fidvi, Khanazad Shaikh Ghulam Nabi, *Sawar.*

****

22
National Archives of India
Document No. B-71, F. 119
Dated 18th July, 1857

Receipt of Rs. 5/- from Amir Khan son of Noor Khan.

Dated 25 *Zilhij*, 1273.
Obediently, Mirza Lal
Bearing seal (Not readable)

****

23
National Archives of India
Document No. B-139, F. 8
Dated 19th July, 1857

Page 2
Ghulam Abbas
Dafadar
4th In: fan Ist troop

To

The King
Asking for some high rank—
Reply that
Mirza Mughal will see to it.

Addressed to the Emperor,

Ghulam Abbas, a resident of Muzaffarnagar, is stating that he was serving as *Sawar* in Regiment IV in the British army. I have resigned and reached here on 29th *Shawwal*/12th June, 1857 to join your service because my ancestors had also served the Mughal Emperors. Now I am waiting when my prayer will be fulfilled.

It shows the dedication and devotion of people towards Bahadur Shah, the Mughal Emperor that they were resigning from their permanent positions when they knew the total uncertainty of the Mughal Empire. Ghulam Abbas was right that his ancestors had served the Mughal Emperors. Aurangzeb writes in his *Ahkam*, "Send to both the brothers (Syed Abdullah and Saiyid Husain Ali) with a mace—bearer, two robes of honour from the royal wardrobe, with two daggers set with plain-work jasper and having pearl straps. The Prime Minister should write a "Letter By Order" full of praise and send it to them. True, love for the high-ranked Saiyids is a part of our faith." But at the same time, Aurangzeb holds opinion, "So relax the reins to the Saiyids of Bareha is to bring on the final ruin." In his last will Aurangzeb directs his sons, "You should treat the Saiyids of Bareha, who are worthy of blessing, according to the Quranic verse," Give unto the near relations (of the Prophet) their dues, and never go slack in honouring and favouring them. In as much as, according to the blessed verse, "I say I do not ask of you any recompense for it except love to my kinsmen, (Quran) love for this family is the wages of Muhammed's Prophetship.

Ahkam-i-Alamgiri. Calcutta, 1988. pp. 61,62.

****

24
National Archives of India
Document No.##,
Dated 21st July, 1857

Kotwal of the city asked all the *Thanedars* that they should prepare a list of Muslims and direct them not to sacrifice cow secretly or openly. They should also take bonds from them to follow these orders. Letters were issued to all the *Thanedars*.

8th *Zilhijja*, 21st July, 1857.

25
National Archives of India, Document No. 38, Collection No. 43, Dated 12th July, 1857 Ist *Zilhijja*, 21 Julus

The King (Bahadur Shah II) to the people of Rohtak.
Commands them to keep peace and order.

****

Order for the Pamphlet

It is notified to the people of Rohtak that I have directed *ahdis* not to torture the people. In near future army will take up the administration and everything will be in order. Now it is ordered that whosoever is found doing injustice or torturing people will be given exemplary punishment. It is your duty to notify this order so that all people should know our intention.

Recorded on Ist *Zilhij*, 21 *Julus*.

****

26
National Archives of India
Document No. B-115, F. 50
12th *Zilhijja*, Year is not Mentioned

Yaddasht

List of the soldiers from Amroha enlisted themselves is Shahjahanabad in the army of the Mughal Emperor:

1. Ali Dad Khan
2. Ali Bakhsh
3. Muhammed Husain
4. Dayam Ali
5. Ilahi Bakhsh
6. Osal Khan
7. Husain Bakhsh
8. Muhammed Bakhsh
9. Mehrban Ali
10. Najaf Ali
11. Bunyad Ali
12. Ilahi Bakhsh II
13. Najeebullah
14. Muneer Ali
15. Karim Bakhsh
16. Muneer Khan
17. Karim Bakhsh II
18. Azeemullah
19. Daud Khan
20. Shaikh Abdu
21. Ghulam Ali
22. Shahab Khan
23. Khuda Bakhsh
24. Mohibullah Khan
25. Peer Muhammed
26. Shujaat Khan
27. Mir Tipu
28. Ali Bakhsh
29. Ali Husain
30. Zahoor Ali
31. Muhammed Khan II
32. Karim Khan
33. Fazle Husain
34. Muhammed Khan
35. Munnu Khan
36. Naeemullah
37. Peer Bakhsh
38. Karim Khan II

People of Amroha had also served the Mughal government and *Qasba* of Amroha was a part of *Suba* Shahjahanabad. Some persons of Amroha also resisted the British government at Amroha itself. Once the revolt was over they were hanged and their houses were demolished and on that piece of land police post was constructed. Thirty-eight persons from Amroha were serving in the Mughal army. It is quite surprising that they were all Muslims and no Hindu from Amroha joined the army of Bahadur Shah. If we just see the list of the army men and others who revolted against British Raj in Amroha, the percentage of Muslims was higher than the Hindus, while Hindus were in majority and Muslims were in minority. That is why, British government also saw this revolt specially designed by Muslims and mostly they were punished very badly.

****

27
National Archives of India
Document No. B-120, F. 137
Dated 25th July, 1857

Seal of *Thanedar* Faiz Bazar
Khas Darul Khilafa Shahjahanabad 21 regnal year.
Addressed to Saif Ali Karrar Khan and others.

Last night servant of Ghulam Mohiuddin Husain Khan abducted Mrs. Dilpasandgir Imami. Her description—medium height, heavy body, black eye brows. Rings in the ears, black colour, age—

Signatures of

Mirza Muhammed Imami, Bhojla Pahari
Bears seal of *Thana* Bhojla Pahari
Khas Darul Khilafa Shahjahanabad 21 regnal year.

Muhammed Razaullah Khan
Thanedar of Turkman
Seal (Not readable)

4th *Ziqad* 21 regnal year. Received in the evening. Signature of Muhammed Amir Ali *Thanedar* Nigambod. Seal (Not readable)

4th *Zilhijja,* 1273 AH. Sent at 2 p.m. quickly. Signature—Mir Amanat Ali Khan, Goralabad.

Seal (Not readable)

4th *Zilhij,* 4 p.m. Signature Muhammed Ikramullah, *Thanedar,* Kashmiri Gate.

Seal (Not readable)

Signature—Mirza Majeed Khan Beg, *Darogha* Qasim Khan Road. 4th *Zilhijja.*

Bears seal of *Thana* Qasim Khan, *Khas Darul Khilafa* Shah jahanabad 21st regnal year.

****

28
National Archives of India
Document No. B-84, F. 22
Dated 26th July, 1857

Seal of *Kachehri* Salar Bahadur 21 Julus Mukarram Darwaza.

Addressed to officers of Husaini battalion should report the Emperor and consider it obligatory.

Recorded on 4th *Zilhij,* 21 *Moalla.*

****

29
National Archives of India
Document No. B-120, F. 142
Dated 27th July, 1857

Addressed to all the *Thanedars* of the city of Dehli.

When you write letters to the Emperor so there you address the Emperor with the title of *Hazrat Jahan Panah Salamat.* Now you address the Emperor with *Gharib Parwar Salamat.* Do not write *Hazrat Jahan Panah Salamat* in future. Consider it obligatory.

Letter signed by Khuda Bakhsh Khan on behalf of *Kotwal*. Dated 5th *Zilhijja*, 21st regnal year 27th July, 1857.

Note received on 6th Zilhijja, 21st regnal year at 4 p.m. Signed by Muhammed Ikramullah Khan, *Thanedar* of Kashmiri Gate.

Note received on 6th *Zilhijj*, 21st regnal year at 5 p.m. Signed by *Thanedar*, of Nigambod.

Mughals followed Turko-Mongol theory of Kingship and there they adopted high sounding titles. Now Bahadur Shah II did not like such titles to be used for him. It shows his drift from that authority. As we see that Sufis called Moinuddin Chishti of Ajmer as "Gharib Nawaz". Promoter of the poor people. In the sufi spirit Bahadur Shah II directed that he should be addressed as "Gharib Parwar." Care taker of poor people, instead of *Jahan Panah* Shelterer of the world. Sultan Muhammed-bin Tughluq (1325-51) named his residence in Delhi as *Jahan Panah.*

****

30
National Archives of India
Document No . B-122, F. 17
Dated 28th July, 1857

Bearing seal of *Thanedar* of Bhojla Pahari *Khas Darul Khilafa*, Shahjahanbahd 21st *Julus*.

Addressed to the Emperor,

Today in the afternoon, Mendhu, sweeper, working in the *Kocha* (residential unit) of Mir Ashiq reported that a blind beggar, by profession a *Kahar* (Doli carrier) was suffering from fever and dihorria for the last fifteen days. In his possession there were two and quarter rupees. His dead body was given to the people of the *mohalla*. He was cremated according to the Hindu rites. It is submitted for your kind information.

Dated 6 *Zilhij*, 1273 *Hijri-i-Nabavi*.

****

31
National Archives of India
Document No. 1, Bearing seal of Hafiz Aminuddin
Dated 28th July, 1857

Relating to the movement of *barqandaz*.

Submitted by Mir Amanat Ali Khan, *Thanedar* Badarpur, Muhammed Mirza and Muhammed Ahsanullah, *Thanedar* Turkman.

Bearing Seals (Not readable)

****

32
National Archives of India
Document No. B-103, F. 134
Dated 29th July, 1857

Murshid Buqqa-i-Afaq Sahib Alam-o-Alamiyan Salamat.

It is brought to the notice of the Emperor on a quarry about the arrest and confinement of a *kababi,* in the *Kotwali*. Who was the person who arranged his arrest. Information about their names and addresses is required. It is the reality that Abdur Rehman son of Muhammed Panah Shaikh, having the profession of *Kababi,* a resident of Chah Shirin Katra and Ghulam Muhammed Khan and Mimman son of Azeemullah resident of Qadam Sharif, got arrested on the complaint of Debi Prasad Saksena, *Havaldar* Company I, posted at Lahori Gate. After taking a bribe of Rs. 500 from Britishers he rumored that these persons have slaughtered cow so that Hindus and Muslims got divided. Just for this reason they were arrested.

Note submitted on 18 *Ziqad,* 21 *Julus.*

Bearing Seal (Not readable)

It shows that the British had spies in Delhi and they were doing their best for creating division among Hindus and Muslims. They were spending money for this purpose. In 1857, Rs. 500 were of great value. Even today we also come across such cases and people are handsomely paid for such job.

****

33
National Archives of India, Document No. B-111 C, F. 44, Dated 29th July, 1857

Addressed to the Emperor,

I submit in relation to the sacrifice of the cow. Those Muslims who are having cows in their custody they should bring it to the *Kotwali* and those can be kept there upto *Iduz Zuha* so that there should not be any problem. If their possessors does not agree with it because some are having for the purpose of milk, so *Thanedars* should take *muchalka* (bonds) from them.

Saiyid Mubarik Shah Khan, *Kotwal*
Dated 7th *Zilhij,* 21st Julus/29th July, 1857.

****

34
National Archives of India Document No. 8, F. 38 Dated 30th July, 1857

Hazrat Jahan Panah Salamat
(Addressed to Bahadur Shah)

It is submitted, yesterday night Father of Mirza Muhammed Bahadur Bakht died. I request you to arrange to issue an order to the security persons to allow him to bury him in the tomb of Humayun and for the procession of the dead body they provide four elephants and four *Taman*. It was obligatory, so I submitted for your kind approval. I pray to God that the sun of your authority should remain shining forever.

Applicant
Servant—Dilawar Bakht alias Khuda Bakhsh.

****

35
National Archives of India
Undated—but looks to be of before 11th May, 1857

Letter addressed to Mughal Emperor Bahadur Shah II Raja, Nahar Singh of Ballabhgarh is saying that I am your most loyal supporter. I do not have any connection with Britishers. He had quoted Persian verses which reflects his loyalty with Bahadur Shah. Muslims were living in Ballabgarh but there was no mosque. I have constructed one mosque inside the fort of Ballabhgarh and one huge Jama mosque in the town as well as one Idgah on the outskirts of the town. Those who are my enemies they have circulated this news that I have aligned with the Britishers. Since generations I am loyal to you. They have written fake letter to British officer with my forged signatures that I am supporting them. You can enquire about the reality from Maulana Muhammed Shah Nizamuddin.

Applicant—Raja Nahar Singh Bahadur *Vali* (In-charge) of Ballabhgarh.

****

36
National Archives of India
Document No. B-20, F, F. 161
Dated 2nd August, 1857

Bearing seal (Not readable)

Addressed to *Kotwal Sahab* and the *thanedars* of the city of Delhi. After Salam, I submit that around 3 p.m., Prem Sukh, *Hajjam* (barber) resident of mohalla Bhar Kharli, came to *thana* and stated that "Mrs. Kalali my wife since yesterday evening due to misguiding of Chanda Khalasi, resident of above said *mohalla*, alongwith following items left the house. I am recording her *hulia* (descript) in the following lines. I request for her search, I am submitting request to all officials to enquire about her where about through sweepers and *chaukidars*. Whenever you get hold of her, please send her to me."

That is all—11 *Zilhijja*, 21 *Moalla*.

Cash	**Gold**	**Big Tray**	**Hobargan**	**Karan Phool of Silver**
	Two	One	One	One pair

Silver Ring in left hand

Her Description

Mrs. Kalali, *Qaum* (Caste) *Nain*—Age—young—colour—wheatish —open forehead, Low Voice—Joint eye brow, medium body,

Writer—Muhammed Amir Ali—*Thanedar* Nigambod.

Dated 11th *Zilhij* 21 received in the evening and after making copies of it sent to concerned officers.

Obediently—Mohd. Ikramullah *Thanedar*, Kashmiri Gate. Seal.

Obediently—Mir Nazr Ali, *Thanedar* Chandni Chowk—Seal. On 12 *Zilhij*, 1273, received at 6 p.m. and immediately was sent.

Obediently—Mir Amanat Ali Khan, *Thanedar* Guralabad. 11 *Zilhij*, 73 Muhammed Bakht Khan *Thanedar*—Seal, 11 *Zilhij*, received envelop late at night.

Obediently Mirza Ahmad Beg, Moharrir (writer) of *Thanedar*.

Obediently—Mirza Muhammed Khan Beg *Thanedar*—Qasim Road.

****

37
National Archives of India
Dated 3rd August, 1858

13th Cavalry

Dated 3rd August, 1858, order has already been signed according to the order of *Sahab* Assistant Commissioner *Bahadur* and is also included.

****

38
National Archives of India
Document No. B-111 d, F. 17
Dated August, 1857

Addressed to *Kotwal* of the city,

One room of the government situated in the market of Chandni Chowk is under the occupation of Lady Faiz Bakhsh, *Tawaif*. She is living in that room as a tenant. Whenever, the rent collector goes to collect rent from her she does not pay it. An order was issued that Lala Ranjan Lal should prepare the report about the arrears of the rent of the above said accommodation and submit it. Dated 13th Muharram, 21 Julus.

Copy of the note is also sent to *Thanedar* of Chandni Chowk for necessary action.

Official room was given on rent to Ms. Faiz Bakhsh, *Tawaif* but she did not pay the rent of the room. As we come across in other documents that people of Delhi were passing through a crisis and life had become difficult so all these circumstances were responsible for a troubled life. Ms. Faiz Bakhsh must also be facing difficulties and had lost her income and was also not in a position to pay rent of her room.

****

39
National Archives of India
Document No. B-102, F. 40
Dated 4th August, 1857

Bahadur Shah wrote that someone reported that some people had started cultivation just under Qutub Minar in Mehrauli. It is ordered they should be stopped in doing so.

****

40
National Archives of India
Document No. B-139, F. 10
Dated 7th August, 1857

(Second Page)
Issued
The king 11 August, 1857 20 *Zilhij*
To,
Rawal Ranjit Singh, Rais of Jaisulmer.
No signature

Says that the news through him by Girdhari Singh Houlahdar 16th Bombay n.i. of their having slain all the xtians has given him the great delight—and requests that he will slay all the infidels who may come in that direction by the River, in the same way.

20 *Zilhij,* 11 August, 1857, No. 62
Murder—11th August, 1858 No. 3

****

41
National Archives of India
Document No. B-139-9
Dated 7th August, 1857

Rao Bhara, Rais of Katchh Bhuj's activities are informed by Girdhari Singh through Mushirud Daula Mumtazul Mulk Muhammed Bakht Khan, that he killed all the British of his region and cleared his area from the presence of British. Emperor got pleased from this news and said that he should also take the administration of that area in his own control and if other British arrive in his region through sea they should be killed too.

The King
To
Rao hara Rais
of Katchh Bhuj
Same as

16 *Zilhij,* 7th August, 1857, No. 62
Murder—7th August, 1857, No. 2

****

42
National Archives of India
Document No. B-43/50
Dated 9th August, 1857

Shuqqa (Letter) addressed to Raja Nahar Singh,

Our most obedient person Raja Nahar Singh Bahadur should not feel hurt for sending eight *Asharafi* as *nazr* (gift) on the occasion of *Id-al-Azha*. I have accepted your *hazr*. I know that you are faithful to Mughal Empire like your ancestors. I am satisfied with your performance.

Shuqqa dated 18th *Zilhijja,* 21 *Moalla.*
Second Page in English by some Britisher.
Re kind to the Rajah of Bulubgarh.

(Signature)

Dated 9 August, 1857
No. 72.

Dayandan Pandit, *Vakil* of Raja Ballabhgarh was having his *haveli* and *Diwan Khana* near Delhi Gate. In Faiz Bazar near Zinatul Masajid, situated the house of Raja Kanwar Raj Singh of Ballabhgarh.

****

43
National Archives of India
Document No.B-135, F. 167-170
Dated 9-11th August, 1857

Order issued for all officers
I have not cared for me at all. I have done an agreement with

the military that you are just like my sons and daughters. Even our own children take some hard decisions. I have fulfilled all your desires. Whatever you said I did that? But alas! You did not care for me. Now you can see the condition of my health. I am not feeling well. Hakim Ahsanullah Khan takes care of me and my health. He is always conscious of my position. Hakim is a sincere person. Why you did not allow him to come and check my health? I know who is sincere with us and who is not? So many things have been stolen. I know with whose connivance it all happened. I shall punish them. If you do not have any attachment with me so you escort me upto the *Dargah* of Khwaja Sahab, I shall sit and serve the *dargah* for the rest of my life. And if you do not agree with it then I shall leave it and shall go anywhere whenever I like? Who can stop me? If I may not be killed by British, I shall be killed by you. I know whatever atrocities are inflicted on my subjects? It is not on them but it is on me. If you can't govern and save them you give me an answer. I shall eat the diamond and shall sleep for ever. When my belongings were looted even the box having seals were also stolen.

Dated 20th *Zilhij*, 21 *Julus* 9th August, 1857.

44
National Archives of India
Document No. B-135, F. 167
Dated 9th & 11th August, 1857

Order

It is the order of the Emperor. We feel happy when our soldiers are happy. My soldiers are just like my own children. I have accepted all their demands but they have nothing to do with me and never care to realize that I am an old person. I know what my own physical condition is. My personal physician, Hakim Ahsanullah Khan is fully aware of my health. You know, what is the value of my decisions?

* * * * * * * * * * *

45
National Archives of India
Document No.B-15, F. 4
Dated 10th August, 1857

My (Emperor's) condition is peculiar. My enemies teach you things against me. Those who had done wrong they will be punished according to *sharia*. If you do not agree with me then you drop me at the *dargah* of *Khwaja Sahab*. I shall serve there as the care taker of the *dargah* and shall live alone there otherwise I shall leave from there myself. Whosoever want can't stop me. If I am not killed by them I shall be killed by you. Whatever atrocities you are doing on people those are not on people but on me. I am really fed up with the present condition. I shall commit suicide by taking diamond. One of my box is also stolen.

****

46
National Archives of India
Document No. B-135, F. 170
Dated 11th August, 1857

Mughal Emperor is again complaining ill treatment of his nobles and other officers. It shows that at this stage even his officers were not listening to him and also creating problems for him as they did not allow Hakim Ahsanullah Khan's personal physician to come inside the fort. At this age Bahadur Shah needed regular check up by a Hakim.

****

47
National Archives of India
Document No. B-60, F. 55
Dated 12th August, 1857

Bearing seal of Isalat Khan.

Animal's house dated 12th August, 1857
List of food items required in the animal's house.

****

48
National Archives of India
Document No. B-139, F. 12
Dated 17th August, 1857

10th *Zilhij*, 17th August, 1857
The King
To,
Ranjit Singh
Rais of Jaisalmer

Saying that Chaman Singh Thakur brother of the deposed Rajah has arrived and requesting him to kill any xtian that may yet remain concealed in his domains—

20 *Zilhij*, No. 63

Ranjit Singh Rais of Jaisalmer submitted that Chaman Singh Thakur brother of Rais of Jaipur, through Mushirud Daula, Mumtazul Mulk, Muhammed Bakht Khan Lord Governor-General wrote to the Emperor that in our area there is no trace of the British. If anyone has concealed himself they should also be killed and you should take the reins of government in your hand.

Dated 20th *Zilhijja*, 21 Julus.

****

49
National Archives of India
Document No. B-130, F. 167
Dated 19th August, 1857

Thanedar Sahab of Sakralahbad,

Regarding the VIIth Risala of Lucknow. Sixteen days have passed so ask him that he should go alongwith Adund Khan.

Dated 29th *Zilhijja*, 1273
Khuda Bakhsh Khan
Naib Kotwal, City of Delhi.

****

50
National Archives of India
Document No. B-15, F. 9
Dated 20th August, 1857

This document contains information relating to army of the king. It is related to towns like Agra, Mathura and Jhansi. Army which came from Jhansi got Rs. 12000/- from Gorgaon. This money was distributed among soldiers. Those who were living in the western part they came here and those living in Haryana they went to their own home towns. Muhammed Azeem is in Bhawani. People of Bareilly also revolted. Khan Bahadur, Rais of Bareilly also helped revolters. They had sent an army on the road coming from Naini Tal so as not to allow any British to come down from there. But we have come to know that Nawab of Rampur is helping the British by sending food etc. Today Hira Singh, Brigadier Major, met *Badshah*. *Badshah* assured him full support and assured to provide him long range guns and also gave him Rs. 2000/- Army of Gawalior is ready. Some *Nawab* had sent an application to Emperor saying that if he was appointed as Officer of army so I shall kill all the British living in Agra fort. Emperor replied that we shall provide all the support to the concerned person.

It shows that people were fed up with the atrocities of British rule and they themselves were offering their services to Bahadur Shah. This was an important aspect of the revolt of 1857.

****

51
National Archives of India
Document No. B-111 d, F. 243
Dated 21st August, 1857

Seal—not readable.

Addressed to Shujaat Nishan Mubarikh Shah Khan, *Kotwal* of the city. It is ordered that you contact the big merchants those who are also residents of Khari Baoli. You take the prices of the following items from them. Shaikh Qutubuddin will contact you alongwith this *parwana*.

Dated 4th *Zilhij*, 21 Julus
Order was followed and action taken
Dated 5th *Zilhij*, 21 Julus

****

52
National Archives of India
Document No. B-111 d, F. 243
Dated 21st August, 1857

Seal—not readable.

Addressed to Mubarak Shah Khan, Kotwal of the city, you are directed to supply following items.

On the second page it is recorded.
Order was followed
5 *Zilhij*, 21 Julus.

****

53
National Archives of India
Document No. 2, Ist *Muharram* 1274
Dated 21st August, 1857

This is submitted that we searched the opium shop but we have to wait till the shop re-opens.

Sent to Mir Muhammed—Ist Muharram, 1274 *Hijri*.

****

54
National Archives of India
Document No. B-74, F. 51
Dated 22nd August, 1857

Record of the expenditure of medicines of the Jarnaili hospital, situated in Darya Ganj, under the supervision of Imam Bakhsh, Doctor, dated 13 *Zilhij*, 1273.

7th Day

Mom	*Parcha*	*Tarpin Oil*
Lemon Sikanjabin	*Arq-i-Gulab*	*Dry Podina*
Small Ilaichi	*Kar*	*Noshadar*
Lakri	*Meda for Pultis*	*Arq-i-Badiyan*
Sana-i-Makki		*Sana-i-Makki*
Chiraita	*Biranjan*	*Roghan-i-Alsi*
Phitkari	*Johk Taza*	*Tohk Basi*
Pukhta Hawai	*Ral*	*San*
Charbi	*Kohl Pai*	

List of Shaikh Imam, Doctor of Hospital Jornaili Recorded on the date.

****

55
National Archives of India
Document, Nos. 104-45

Addressed to *Kotwal*,

I had called Suji Ram and Raghunath Singh. Now Raghunath Singh came and reported that his brother Suji Ram is un-well, so I am sending Raghunath Singh alongwith the peon to escort him to *Kotwali.*

(Un-dated document).

****

56
National Archives of India
Document No. 1
Dated 23rd August, 1857

The king had gone to Telee Wara.

General Order 23rd August, 1857
Officers of the Sikh that 2nd Muharrum
Military
August 23rd, 1857
Nos. 33,34
2034

Hukum Nama addressed to officers of Sikh Paltan. I hope that Sikh soldiers will fight the British. Emperor has praised you very well. On the back of the document it is submitted to Janab-i-Aali, through *parwana* that we visited garrison of Teliwara at 4 p.m.

****

57
National Archives of India
Document No. B-111 d, F. 15
Dated 24th August, 1857

Seal of Colonel Sahab,...office of Kachehri,

Dated 3rd Muharram, 21 *Moalla,* regarding the receipt of letter and its reply to Muhammed Hasan Khan.

Dated 3rd Muharram, 21 Julus.

****

58
National Archives of India
Document No. 70, F. 243
Dated 30th August, 1857

Second Page

From the officer of Brigade of King that they were fed up and wanted to leave the king if he did not pay them. All the people of the city are in league with the English.

****

59
National Archives of India
Document No. B-111 d, F. 109
Dated Ist September, 1857

Murshid Zadeh Afaq Sahab-i-Alam-o-Alamiyhan Dam Iqbalah. Submitting request to you.

As per your order the rain drain channel flow from the house of Mir Jan *Tawaif* (Dancing girl) falling in the house of Mirza Ghiyasuddin Bahadur, is now sealed by the thanedar of Nigambod. I am submitting this *arz dasht* (action taken report) to you kind self. I am also enclosing the report of work done by the *Thanedar.* With great respects. With the grace of God the Sun of the Sultanat should always remain shining.

Submitted by the servant Saiyid Mubarik Shah Khan *Kotwal,* Delhi. Application dated 14th Muharram, 21 *Julus.*

****

60
National Archives of India
Document No. B-111 d, F. 122
15th Muharram 21, Julus, Dated 7th September, 1857

Bearing seal of Khizr Muhammed Khan 1274 AH,

Addressed to the *Kotwal* of the City. It is reported that the *Bagh-*

i-Asad Khan which belongs to Badruddin Ali Khan is being devastated by the miscreants. They are cutting the trees so you visit the place as soon as possible and take action so that the garden can be saved. Take some measures so that in future no one cut trees.

It is quite surprising that Mirza Sangin Beg in his work *Sairul Manazil*, had given a list of *Baghs* (gardens) of Delhi but there is no mention of *Bagh-i-Asad Khan*. It seems that Bagh-i-Asad Khan might have been planted at a later stage.

Dated 7th September, 1857

****

61
National Archives of India
Document No. 15, F. 23
Dated 8th September, 1857

Letter addressed to a person but his name is not mentioned but the letter contains two names, Mansoor Sahab and Mirza Sahab and one by designation of Mufti Sahab. It is stated that people belonging to different categories inhabit the city. Following categories are there: (1) Labourers; (2) Craftsmen; (3) Mahajan and Traders; (4) Rich people and among those are—(*a*) *Jagirdar* and the *Zamindar* and (*b*) Those who are property owners. But due to all these disturbances all are fed up whether they are labourers, craftsmen, traders, *Jagirdars* or owners of properties. Everywhere there is loot and plundering. Now people are waiting for the implementation of administration of British Government. People are totally fed up with the prevailing condition. People are praying day and night that God show them a day when the administration of British Government is established. Because there is no opportunity to talk on this matter otherwise people will declare me as mad. Time has come that the administration of British Government is established. Document is dated 8 Sammat (8th September, 1857).

Note: Since it was highly confidential letter so it is written on a small piece of paper so that it should be delivered secretly. This letter reflects the feelings of a larger section of the people of Delhi that they were fed up with the law and order situation and loot and plunder. When the situation became hopeless, they started praying to God for peace as well as implementation of British administration, so that they remained safe and could work in a peaceful atmosphere.

****

62
National Archives of India
Document No. B-130, F. 248
Dated 12th September, 1857

Addressed to *Thanedar* of Dariba

Court of the Emperor,

It is directed to collect two hundred rupees from Mrs. Mubarikun Nisa Begum, owner of Mubarik Bagh (Garden), [Near the eastern gate of *Dargah-i-Shah-i-Mardan,* there is the tomb and garden of Nawab Mubarak Mahal Begum *Sahiba,* mother of Muhammed Akbar Shah Badshah II, *Ghazi* Mirza Sangin Beg *Sairul Manzil,* p.90, (Delhi, 1982)] resident of Kabuli *Darwaza,* relating to watering charges due for the *Fasl-i-Rabi,* 57. It is directed to collect the same amount from her. If it is delayed they will be answerable for the same.

Khuda Bakhsh Khan, Naib *Kotwal* of City of Dehli.

Near the eastern gate of Dargah-i-Shah-i-Mardan, there is the touch and garden of Nawab Mubarak Mahal, Begum Sahiba, mother of Mughal emperor Akbar II, Mirza Sangin Beg. p. 90

****

63
National Archives of India
Document No. B-111d, F. 173
Dated 13th September, 1857

Seal of *Adalat-i-Faujdari*

Taliqa-i-Khas Qila-i-Mualla

Addressed to Muhammed *Qazi* Faizullah Khan, *Kotwal* of the city. All the Hindus and Muslims are the subjects of the Emperor. Do not allow anyone to fight with each other.

Recorded on 27th *Ramazan*, 21st *Julus*, 13th September, 1857.

Order of the Emperor will be obeyed.

Qazi Faizullah Khan, *Kotwal* of the city.

****

64
National Archives of India
Document No. B-15, F. 19
Dated 13th September, 1857

Battle at Qudsiya *Bagh*,

This document is related to the details of encounter of Indian forces with British army at Qudsiya *Bagh*. They fought throughout the night. It is reported that wounded persons were brought from the field in the *dolis*. Due to this fight Indians were very much disturbed. Indians became successful in capturing three guns of British army. But Talangas were abusing Indians. Some Indians fled away. One commander of Sikh regiment came to our side without having any weapons with him. He talked to some persons of our side and left. It remained unsolved as to why he came and went away. Gojars have informed that three companies of British army are coming from Murad Nagar, and proceeding towards Delhi. Suchara Singh informed that they will come through Alipur. Rao Tula Ram had sent a letter that he has collected three lakh rupees. Send Shabbu Bakhsh to come and collect the money. At Ajmeri Gate Mirza Mughal was holding the charge of the army.

****

65
National Archives of India
Document No. B-111d, F. 137
Dated 13th September, 1857

Bearing seal of the office of Colonel Muhammed Khizr *Sultan*

Bahadur, addressed to *Kotwal* of the city. Hindus and Muslims are free to follow their religion. If anyone is having any problem he can report it to me personally by visiting Sahab-i-Alam Bahadur at Kashmiri Gate.

Dated 23rd *Muharram*, 21 *Moalla*.

****

66
National Archives of India
Document No. 35/2
Dated 4th November, 1857

Nawab Sahab *Mushfiq-o-Mehrban Mazhar-i-Lutf-o-Karam Farmai Mukhlisan Sallamahu Tala.*

Received your letter dated 2nd October, 1857 and came to know about the prevailing situation. I am your old hereditary servant. I am at your service whenever and wherever you want. I offer my life and belongings to you. Recently I have received a document relating to some ordinances in Persian alongwith its translation into English. I am sending it to you alongwith this letter. I am having all the copies of it in my office at Jhajjar. Dated 4th November, 1857.

Bearing seal of Abdur Rehman Khan, Asadud Daula wa *Mumtazul Mulk Hizabr-i-jang Bahadur.*

****

67
Dated 5th November, 1857

Rajasthan State Archives (RSA) Stack No. 1, Pad No. 2–M-06-1 (Parts) Major Head Military Record No. 1, Part 5-3 Mutiny Papers—Regarding protection of Jaipur during 1857, Rajasthan

Dated 5th November, 1857

Rajasthan Sate Archives, Bikaner.

Addressed to Captain William Fredrick. It is reported on 5th November, 1857, that around three hundred people came from

Shaikhawati, a part of Raj Jodhpur. Make necessary arrangement to check them.

Bearing signature in English (not readable)

Reply of the letter—
Precautionary measures have already been taken. We shall be in touch with the *Vakils* of the Raj.
Dated 7th November, 1857.

****

68
Rajasthan State Archives
Document No. 484-2

Report relating to Raja Sawai Chittor to Captain William Fredrik agent of the Raj dated November, 1857. Report of the army cantonment of Airanpur that the revolters belonging to Jodhpur and Shaikhawati reached upto Bakala village. It will be tackled very easily. They are directed to report the matter daily.

****

69
Rajasthan State Archives
Document No. 485-1

Report of Captain William Fredrick, agent of *Raj Sawai* Jaipur, 3rd November, 1857, that Bhopal Singh, administrator of Sawai Ram Garh and Shaikhawati relating to the revolters belonging to the region of Jodhpur.

Bearing signature in English.
Information dated 7th November, 1857
Bakhshi of the army will make the necessary arrangements.
Dated 7th November, 1857.
Dated 5th November, 1857, No. 170.

****

70
Rajasthan State Archives
Document No. 491-1

Report of Captain William Fredrik, Agent of *Raj Sawai* Jaipur, dated 30th October, 1857. It is reported by the *Vakil* of the Tonk Sate that some revolters who fled away from Delhi had taken shelter in the villages of Chittor. It is ordered that search should be made to arrest all those revolters. Arrest the revolters. It will bring honour for the Raj.

Signature in English (not readable)
Dated 3rd November, 1857, No. 1591

Sent the report to the *Ziladar* to check the revolters.

****

71
Rajasthan State Archives
Document No. 494-2

Report of the *Raj Sawai* Chittor addressed to Captain William Fredrik, Agent of the *Raj,* dated November, 1857. We have received a report dated 16th October, 1857 that Abdullah Beg, belonging to artillery of Kota is staying in Hindon. Direct the *Ziledar* of Hindon to arrest him. *Kotwal* and *Ziledar* of Hindon reported that we made a research for Abdullah Khan in the city but failed to get anywhere about of him. Sent an order to make all arrangements to arrest him at any moment of time.

****

72
National Archives of India
Document No. B-100, F. 167, Undated

I son of Abu Bakr, make an agreement that I shall not misbehave with my wife. If I do it then the officer and the relatives of my wife can decide the punishment for the recommendation of *Hakim* (Officer). Now it is acceptable to me and I hope that your Excellency and her relatives will fell satisfied after the submission of this bond by me.

****

73
National Archives of India
Document Nos. 43-62,
Undated

My dear Colonel,

The enclosed note I picked up from the floor of the palace affords some information about the King's intentions.

Bearing seal (not readable)
Undated letter of Bahadur Shah II to *Nawab* of Jhajjar.

Letter is addressed to *Asadud Daula, Mumtazul Mulk,* Muhammed Abdur Rehman Khan *Bahadur Hizabr-i-Jang*. Now I have become too old and have become too weak so I have decided to follow the path of Darwaishi (Sufi Path). I have decided that I should, alongwith the family members of the *Taimuri* dynasty, first of all, go to the *dargah* of Khwaja Qutubuddin Bakhtiyar Kaki and then to *Harmain-i-Sharifain* (Mecca and Madina) and there I shall spend the rest of my life in prayer. Since you are my well wisher, you provide me some persons and horsemen of confidence who will accompany me in this journey. I have lot of belongings with me but it is not possible at the moment to take all that with me. I shall leave all that in my residential portion inside the fort. My servants will look after my belongings in my absence and when I reach there please arrange four/five hundred carts and five or six hundred camels so that those belonging can be transported from Delhi to Mecca as follows:

---

1. On the back of this some British army officer wrote that he found this paper in the palace of Bahadur Shah but they were not

aware of this plan of Bahadur Shah. It appears that Bahadur Shah wrote this letter to *Nawab* of Jhajjar but he could not send it to *The Nawab* and when the revolt of 1857 was suppressed and British army occupied the Red Fort there they must have found this letter of Bahadur Shah II. This is a significant letter because it reflects the disillusionment of Bahadur Shah and why he decided to migrate from Delhi to Mecca and wanted to lead rest of his life as a *sufi*.

****

74
National Archives of India
Document No. B-100, F. 177
Undated

"Letter addressed to Mirza Chhote Sahab",

You told me that you will be there on Wednesday, but I want to say that on that day there is *Urs* of *Hazrat Janab Aali* so it will be difficult to discuss anything. If you come on 18th in the afternoon it will be better.

****

75
National Archives of India
Document No. B-102, F. 103
Undated

Addressed to Hazrat Ghulam Nizamuddin, Saiyid Abdullah, Maulavi Muhammed Salim, Alaud Daula, Saiyid Moinuddin Khan, Saiyid Hasan Askari and Mian Niaz Ahmed should know that a rumour is circulated that the Emperor after forsaking Sunni sect converted to Shii sect just to defame him and to create division among his supporters. Emperor can never think of it. It was basically done by Mirza Haider Shikuh and Mirza Nooruddin. Just because of enemity they had done it to defame the Emperor. It is totally a false information.

---

1. Persons addressed in this letter may be some influential persons of the society. Mirza Hyder Shikuh and Mirza

Nooruddin may be the agents of the British and on their direction they will be doing it to create division among the supporters of Bahadur Shah. If we see the list of the supporters of Bahadur Shah or at other places, people who sacrificed their life fighting against the British were overwhelmingly Sunni Muslims. We come across only few persons belonging to Shii sect. In the *Qasbas* where Saiyids were holding important positions almost all of them supported the Britishers. Though Sunnis like Nawab of Jhajjar and few others also provided support to the British, the number of Shiis supporting the British was higher. In Delhi, Meerut, Muradabad, Aligarh Sunnis were supporting Bahadur Shah. Now there was Shii-Sunni tension also since the second half of 16th century and lot was written on polemics. If at this juncture it was rumoured that Bahadur Shah had accepted Shii faith, automatically he would have lost the support of Sunnis.

2. Mir Askari had built an *Imambara* in *Kucha Natwan*, Chandni Chowk, near the Kothi of Begum Samru, Mirza Sangin Beg: *Sairul Manazil*, Delhi, 1982, p. 36.

****

76
National Archives of India
Document No. B-100, F. 167
Undated

Addressed to Mirza Zaheeruddin,

Informing that the son of late Zaman Shah did not come for two or three days. Today he died. Sent one hundred rupees to his descendents so that they could live peacefully.

****

77
National Archives of India
Document No. B-104/45
Undated

Addressed to the *Kotwal Sahab,*

Raghunath Singh informed that his brother Suji Ram is ill and could not attend to his duty.

****

78
National Archives of India
Document No. B-195, F. 05
Dated 23rd March, 1857

Copy of *Sadiqul Akhbar* No. 12, Published on 23rd March, 1857, Vol. 3, from the Press of Jameeluddin.

Some notorious person has put up a pamphlet on the back wall of Jama Masjid of Delhi. It says that Muslims and Hindus should keep themselves aloof from supporting Christians. In near future I (ruler of Iran) will come and conquer India and shall reward Indians. Name of the author of this pamphlet is recorded as Muhammed Siddiq Khan. Whosoever will arrest this person will get reward from the government. He will be given an exemplary punishment.

****

79
UP, State Archives

F. No. 1, Page 25, Etawah file.

From: The Magistrate of Etawah

To: The Civil Surgeon of Etawah.

Sir,

I have to request the favour of your examining Ally Ahmed Khan, a wounded person sent to the hospital on the 17th Ultimo....This rebel was wounded in Hurchand poor affair.

Order addressed to...Singh, Darogha of Prison, Distt. Etawah, dated 19th April, 1858, Parwana No. 232, Names—Baldev and Ali Ahmed, arrested for revolting and looting. Special Commissioner of Distt. Etawah, ordered on 15th April, 1858 for rigorous punishment for seven years.

****

80
Sir Charts Dulk, Gazeeteer Britain Published 1885, London. p. 723

It is certain that during the revolt of 1857, the British had hung hundreds of Indians who were not aware of any Indian language. They were also not in a position to follow the statements of the witnesses nor could they understand the statements of the victims for their non-involvement in the revolt. I have asked one officer who was posted in the cantonment of Sahardal near Banaras that he must be having the fear of attack of the people of Banaras. In response to this query he said that he wanted it by heart that they should attack them, so that they could get an opportunity to loot the city of Banaras which had not been plundered for two centuries.

It reflects the intention of British officials during 1857. They just project themselves as the champion of justice. If we see their statements, it is very much clear that they were great tyrants.

****

81
UP, State Archives, Letter No. 32

From:

George Copper, Secretary Chief Commissioner of Awadh

To:

G.F. Adminston, Secretary, Government of India, Lucknow dated Ist December, 1857.

Sir, Governor, General Bahadur on 14th September, sanctioned fifty thousand rupees to use this money for helping Hindus of Bareilly to fight against Muslim revolters. I want to inform you that we failed in this attempt and we have to abandon the idea completely.

Yours Obediently,

George Copper, Secretary, Chief Commissioner, *Alam Bagh,* Lucknow

Ist December, 1857.

This is the direct evidence from the official note of George Copper, Secretary, Chief Commissioner of Awadh that he had sanctioned rupees fifty thousand in 1857 for its distribution among the Hindus of Bareilly to encourage them to fight against Muslims but the project failed. It reflects the bad intentions of British officials. It also reflects the example of Hindu-Muslim unity.

****

82
UP, State Archives
Document No. 13, Box No. 1,
Etawah File

My Lord,

I have received a *parwana* dated 8th January, 1859 regarding the arrest of Baldev Singh, revolter on 11th December, 1858. There are no papers with me relating to the case of Baldev Singh. As directed I had sent Baldev Singh to Etawah and whatever was required I have recorded.

Letter dated 9th January, 1859.

****

83
UP, State Archives
Document No. Nil
Dated August, 1857

List of absconding criminals who joined the service of the *Badshah* and revolted, w.e.f. August, 1857.

From Proper Delhi—Roshan Khan, son of Akbar Khan, Pathan, Distt. Mathura. He worked as Barq Andaz Crime—Joining the services of Badshah as follow:

Total number of persons is 1160. Last name in the list is that of Najaf Ali. Majority of names are of Muslims, only few names are of Hindus.

****

84
UP, State Archives
Document No. Nil, *Hukum Nama*
Dated 8th November, 1857

With the exception of those people who were not involved in the killings they can be forgiven. But those who intentionally given shelter to murderers they can't be forgiven. But those who unknowingly got involved will be forgiven in due course of time but they should go and get themselves involved in their own professions. Once there will be peace in the country we shall pay our attention to the development of the country so that country should make progress. We shall construct roads and dig canals for irrigation.

Commissioner Bahadur of Panipat vide government's letter dated 8th November, 1857, acted on Queen's order for forgiving the people. Persons who were forgiven their names are mentioned as below:

Hasan Khan, Peon, Isalat Khan, Har Narain, Abdur Razzaq, Saadullah, Muhammed Husain Khan, Ahmed Ali Khan, Aleemudin, Kallu, Zabardast Khan, Maugli, Sarjan, Harchand, Pat Ram Jat, Roop Ram, Mughaldar Rangar.

****

85
UP, State Archives
Copy No. 91
Dated 25th March, 1861

From Under Secretary Sahab, Government of India addressed to Secretary Sahab Bahadur Bengal. I am writing this *Chitthi* (letter) No. 138, dated 13th running I want to draw your attention to the publication of regnal year of *Sultanat* meaning by *Shahanshah-i-Mughal* or *Badshah* of Delhi creates problem. I am submitting it for your kind attention to forbid the publication of regnal year and in place of that year of Queen in new Jantaris should be published.

Signed by—M.U. Saron, Under Secretary, Government of India. Wagasṭ No. 672, dated 3rd April, 1861. Arrange to inform and instruct the commissioners not to publish the regnal year of the Emperor and to publish the year of *Malika-i-Muazzima.*

On order
H.R. Dabos
Secretary, Government of Punjab.

****

86
National Archives of India
Document No. 43
Dated 31st July, 1857

Addressed to Bahadur Shah,

Some people have conveyed to Bahadur Shah that Nahar Singh, the ruler of Ballabhgarh is not faithful to him and he is in agreement with British. Nahar Singh clarified his position and re-asserted that he can't think of any one except the Emperor.

From: Raja Nahar Singh Bahadur, Wali (Governor) of Bahadurgarh.

In 1679, Gokla Jat revolted against Aurangzeb. These Jats created problem in the region of Mathura and Agra. They even dug out the grave of Akbar, the Mughal Emperor (1556-1605). But in 1857, the Jat Raja Nahar Singh was very much with the Mughal Emperor Bahadur Shah II. He fought against the British and was hanged by the British. While some Muslim Nawabs like *Nawab* of Jhajjar did not support Bahadur Shah and supported the British.

****

87
Khair

Rao Bhopal Singh of Khair was hanged.

****

88
Aligarh

A meeting was held on 4th July, 1857 in the *Kotwali* of Aligarh. Munshi Daya Shankar, Deputy Collector, Thanesar, Lala Chhote Lal, Nand Kishor, Jani *Aga* Shankar, Lala Tulsi Prasad, Munshi Muhammed Daud, Hakim Tafazzul Husain, Shaikh Ziaullah and Khwaja Najaf Ali were appointed as *Panch*. Munshi Muhammed Daud and Munshi Daya Shankar were appointed as *Sarpanch* Munna Lal son of Chunni Lal was appointed. On 6th July, 1857, Dr. Karim Bakhsh, who revolted from 9th British battalion, was appointed as *Kotwal* of the city. On 10th July, the *Sawars* and infantry who revolted in Jhansi cantonment entered in Aligarh alongwith three long range guns. Persons from Pilla Sahibabad, Sindholi, Isanpur and Daud joined service. On Friday, 21st August in the Jama Mosque, Maulvi Abdul Jalil delivered *Khutba* and asked Muslims to declare *jihad* against the British. Maulvi Abdul Jalil died fighting against British. On 29th August, property of Maulvi Nasimullah, Maulvi Abdul Jalil, Niaz Ahmad Khan and Muhammed Yusuf was confiscated. Maulvi Nasimullah recruited his army from Akbarabad, Bhikanpur, Dataoli, Etah, Atrauli and Chandpur. Nasimullah had taken position at Sarai Hakim and Banna Debi. On 19th October, 1857, Maulvi Nasimullah was gunned down by the British army and Aligarh was re-captured by British forces.

****

89
UP, State Archives
No. 1022
Dated 25th June, 1857

On order of Mr. Hensry Devis Dalak Sahab Bahadur, addressed to Parshan Singh, *Thanedar* that Hate Sahab, Commissioner Bahadur, vide letter No. 1022, dated 22nd (June) alongwith the copy of the letter of Secretary of the Government, for the sanction of rupees five thousand for the reward to be given whosoever arrest Maulvi Liyaqat Ali, revolter. You issue a pamphlet of the said contents and get it pasted everywhere for the knowledge of the people. Order dated 25th June, 1858.

On the back of the document it is recorded:

As ordered, I have announced the reward of rupees five thousand to be given to a person who arranges the arrest of Maulvi Liyaqat Ali. I have arranged the display of this pamphlet on roads, *Bazaars* and *Thanas*. I am submitting it for your kind attention. Dated 26th June, 1858.

Slave
Parshan Singh,
Thanedar of all *Thanas*.

****

90
Aligarh Documents
UP, State Archives, File No. 13

List of Rebels of 1857
Following persons were identified as revolters from Aligarh. Ejaz

Ali, Husain Khan, Hasan Khan, Kotwal, Mehbub Khan, Kol., Daud Khan, Jamadar, Imam Bakhsh, Husaina, Hasana, Peera, Khuda Bakhsh. Order of Major Sahab.

****

91
Dated 8th March, 1858
List of revolters

Rasool Khan, Khuda Bakhsh Kallu, Abdul Jalil, Upper Fort, for declaring *jihad* and fighting against the Britishers. Nasimullah, Upper fort, Murtaza Khan, Upper fort, Boli Khan, Chah Garmaya, Kol, according to the list of Rubkar 29th August, 1857 *Ijlas*. List of persons whose houses were demolished Ghaus Khan, *Kotwal* of the city, Mohalla Afghanan, Medu, Tailor, Khub Khan, Imam Bakhsh, Jamadar, Iradat Khan, Mir Khan Kochwan, Naib Khan, Aminuddin, Bolaqi, Baqar, Mian Ganj, Salimuddin, Madar Darwaza, Mian Jan Sawar, Damahi Darwaza, Mufti Inayat Ahmed, Upper fort, Gulab Khan, Ahmed Khan, Mohalla Sarai Sultani, Kol, Shaikh Lal Muhammed, Upper fort, Amiruddin, Taj Ganj, Agra, Ahmed Davi, Mamun Bhanja, Kallan, butcher, Ahmed Khan, Nannu, Jolaha, Zahori son of Imami, Julaha, resident of Upper fort, Kol, was arrested for committing loot and plunder, vide warrants dated 4th November, 1858. List of Muslim Ghaddaar for revolting and taking part in *jihad*, dated 8th November, 1858.

****

92
UP, State Archives
File No. 37
Dated 8th November, 1857

List of Muslims who participated in the mutiny—Karim Bakhsh verses government. He took part in Jihad.

****

93
National Archives of India
Document No. B-101, F. 13
Dated 12th July, 1857

Request of Zeenat Mahal addressed to Bahadur Shah that Mirza Mughal Bahadur has prohibited the sale of lime. She needed some quantity of lime for the repair of her *haveli*. You please personally direct him or the release of few *chhkras* of lime so that this lady could carry out the repair works etc.

Ordered that according to *Hasbul Hukum* of the Emperor, *Parwana* (order) should be issued to the officers of the battalion posted at Ajmeri Gate to give *parwana* for five carts of lime to Ghulam Ali, *darogha* of Farash Khana.

Dated 20th Ziqad, 21 Julus/ 12th July, 1857.

****

94
Atrocities of Kuffar

We hear that these Christian *kuffar* are committing atrocities on Indians and specially on followers of Islam. Wherever, they find Muslims they hang them. They have devastated so many villages. In Sonipat they hanged one Maulavi. They tortured the Saiyids of Gulaoti.[1] They have collected revenue of this year and are now demanding revenue of the next year also.

1. Gulaoti is a town in Bulandshahr district.

****

95
Delhi

Experienced people are of the view that there is no need of army from Mumbai and Indore for their coming to Delhi. It will be better that they take their positions at their own places only. And there, they confront with British army, only then we shall be able to defeat them. As far as Delhi's army is concerned it is of no use.

Once they drink water of Delhi, and take a round of Chandni Chowk, Dariba-i-Kalan, Jama Masjid and taken the Qalaqand of Ghantewale, the soldiers are finished. Then they were totally aimless. Our history and experience tell us this. They have become easy going people and only enjoy life. Experienced rulers and governors did not like to stay in this city.

****

96
Akhbaruz Zafar Delhi
Document No. 24, Vol. 19,
Dated Sunday, 2 Muharram, 1274.

Pamphlet

A declaration was issued to declare *jihad* against Christians. Cost of the pamphlet was 4 annas but it is requested that rich persons could buy it for a higher price by paying Rs. 100/- or Rs. 200/-. But their attitude was cold and the buyer was not available. In the end it is stated that whatever we are facing today is the result of our own doings and we are under punishment by God as follows:

> This shows the attitude of rich people that they were not helping those who were doing some work for the welfare of Indians. It is quite common among religious people that they do not own any responsibility but relate everything to God.

Mumbai

We have heard from the pilgrims of Mecca that in Mumbai Indians killed so many Christians. Some Christians who tried to fled through ships so even those were drowned in the sea.

****

97
Gawalior

We have heard that Bijabai did not revolt against the British openly. The army coming from Jabalpur and Indore, arrested Bijabai and

Gawalior's army had also joined Islamic army. Some say that Bijabai had sent a letter to Agra stating that army is not under my control. Someone has informed that Gawalior is also looted. I think it should not be like that of Jaipur. But it is certain that Bijabai was not a supporter of Christians by heart.

****

98
Jabalpur

In Jabalpur Christians were also killed.

****

99
Jhajjar

One friend had come from Jhajjar who told us that earlier we were having the view that once direction is given from *Takht-i-Islami* (Delhi) so they will also reach Delhi to support but when some people went to Jhajjar on the direction of the Emperor, so the secret became open. Proposal for sending army to Delhi was turned down because he required army for the administration of Jhajjar itself. Emperor asked for the payment of five lacs so only one lac was paid by the ruler of Jhajjar.

****

100
Daily Report of Khulasatul Akhbar relating to Hazrat Zille Subhani Khalifatur Rehmani Saturday, 17th (Muharram, August, 1857)

After morning prayer and other *aurad* and *manajat*, Samsamud Daula Nawab Ahmed Quli Khan Bahadur, Moinud Daula, Sarfarazud Daula, Nawab Hasan Ali Khan, Nawab Aminuddin Ahmed Khan, Mir Adl and other officials and officials visited the court. They conveyed regards to the Emperor. Because the Emperor was upset he did not attend the court. Then Mirza Khizr Sultan Bahadur, Mirza Abul Hasan, sons of the Emperor visited the Emperor and reported the matter. Because of the incident of Ehtramud Daula Bahadur, Emperor was totally upset. Due to this tension his digestion also got upset. Emperor ordered the Princes not to leave Ehtramud Daula alone. Emperor directed Mirza Muhammed Zahiruddin Bakht Bahadur that he should send all the belongings of Ehtramud Daula through Police and present everything in his presence. Even upto the time of *asr* (afternoon) Emperor remain upset and he could not sleep at night also. Hakim suggested some medicines which were used by the Emperor.

****

Wednesday 21st (Muharram, August, 1857)

After prayer, Emperor attended the *Darbar*. Everybody wished the Emperor. Emperor directed Mirza Zahiruddin Bahadur that Nawab Saiyid Hamid Ali Khan, Ahmed Mirza Khan, Debi Singh and Salig Ram were forbidden from entering the Qila-i-Mubarak (Red Fort). Order was executed. Before prayer Emperor also had audience and then Hakim was called and he checked Emperor's health and then he left.

****

101
Sonipat

It is heard that Maulavi Sahab who killed British ladies and children was hanged. It is ordered by the British officers that they should vacate a residential area known as Kot. If people of that area will not vacate the area, their houses will be blown. The British had selected that area because that was on the highest point of the city so they wanted to make that point as their army headquarter of Sonipat city. People of Sonipat are highly disturbed from this order of the British officers. Actually we could not plan for the protection of the people of adjoining towns.

****

102
Punjab

People who come from Lahore report about the killing of some *Pagans* (Christians). But we know that they are leading a peaceful life there. As the Christians were de-rooted from the west it is not the case in Punjab. Specially the ruler of Punjab is supporting Christians like anything.

Army of Iran

Some people say that Iran's army has reached upto Atak. But this news does not seem to be authentic. It seems to be a rumour only. But we can't rely on rumour.

Indore

It is heard that the army of Indore had killed Christians and some Pindaris had also reached there.

Delhi Urdu Akhbar is published, under the supervision of Saiyid Abdullah.

****

103

Order was issued by Mirza Zahiruddin to ban the entry of Nawab Saiyid Hamid Ali Khan, Ahmed Mirza Khan and Raja Debi Singh in the Qila-i-Mubarak.

****

104

It is heard that Iran's army is coming to invade India to defeat the British.

****

105

A report published in Delhi Urdu Akhbar that Indian army had killed large number of soldiers of British army.

****

106

UP, State Archives
Allahabad, F. No. 1568

Letter addressed to some higher officer No. 78, dated 25th July, 1858, regarding the delay in the demolition of the fort of Jahangirabad, due to heavy rains.

Once the British became successful in the suppression of the revolt of 1857 so apart from killing the participants they also carried out the demolition of houses, *Garhis* and the forts of those who actively took part in the revolt of 1857. There is a long list of *Garhis* of Muhammed Mehmud Ali Khan, Muhammed Faiz Ali Khan, Imdad Ali Khan, Ahmed Ali Khan residents of *Qasba* Chhatari, *Qasba* Pahasu were demolished.

****

107

Mubarak Shah Khan, Kotwal of the city, should know that yesterday special order has been issued for the prohibition of the sacrifice of cow on the occasion of Id az-Zuha. The traders who are involved in selling cows should not be allowed to sell cows. Even if somebody is having a cow in his home, he, too, should not be allowed to sacrifice a cow. If somebody secretly or openly sacrifices a cow that person shall also be killed. Do not allow anyone coming to the city to sell cows. On the occasion of Id az-Zuha, be vigilant so that nobody should involve himself in selling or sacrificing the cows in the city. It is according to the will of the Badshah. We have sent all the details.

Recorded on 7th *Zilhijja*, 21 *Julus*.
Next page—copy of the *parwana* is sent in the city.
7th *Zilhijja*, 21 *Julus*, Reply has also sent. Rest is OK—As follows.

****

108
Haryana State Archives, Haryana
Document Nos. 123-24.

Register prepared on the orders of Deputy Commissioner Bahadur of Panipat dated 8th November, 1857.

According to the order of Secretary, Government of Bengal, Her Excellency the Queen of England forgiven the crimes committed by the following persons. (Ref. Table 1 on p. 84)

****

109

We have reported about the condition of Aligarh and Babugarh. We shall send the treasury of Aligarh under the protection of army.

****

110

Bearing seal of Roshan Singh, Dated 1253. Royal order. Mirza Mughal should send infantry according to the request of Jawahar.

****

111
Addressed to the Emperor

I have reported on 23rd June, 1857. Now I am ready to serve you, because my ancestors had also served the Mughal Empire.

Bearing seal of Ghulam Abbas.

112. Imperial Order

Table

S. No.	Name	Position	Age	Caste	Posting	Reporting Date	Reason for Absence
1.	Hasan Ali Khan	Peon	30	Balloch	Sonipat	26.11.57	Warrant of Arrest was issued against Hasan Ali Khan of Hissar. I thought that someone might not arrest me so just for having this fear, I was absconding.
2.	Asalat Khan	Camel Driver	45	Dogar	Sonipat	29.11.57	When the British conquered Delhi so I left the duty with a fear of death that others are being killed, so I will also be killed.
3.	Har Narain S/o Roop Ram		55	Beragi	Bhindari	29.11.57	No reason.
4.	Abdur Razzaq		30	Chhapni	Panipat	29.11.57	Had gone to Ludhiyana to sell books during this period revolt had taken place and my name was registered as absconder. Having this fear in mind I did not join my duty.
5.	Saadullah Khan		40	Pathan	Panipat	8.11.57	Some reported against me that I had gone to Delhi. Having this fear in my mind I did not join my duty.
6.	Mohd. Husain Khan		26	Pathan	Panipat	29.11.57	When Commissioner of Panipat, Kotwal, Bakkshi and Sud Pal Singh, Deputy Collector of Panipat arrested people of Panipat so having this fear in my mind I left my office and remained wandering here and there.
7.	Ahmed Ali Khan		20	Pathan	Panipat	29.11.05	I had gone to Delhi to sell horses. When I could not sell my horses I had gone to Kanpur and during this period revolt broke out. When I came back to Panipat my relatives told me that your name is recorded as absconder so since then I was wandering from here and there.
8.	Aleemuddin		40	Shaikh	Khewra	30.12.58	I was serving as Chokidar in Sinoli and due to illness I had gone to my home town and people of Sinoli registered my name as absconder.

(Contd.)

S. No.	Name	Position	Age	Caste	Posting	Reporting Date	Reason for Absence
9.	Kallu		25	Baloch	Khapwara	30.12.58	Somebody reported that I had gone to Delhi. Having this fear in my mind I remained loitering here and there.
10.	Zabardast Khan		25	Baloch		30.12.58	I was serving in Qimashpur and when I fell ill so I had gone to my home town. Somebody reported that I had gone to Delhi. That is why I did not report to my duty.
11.	Mangli		26	Baloch	Shamli	15.12.58	Kapoor Singh, Contractor reported that I joined the revolters. But I was not at all involved in the revolt.
12.	Mughla Ramgar		40	Gharonda		30.12.58	I had to sell my Oxen to Rohtak. People of Gharonda burnt my village. Due to this fear I did not come back to my village.
13.	Sarjan Mandi		50	Jat	Oldipur	29.4.58	On orders of Commissioner of Delhi, dated 4.1.59, he was freed from prison.
14.	Har Chand Mogi		45	Jat	Oldipur	29.4.58	—do—
15.	Pat Ram Madi		40	Jat	Bacathdina	29.4.58	—do—
16.	Room Ram Madi		40	Jat	Rasoi Rasoli	29.4.58	-do-

Addressed to all Hindus and the Muslims. Those who believe in the welfare of religion and the nation they should be ready to join the emperor who is fighting these *pagans* (Christians) for the sake of Islam. Those who will support Christians will be ruined.

Dated 11th August, 1857.

****

113
Following Items are Required

Rais of Jiuri had given five thousand rupees. Rais of Qasba Parera has given ten thousand rupees. Rais of *Qasba* Dharampur has given Rs. 5,000/-. Rais of Bhikanpur Rs. 10,000/- Rais of Badaun Rs. 10,000/-. Traders of Mathura city Rs. 5,000/-. Raja Ballabhgarh Rs. 10,000/-. Ghulam Husain ruler of Atrauli Rs. 20,000/-. Raja of Bharatpur Rs. 5,000/-.

****

114
Addressed to the Emperor

I have come from Tonk and I have formed a company of five hundred soldiers and brought with me 15,000 *mujahidin* with me, those who are ready to sacrifice their lives.

Applicant—Ghulam Mohiuddin Khan, *Risaldar Khas*.

Emperor is also having full confidence on Sikh regiment and they will fight very well.

Dated 23rd August, 1857.

****

115
Addressed to Emperor

"Gharib Parwar" (Raiser of the poor). After meeting you I reached Ghaziabad and there I came to know that with the help of some Jats, the British had ruined and burnt Pilakhwa. Around 300 Jats supported the British. Around fifty British alongwith Jats got assembled in Begumabad to destroy the Hindon bridge. They have also become successful in cutting the supply of food etc. to Delhi.

Letter of slave—Ahmed Khan, resident of Ghaziabad.

Dated 9th September, 1857.

* * * * * * * * * *

116
Addressed to the Emperor

The British have disarmed the 95th Battalion stationed in Amritsar. Those who got opportunity they just flee from Amritsar. They have also disarmed me and whatever money I had, they took all that. Whatever I had with me was also looted by the Gujars. Now I have nothing in my possession.

Letter of Qasimuddin, soldier.

* * * * * * * * * *

117
Order Under the Seal of the Emperor,

Zillus Sadat Saiyid Abdul Husain

Since then you have left for Rohtak, you have not sent any letter regarding your condition. When you receive this *farman*, immediately inform me about the condition of Rohtak.

Dated 25th May, 1857.

* * * * * * * * * *

118
Addressed to the Emperor

We humbly submit that we the residents of Jai Singhpura, Shah Ganj known as Paharganj and other places are living under your shelter. *Qasba* Shah Ganj was always called with the name of the Emperor. Now Imperial forces come out from Ajmeri Gate and take away commodities from the shops with force. They even enter in the houses and take away clothes, utensils etc. Those who resist they are beaten badly by soldiers. We are really fed up with their atrocities and request you to forbade them from doing injustice with us.

Applicants—Chand Khan and Gulab Khan.
Dated 19th June, 1857.

****

119
Emperor's Order in His Own Hand Writing

Mirza Mughal—Do something so that these persons can be forbidden from doing such things with the people.

****

120
Addressed to the Emperor

We humbly submit that for sometime Mirza Abu Bakr comes to the house of Princes Farkhunda Zamani situated on Tiraha Bairman Khan. Here he drinks and does all that which we can't explain. Yesterday he came and left only at night after enjoying there.

Applicant—Ahsanul Haq.
Dated 4th July, 1857.

****

121
Addressed to the Emperor

We humbly submit that *sawars* are staying in Chandni Chowk and keep their horses just in front of the shops. Some shopkeepers have vacated their shops and others are going to follow it. It is a great loss for this market.

Applicant, Ratan Chand, *Darogha* of Royal gardens etc. of Sahibabad.

****

122
Order of the Emperor

Address to Mirza Mughal—you are directed to remove these *risaldars* from there and ask them to stay some where else so that the people should not suffer.

****

123
Addressed to Mirza Mughal

Dear Son,

As you know that Saiyid Husain Ali Khan, police officer, submitted a note that few policemen of Aliganj, Palanji, Hasangarh and Alapur got wounded by Gujars. Today we have come to know from the report of the Police Officer of Mehrauli that same group of Gujars are creating problem there also. They have looted some villages also. Breaking of law in such a way is very dangerous. I direct you that you send a battalion of fifty soldiers with horses to arrest the Chief Numbardar of these Gujars.

Dated 17th July, 1857.

****

124
Bearing Seal of Abul Zafar Sirajuddin Bahadur Shah Badshah Gazi 1253 Hijri and Ist Regnal Year

Addressed to Muhammed Mehmud Khan Bahadur to control the loot and plunder going on in the *parganas*. You recruit more policemen so that the situation can be controlled.

Dated 28th *Ziqad*, 21st regnal year/21st July, 1857.

****

125
Addressed to the Emperor

It is submitted that Jawahar Bakhsh, serving in intelligence services, stole my female asses from Hauz-i-Qazi. When I identified so, only after taking eleven rupees, he returned my asses. After three days he again came to my place with a person serving in intelligence police, who is serving in the area of Turkman police station. It is such a high handedness which we are facing through police personnel. Please arrange to inquire into the matter so that justice could be done to me.

Applicant—Karim Bakhsh known as Nathua, owner of assess.
Dated 22nd July, 1857.

****

126
Addressed to the Emperor

With respect, we want to inform you that a gang of ruffiance comes to our shops located in Kashmiri Gate. Sometimes they also come alongwith Chief Police Officer, and accuse us that we are in alignment with enemies and demand that we supply them food etc. We are fed up of their activities. We shall be ruined. We request you to arrange to lock our shop with government locks so that we could live in peace and our shops remain safe.

Applicant—Shiv Dayal and Shadi Ram, shopkeepers.

Emperor himself wrote with pencil.

Mirza Mughal—Give protection to the persons concerned.

On the bach—Note no. 557 is recorded.

Order of Mirza Mughal, dated 17th July, 1857.

Today I received the application. Applicants request that their shops be sealed with government locks. So I order Chief Police Officer, that the shops of applicants be sealed with government locks.

Dated 17th July, 1857.

****

127
Order Bearing Royal Seal (Not Readable)

From the Office of Chief Police Officer, Dated 22nd July, 1857

You have sent five convicts but files of two are available in our office and the files of three are not available in our office. If you have any record of those missing files so you inform me. Be careful in future that whenever you send any convict, he should come alongwith the file. List of cases is available.

****

128
Addressed to the Emperor

Zille Subhani Jahan Panah, Feet of my horse wounded very badly and I can't ride on it. Please grant me a leave of one month so that I could search and purchase a horse.

Applicant—Khanazad Imamullah Khan *Bargir*.

(Emperor himself wrote with pencil) Officers of salary section are directed to sanction him a leave of one month.

****

129
Addressed to the Emperor
Dated 18th August, 1857

You have ordered and sanctioned Rs. 200/- for the repair of the bridge, so we pay daily-wages to labourers in the evening working there. Since we have not given the repair of this bridge on contract so the job will be completed in less than Rs. 200/-. It was necessary to bring this fact to your kind notice.

Applicant—Slave Zahooruddin.

****

130
Bearing Royal Seal
Dated 12th August, 1857

Addressed to Mirza Safi Tehmasp, Sultan Hyder, Mirza Ziauddin Bakht and Mirza Usman, that you faced lot of hardship in Awadh. Everything is drastically changing and we are really shocked. But everything depends on the will of God, we have to be thankful in every situation. Do not keep envy with each other. You stay in Aminabad and try to avoid all dangerous situations. God will pardon us. The restless situation through which we are passing will be over in a short period of time with the grace of God. We shall remain careful and thankful to you.

****

131
Addressed to the Emperor

I submit most humbly that justice is the most liked act of God. Forbid high ranking office not to do injustice to the people. High ranking army officers are demanding the permission of killing of Christian women, men and children in their custody. If you will allow them then you will be away from religion. First of all these officers should take *fatwa* (decision) on the killing of women and children and if *ulema* allow only then they can kill them. I request you not to order for anything which goes against the *shariat* (law) of Prophet Muhammed.

Applicant—Nabi Bakhsh Khan, Clerk of the Emperor.

****

132
Imperial Order

Bearing Seal,

Addressed to special servant Raja Nahar Singh Bahadur. I have come to know that you have appointed a *Thanedar* in Badarpur and Naziruddin Khan is appointed as *Thanedar* of Badarpur by the Mughal government, who is presently posted at Arab Sarai. You are directed to remove your appointee.

****

133
Addressed to the Emperor

I humbly submit that there was no peace on road of Delhi, so according to your direction I tried my best to maintain law and order in the area. Resident of *moza* Pali were doing loot, plunder and killings in the area. I am trying to bring peace in the area so that the road from Ballabhgarh to Delhi should become safe. Some one must have told you about my attitude towards you that I am not faithful to you and wanted to gain authority in the region. Somebody told you that some Christians also hiding in Ballabhgarh. Twelve years back there was my Indian servant who got converted to Christianity but due to your dislike towards Christians I have also removed him from my services but now this person accepted Islam so he could be accommodated. If you permit, I can again employ him.

Applicant—your old obedient—Nahar Singh, Raja of Ballabhgarh.

Bearing seal of Raja Nahar Singh.

****

134
Addressed to the Emperor

I humbly submit that I received your order for visiting the Darbar and taking the charge of Delhi Police but at the same darbar and taking the charge of Delhi Police but at the same time I received the order for assigning me the task of maintaining law and order on the high way. I feel honoured after receiving all these orders. I am grateful to God. Residents of *moza* Pali and Palwal are involved in loot, plunder and killings in the area. Once I am able maintaining law and order in the region, I shall visit Delhi to pay homage to you.

Applicant—Khanazad Nahar Singh, Raja of Ballabhgarh.

****

135
Addressed to the Emperor

It is submitted that Raja Sahab arrived in Delhi. Now he wants to bring clothes from Ballabhgarh so please arrange to issue *parwana-i-Rah dari* (permission letter) so that bullukcarts can come to Delhi and bring all the things required by the Raja and nobody should stop it at Delhi Gate.

Applicant—Ahmed Ali, Clerk, Raja Ballabhgarh. Bearing seal of Ahmed Ali.

Imperial order. Mirza Mughal, you are directed to issue *parwana-i-Rah dari*.

****

136
Addressed to the Emperor

I had sent several applications but I was not honoured by reply. Some ruffians of moza Pali have created lot of problem and harming the people of that area. Though I am trying to control that but without your order I can't interfere in these matters directly. I am also trying to enhance the soldiers to bring to the suffiaus of this region into order. I am sending Qalander Khan Resaldar alongwith some soldiers to your presence. Whatever order I shall receive from them, I shall follow that.

Application of eater of the salt and slave—Nahar Singh, Raja Ballabhgarh.

Bearing seal of Raja Nahar Singh Bahadur.

* * * * * * * * * *

137
Addressed to the Emperor

I am submitting that as per your order I am maintaining law and order of the highway of Delhi as well as Police Station of Badarpur. If you have appointed someone else as the *Thanedar,* then I shall remove my appointee from there. I had sent Qalander Bakhsh Khan, Risaldar, but the persons looking after security at Delhi Gate, did not allow them to enter in Delhi.

Application of an old servant—Nahar Singh Bahadur, Vali of Ballabhgarh.

Bearing seal of Raja Nahar Singh.

* * * * * * * * * *

138
Addressed to the Emperor
Dated 22nd May, 1857

This slave was honoured by your order sent to me. I have controlled the administration of *mauza* Pali, Palwal and Fathpur.

Please direct the policemen of Delhi not to interfere in the work of Ballabhgarh.

Application of an old servant Nahar Singh Bahadur, Vali of Ballabhgarh.

Bearing seal of Raja Nahar Singh Bahadur.

****

139
Addressed to the Emperor

Received your letter. Please arrange to direct the security persons of the gate not to tease the people of Ballabhgarh. Today I had gone to Dilkusha Bagh and there I saw Id's moon and all the people of this region had seen Id's moon. I extend my greetings of Id. I hope this Id will bring good blessings for you.

Bearing seal of Raja Nahar Singh Bahadur.

****

140
Addressed to the Emperor
Dated 25th May, 1857

I humbly submit that yesterday I had sent an application regarding the condition of the state. I have controlled the administration. There is a need to appoint some soldiers in Hanuman *thana* and one *thanedar* and twenty-five policemen in Mehrauli.

Bearing seal of Raja Nahar Singh Bahadur.

****

141
Addressed to the Emperor
Dated 27th May, 1857

I humbly submit to appoint twenty policemen in the police

station of Mukunda and Shahdari. With the grace of God I shall control the administration.

Application of Khanazad Nahar Singh, *Vali* of Ballabhgarh.
Bearing seal of Raja Nahar Singh.

* * * * * * * * * *

142
Addressed to the Emperor
Dated 30th May, 1857

I have come to know that some bullackcarts were looted. I shall try to enquire into the matter.

Applicant—Khanazad Nahar Singh, Vali, Ballabhgarh.
Bearing seal of Raja Nahar Singh.
Recorded in pencil by the Emperor.
I have read the letter, this person is our well wisher.

* * * * * * * * * *

143
Addressed to the Emperor
Dated 28th May, 1857

I have controlled the administration of the district. I am sending five *asharfis* as a *nazr* (gift) on the occasion of Idul Fitr. Kindly accept it.

Applicant—Nahar Singh.
Bearing seal of Nahar Singh Bahadur.
Something is written by the Emperor which is not readable.

* * * * * * * * * *

144
Addressed to the Emperor
Dated 31st July, 1857

I have given charge to old officers and they have eaten around one lac. When I asked them to submit an account so they left for Delhi. They are involved in rumouring against me that I am siding with British. They are not your well wishers but your enemies.

Applicant—Nahar Singh.

****

145
Addressed to the Emperor
Dated 5th August, 1857

Those who are working with you, it is really a great privilege. I am very far from you and can't enjoy that honour. I am sending eight *asharfis* as a *nazr* (gift) on the occasion of Id. I hope that you kindly accept that. One for you and two for the queen and one for Prince Mirza Jawan Bakht.

Applicant—Raja Nahar Singh Bahadur, *Vali* of Bahadurgarh. Bearing seal of Raja Nahar Singh.

****

146
Royal Order with Seal and the Signature
Dated 8th August, 1857

Received your application alongwith eight *asharfis*. We accept it because you are one of the most loyal servants.

****

147
Addressed to the Emperor
Dated 14th August, 1857

Received the receipt of the acceptance of my Id's gift. It is a great honour for me. My ancestors had also served you. I also request you to grant me *naqqara* (Drum) and *alam* (Flag). Since I have come back from Delhi, I am very busy in maintaining law and order.

Bearing seal of Raja Nahar Singh.

****

148
Addressed to Raja Nahar Singh
Vali of Ballabhgarh
Dated 14th August, 1857

You appoint some of your most loyal servant as your *vakil* (Agent) in the *darbar* (court), so that we can convey our messages verbally through him to you. Consider it a great honour for you.

****

149
Addressed to the Emperor

My ancestors are serving the Mughal Empire since long time. While British were having their control in Delhi, so you forbade me to stay in Delhi. Now I am having a desire to stay in Delhi but still I am waiting for your permission. I think there are some persons in Delhi, who are misguiding you on my behaviour. Following persons have taken this amount from me and when I am in dire need of money so they are not returning it to me.

1. Hakim Abdul Haq 10 lacs
2. Mukta Prasad Rs. 15,000/-
3. Raja Lal Sahab Rs. 10,000/-

4. Nisar Ali Rs. 10,000/-
5. Jawala Nath Pandit Rs. 30,000/-
6. Shair Khan Rs. 25,000/-
7. Hisaruddin Rs. 5,000/-
8. Amir Ali Rs. 10,000/-
9. Saadat Ali Rs. 8,000/-
10. Ahmed Mirza Rs. 10,000/-
11. Mubarak Ali Khan Rs. 2,000/-

Applicant slave Raja Nahar Singh Bahadur.
Bearing seal of Raja Nahar Singh Bahadur.

****

150
Addressed to the Emperor
Dated 2nd September, 1857

Received your letter, I feel honoured that you have accepted horse sent by me. I submit that you arrange the arrest of Hakim Abdul Haq and Pandit Jawala Prasad and give them under my custody so that I could collect Rs. 25,000/- from them. I am always praying for the longevity of your Sultanat.

Applicant–servant—Raja Nahar Singh Bahadur.
Bearing seal of "Raja Nahar Singh Bahadur."

****

Appendices

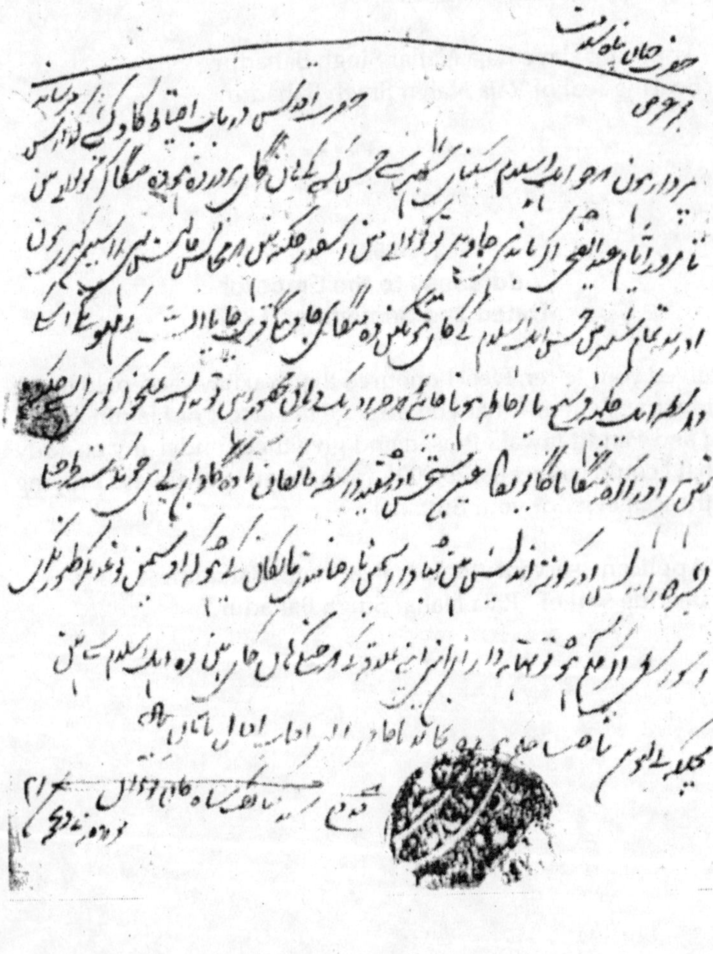

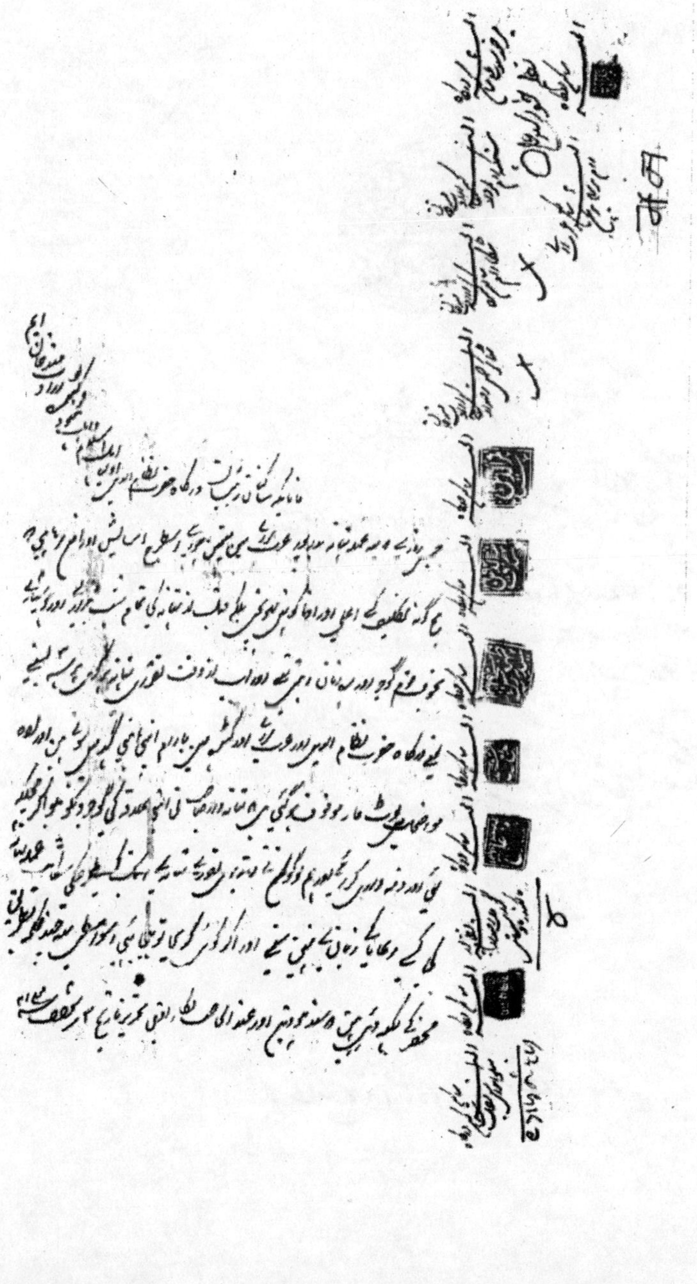

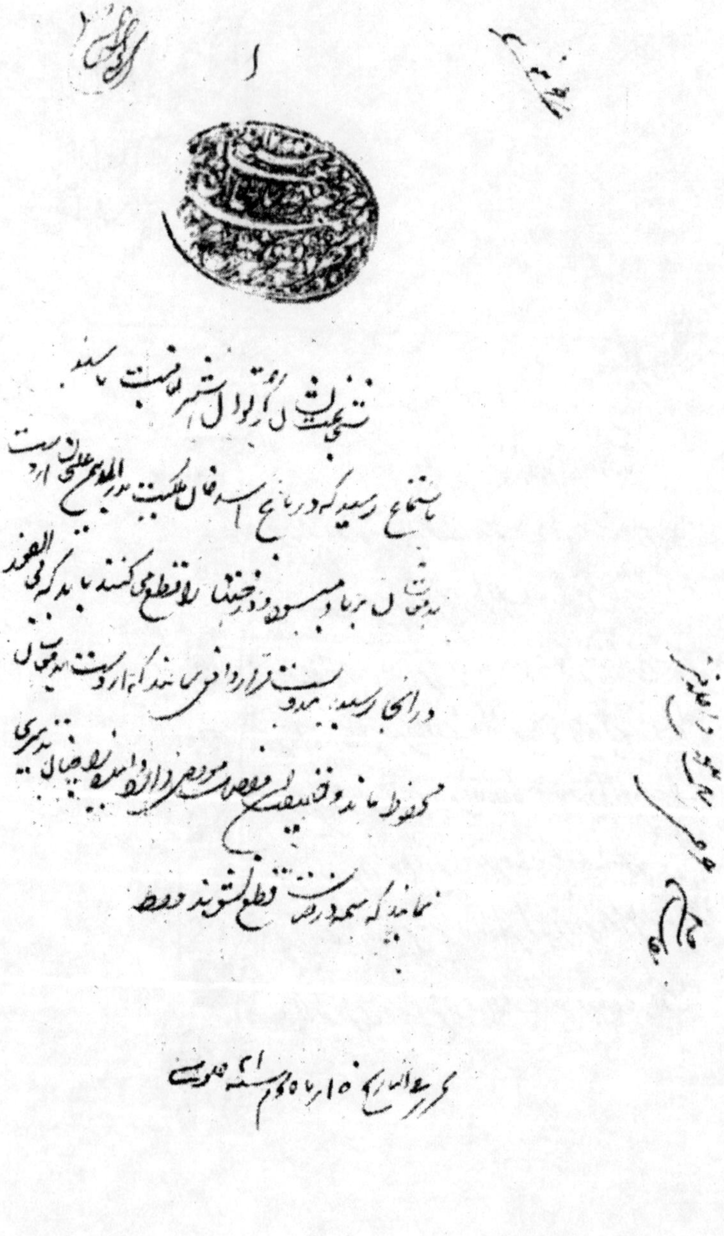

Hand writing of Bahadur Shah

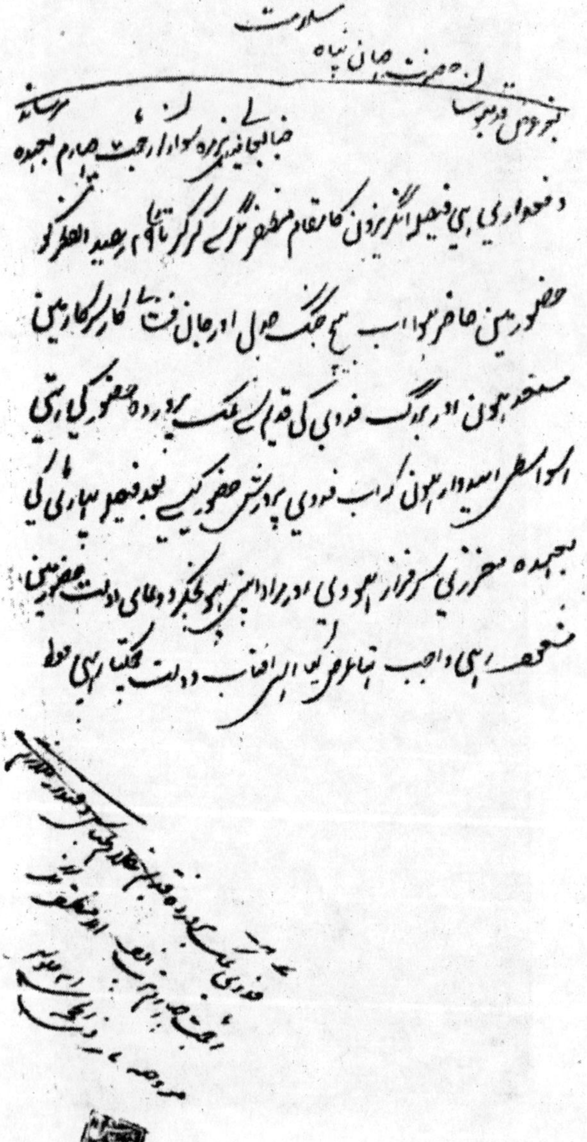
سلامت
از حضرت جہان پناہ
حضور میں حاضر ہوا اب ہم جنگ جدال اور جان فشانی کار سرکار میں
مستعد ہوں اور برگ فدوی کی قدیم سے نمک پروردہ حضور کی ہی
امیدوار ہوں کہ اب فدوی پرورش حضور کی بعد فیصلہ [illegible]
بعہدہ [illegible] سرفراز ہووے اور مراد اپنی پہونچکر دعای دولت حضور میں
مشغول رہے واجب تھا عرض کیا [illegible] آفتاب دولت [illegible]

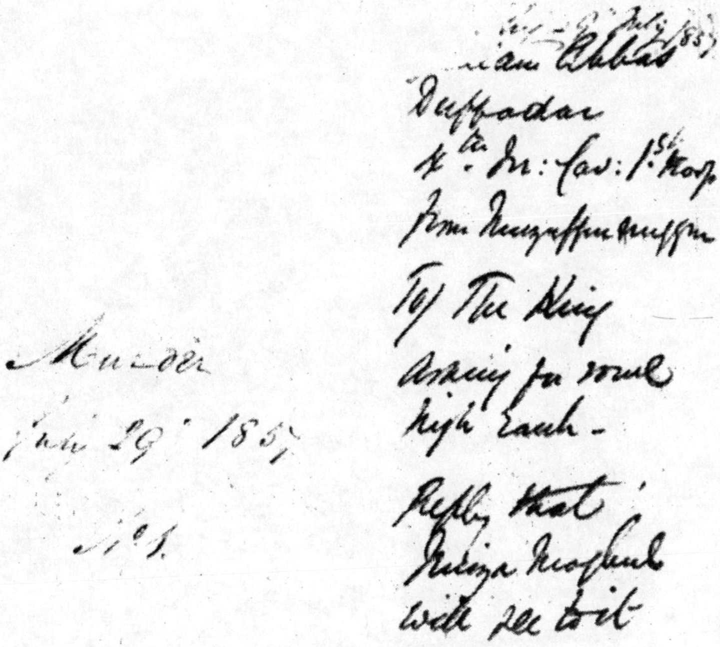

... 29 July 1857
...am Abbas
Duffadar
4th Irr: Cav: 1st Troop
from Muzaffurnuggur
To/ The King
Asking for some
high rank –
Reply that
Mirza Moghul
will see to it

Mu-dir
July 29 1857
No 1.

(۱)

Parwana to Saiyid Khairat Ali

Dated: 1787A.D.

پروانہ بتاریخ ۱۷۸۷ء

یا فتاح

برای نیاز حضرات ائمہ معصومین صلواۃ اللہ علیہم اجمعین۔ پروانہ بہ مہر میاں صاحب الماس علی خاں صاحب مرقومہ بست و یکم شہر محرم الحرام ۱۲۰۲ھ متصدیاں مہمات حال و استقبال پرگنہ بلرام عرف کاسگنج بدانند کہ موضع مبارک پور باسم سید شاہ خیرات علی صاحب معہ فرزنداں از قدیم مقرر و معاف واگذاشت است۔ لہذا نگارش میرود کہ الحال ہم موضع مذکور در تعلق و تصرف مشار الیہ مع فرزنداں واگذاشت دارند و حسب این طور عمل آرند۔

(۲)

TAJWEEZ

relating to Mauza Mubàrakpur

Dated: 1842A. D.

تجویز بتاریخ ۱۸۴۲ء

عدالت صاحب کمشنر خاص متعلقہ اضلاع عظیم آباد و بنارس واقع تاریخ بست و پنجم ماہ اگست ۱۸۴۲ء اجلاس جان مارود الیٹ اسکوائر صاحب کمشنر خاص حسب قانون سیوم ۱۸۴۸ء عزیز الدین حسین و فخر الدین حسین و جعفر حسین و زائر حسین اپیلانیاں بنام سرکار سپانڈنٹ بدعوی واگذاشت موضع مبارک پور و شش بیگہ دہ بسوہ آراضی خام قصبہ خاص بلرام ضلع بدایوں معافی بنام سید بہاء الدین و خیرات علی مرقوم است۔

Documents relating to Imam Bara of Saiyid Shah Khairat Ali built in 1774.

(Copy)

To

The Right Honorable
Francis Earl of Moira K. G
Governor General in Council
Fort William

Revenue Dept.

My Lord

On the 10th July 1810 Government were pleased to admit the claim of Shah Khyrat Allee to a Pension of Rupees 1000 per annum in lieu of the Villages of Nurnowlee and Hatha.

2d. We have now the honor to lay before your Lordship the copy of a letter from the late Collector of Etawah notifying the Death of the said Khyrat Allee, and applying for Instruction relative to the continuance or otherwise of the Pension to the Heirs of the deceased and also in regard to another Village named Mobarickpoor of which the deceased appears to have held rent free possession till his Death.

3d. The Sunnud of the Nawab Vizier on which the claim of Khyrat Allee to the Pension rests, a Translate of which is annexed to the papers submitted with

one-

Documents relating to maafi assigned by Asifud Daula in 1787 which was confiscated by the British in 1804

r address of the 12th June 1810, is to the said Khyrat Allee and his Dependants which expression we conceive to include a hereditary tenure and we should imagine that the Pension which he received in lieu of the lands granted to him by that Sunnud should therefore be considered hereditary also, unless the circumstance of his never having obtained actual possession of the lands should be deemed to take the case out of the purview of Section VII Regulation 24 1803.

4th Your Lordship will observe that from the use of the term &ca on the above Sunnud after the names of the two Villages Nurowlee and Northa therein granted, the late Collector inferred it to have included the Village of Mobarukpoor also, and was therefore of opinion that the deceased had fraudulently continued to occupy a part of the lands the whole of which was intended to be compensated by the Pension of Rupees. We accordingly directed that the Heirs of Khyrut Allee should be called to produce any separate Document which they might have in proof of their ancestors right to the Village of Mobarukpoor independant of the Villages of Nurowlee and Northa, in default of which the Collector was instructed to attach the

the lands, and in the mean time to stop payment of the Pension.

5th. The Parties have in consequence produced an original Sunnud which we have the honor to submit with a Translate, for the Village of Mobarukpoor to Baha oodeen Hossien, who appears to be the eldest son of the late Khyrat Allee, and his Brothers, which as it bears date 7 years previously to the Sunnud for the two other Villages would prove the tenure to be independant of the latter grant, and as the Grantees are themselves alive would establish their right to hold the lands till the death of the last Survivor of them.

Board of Commrs.
Furruckabad.
The 25th. November 1813.

We have the honor to be &ca.
(Signed) E. Colebrooke

P.S. We beg leave to request that the original Document herewith submitted may be returned to us.—

E.A.D.

No. 1296 of 1838

From
J. B. Outram Esqre
Assist. Secy to Government N.W.P.

To
W. H. Lowe Esquire
Secy Sudr Board of Revenue N.W.P.
Dated Allahabad the 8th September 1838

Revenue Deptt N.W.P.

Sir,

I am directed by the Right Honble the Governor General to forward the accompanying correspondence, as noted in the margin, regarding the Pensions of Zuhur ood Deen Hoosein and Uzeez ood Deen Hoosein, and to request that the Board will favor His Lordship with their opinion, and any farther documents which may be forthcoming in their records, relative to the Pensions in question.

From Depy Collr Allygurh	dated 14th June	No. 6 with Enclos
To Offg Civil Auditor N.W.P.	dated 26 June	No. 758
From Ditto	dated 23 July	No. 48 with Enclos
To Ditto	dated 11th August	No. 1098
From Ditto	dated 27th Augt	No. 67 with Enclo:

2nd. I have the honor to request the return with your reply of the original documents now forwarded.

Allahabad
The 8th September
1838

I have the honor to be
Sir,
Your most obedient Servant

[illegible signature]

Assist. Secy to Government N.W.P.

[illegible initials]

In an enclosure at the back of Moti Masjid near the dargah of Khwaja Qutubuddin Bakhtiyar Kaki, Mehrauli, Delhi. There are two graves one grave is of Akbar II, father of Bahadur Shah II, vacant space left was marked by Bahadur Shah Zafar for his own grave. But he could not be buried here.

Jama Masjid of Ballabhgarh built by Raja Nahar Singh.

دستاویزات غدر ۱۸۵۷

مرتبہ

پروفیسر سید محمد عزیز الدین حسین

شعبہ تاریخ و ثقافت

جامعہ ملیہ اسلامیہ

نئی دہلی

ہدیۂ تشکر

سب سے پہلے میں اپنے والد مرحوم پروفیسر حکیم سید محمد کمال الدین حسین ہمدانی کا کہ جو بچپن سے مجھے تاریخی واقعات سناتے رہے اور اسی وجہ سے مجھے تاریخ سے دلچسپی پیدا ہوئی۔ میں اپنے بھائی انل نوریہ کا شکر گزار ہوں کہ انھوں نے ۲۶ جنوری ۲۰۰۰ء میں مجھے مشورہ دیا کہ میں ۱۸۵۷ سے متعلق فارسی و اردو دستاویزات پر کام کروں کہ ۲۰۰۷ء میں ۱۸۵۷ کی ڈیڑھ سو سالہ یادگار منائی جائے گی۔ جیسا کہ میں نے اپنی کتاب ''عہد اورنگزیب کا سیاسی ڈھانچہ'' میں لکھا ہے کہ میرے علمی کیریر کے احیاء میں دو حسنوں کا بڑا اہم کردار رہا ہے۔ ایک استاد محترم پروفیسر سید نور الحسن سابق وزیر تعلیم، حکومت ہند، نئی دہلی اور دوسرے بزرگ دوست جناب پروفیسر مشیر الحسن وائس چانسلر، جامعہ ملیہ اسلامیہ، نئی دہلی۔ ان دونوں کی ذاتی دلچسپی نے میرے علمی کیریر میں حسن پیدا کر دیا۔ میرے پاس الفاظ نہیں ہیں کہ جن سے انکا شکریہ ادا کرسکوں۔ پروفیسر گیان پرکاش شرما کا شکر گزار ہوں کہ انھوں نے DRS کے تحت اس پروجیکٹ کی تکمیل واشاعت کے لیے ہر طرح سے مدد کی۔

اپنے ساتھی سنگھدار وآئے اور محمد مصعب کا شکر گزار ہوں کہ انھوں نے اس کام کی تکمیل میں بڑی مدد کی۔ اپنے احباب میں پروفیسر نرائنی گپتا، پروفیسر سنیتا زیدی، پروفیسر سیما علوی، ڈاکٹر رضوان قیصر، مکل کیشون، ڈاکٹر مینا گوڑ، پروفیسر بھنور لال بھادانی، ڈاکٹر پرمود مہرا کا شکر گزار ہوں کہ انھوں

نے ہمیشہ میری مدد کی۔ اپنے شاگرد اور دوستوں میں ڈاکٹر فرحت نسرین، ڈاکٹر محمد تعظیم، محمد علی، طیبہ منور، اور سید علی کاظم کا شکرگزار ہوں کہ جب بھی مجھے ان کی مدد کی ضرورت پڑی بڑی خندہ پیشانی سے باوجود اپنی مصروفیات کے میری مدد کرتے رہے۔

نیشنل آرکائیوز آف انڈیا، نئی دہلی و بھوپال، اتر پردیش آرکائیوز، لکھنو الہ آباد، خدا بخش لائبریری، پٹنہ، راجستھان اسٹیٹ آرکائیوز، بیکانیر، نٹ ناگر شودھ سنتھان، سیتامئو، آزاد لائبریری، علی گڑھ مسلم یونیورسٹی، علی گڑھ، ذاکر حسین لائبریری، دہلی، رضا لائبریری رامپور کے لائبریرین، ڈائریکٹرس اور جملہ اسٹاف کا شکرگزار ہوں کہ انھوں نے ہر طرح سے مدد کی۔ جناب محمد راشد صاحب کا شکرگزار ہوں کہ انھوں نے اس کتاب کی ٹائپنگ کی۔

میں مدن سچدیوا، مینیجر کنشکا پبلشرس، نئی دہلی کا شکرگزار ہوں کہ انھوں نے نہ صرف اس کام میں بلکہ میری تمام کتابوں کی اشاعت میں ذاتی دلچسپی لی جس کی وجہ سے یہ کتاب شائع ہو سکی۔ یہ کتاب شاہ جہاں آباد سے ہی شائع ہو رہی ہے جو ۱۸۵۷ء میں غدر کا مرکز رہا۔

میں اپنی شریک حیات پروفیسر طلعت عزیز کا شکرگزار ہوں کہ جن کے تعاون سے میں اپنے علمی کاموں کو پائے تکمیل تک پہونچا سکا۔ آخر میں اپنی بیٹیوں ڈاکٹر عطیہ عزیز و زیبا عزیز کا شکرگزار ہوں کہ ان کی محبت ہی سے مجھے یہ قوت حاصل ہوتی ہے کہ جس کی وجہ سے میں ان کاموں کو پورا کر پاتا ہوں۔

۲۹ر مارچ ۲۰۰۷ء

پروفیسر سید محمد عزیز الدین حسین ہمدانی
شعبہ تاریخ وثقافت
جامعہ ملیہ اسلامیہ، نئی دہلی

دیباچہ

میں تو عہد وسطی کے ہندوستان کی تاریخ کا طالب علم ہوں اور ۱۸۵۷ جدید دور کے مورخین کا میدان ہے لیکن میرے بھائی انل نوریہ جن کو ہندوستان کی تاریخ سے دلچسپی ہے اور جدید ہندوستان کی تاریخ پر برابر لکھتے رہتے ہیں۔ آجکل سپریم کورٹ آف انڈیا میں ایڈوکیٹ ہیں اور یاروں کی بستی میں رہتے ہیں انھوں نے ۲۶ جنوری ۲۰۰۰ کو مجھے مشورہ دیا کہ ۲۰۰۷ میں ۱۸۵۷ء کی ۱۵۰ ویں سالگرہ منائی جائے گی اور ۱۸۵۷ سے متعلق فارسی و اردو دستاویزات کثیر تعداد میں نیشنل آرکائیوز آف انڈیا نئی دہلی میں محفوظ ہیں اور ان پر کام نہیں ہوا۔ میں نے ان کا مشورہ مان لیا۔ میرا کیریر بھی آرکائیوز سے شروع ہوا تھا اور ریسرچ کے سلسلہ میں اکثر آرکائیوز جانا رہتا تھا۔ جب میں نے پہلی مرتبہ ۱۲ فروری ۲۰۰۰ء میں

Imperial Record Department. Press list of mutiny papers of 1857. Benig a collection of the correspondence of the mutineers at Delhi, reports of spies of "English officials and other miscellaneous papers, (calcutta,1921).

کا مطالعہ کیا تو صحیح اندازہ ہوا کہ کس قدر مواد ۱۸۵۷ پر فارسی و اردو زبان میں موجود ہے۔ دراصل انگریزوں نے انتظامی و تعلیمی کام ایک سسٹم کے ساتھ کیے۔ ایسا ہی ایک کام ۱۹۲۰ء میں سید ابو محمد جن کو آفیسر بہ کار خاص اس کام کے لیے مقرر کیا گیا کہ وہ ۹۰-۱۸۵۸ء تک اودھ رکارڈس کا انڈیکس تیار کریں۔ ان کا مقصد یہ تھا کہ جب بھی جس سے متعلق انھیں معلومات فراہم کرنی ہو تو وہ بہ

آسانی ہو سکے۔

ان دستاویزات پر کام اس لئے نہیں ہوا کہ یہ عہد وسطی کے مورخین کا میدان نہیں اور جدید ہندوستان کے زیادہ تر مورخین فارسی اور اردو سے نابلد ہیں بقول غالبؔ:

زاہد تنگ نظر نے مجھے کافر جانا اور کافر یہ سمجھتا ہے کہ مسلماں ہوں میں

آزادی کے بعد ان دونوں زبانوں یعنی فارسی اور اردو کو نفرت کی نگاہ سے دیکھا گیا۔ ابھی کچھ دن پہلے میں نے شعبہ تاریخ جامعہ ملیہ اسلامیہ کی ایک میٹنگ میں یہ بات کہی کہ ہمارے ساتھیوں میں اردو داں بھی ہونے چاہیے تو میرے ایک ساتھی نے کہا کہ میں فرقہ وارانہ سوال اٹھا رہا ہوں۔ کلکتہ یونیورسٹی میں بنگالی زبان کو میڈیم کا حصہ بنا کر غیر بنگالی اساتذہ کو اپنے دائرہ سے نکال دیا تو کیونکہ یہ بنگال میں ہوا تو سیکولرزم ہے اور جامعہ ملیہ اسلامیہ میں اردو کی بات کی گئی تو یہ کمیونلزم ہے۔ برٹش راج میں فارسی وار دو اسکولوں کے نصاب کا حصہ تھی لیکن آزاد ہندوستان میں دونوں زبانوں کو اسکولوں کے نصاب سے نکال دیا گیا۔ ۱۸۵۷ پر بہت کام ہوا لیکن فارسی وار دو دستاویزات کا مطالعہ کئے بغیر ہی ۱۸۵۷ پر کتابیں لکھ دی گئیں۔ یہ ہے آزاد ہندوستان میں جدید تاریخ نگاری کے فن کے ارتقاء کا کار نامہ۔ یعنی مغل بادشاہ اکبر (۱۶۰۵-۱۵۵۶) نے جب اکبر نامہ اور آئین اکبری لکھنے کی ذمہ داری ابوالفضل کے سپرد کی تو فتح پور سیکری کے دیوان عام کو مغل آرکائیوز میں تبدیل کر دیا۔ تمام دستاویزات وہاں رکھ دی گئیں تا کہ انکا مطالعہ کر کے ابوالفضل تاریخ لکھے۔ اور ہم نے بیسویں صدی میں دستاویزات کا مطالعہ کئے بغیر ہی ۱۸۵۷ پر بہت کچھ لکھ دیا۔ ولیم ڈالرمپل مبارک باد کے مستحق ہیں کہ انھوں نے ایک ٹیم بنا کر ان دستاویزات کا مطالعہ کیا اور ایک کتاب

The Last Mughal , The Fall of a daynesty, Delhi,1857

۲۰۰۶ میں شائع کردی۔ تین سال قبل میری ان سے ملاقات پروفیسر نرائنی گپتا نے کرائی تھی اور ہم نے ۱۸۵۷ سے متعلق ان دستاویزات پر تبادلہ خیال کیا تھا۔ ورنہ تو ان دستاویزات کو انتظار میں ۱۵۰ سال گذر ہی گئے تھے کہ کوئی مورخ پڑھے اور انکی داستان لکھے۔

۱۸۵۷ کا غدر ہندوستان کی تاریخ میں اہم مقام رکھتا ہے۔ مورخین اور دانشوروں نے اسے غدر، بغاوت اور جنگ آزادی کی پہلی لڑائی کا نام دیا ہے۔ ہندوستان کی تاریخ کے اس باب پر کام ہوا ہے لیکن ابھی بہت کام کی گنجائش ہے۔ ۱۸۵۷ سے متاثر تمام شہروں میں اس سے متعلق دستاویزات کے ذخیرے نہ صرف فارسی واردو بلکہ مقامی زبانوں میں کثیر تعداد میں موجود ہیں۔ تیرھویں صدی عیسوی سے ۱۸۹۱ تک حکومت کی سرکاری زبان فارسی رہی جسکی وجہ سے احکامات، خطوط اور دفتروں کی کارروائی فارسی زبان میں ہوتی تھی۔ جسکی وجہ سے جدید ہندوستان کی تاریخ سے متعلق مواد بھی کثیر تعداد میں فارسی واردو زبان میں موجود ہے۔ یہ اور بات ہے کہ ہم اس مواد کے بارے میں جانتے ہی نہیں اور نتیجتاً مطالعہ ہی نہیں کیا۔ ۱۸۵۷ کے دستاویزات کے مطالعہ سے ہندوستانیوں کے جذبات کی عکاسی ہوتی ہے جیسا کہ ایک شاعر نے کہا ہے

شورش عندلیب نے روح چمن میں پھونک دی　　ورنہ یہاں کلی کلی محو تھی خواب ناز میں

ہندوستان میں ۱۸۵۷ سے متعلق فارسی واردو دستاویزات اور دوسرے ماخذ نیشنل آرکائیوز آف انڈیا، نئی دہلی، بھوپال، دہلی اسٹیٹ آرکائیوز، دہلی، کمشنرز رکارڈس آفس، دہلی، ذاکر حسین لائبریری جامعہ ملیہ اسلامیہ، نئی دہلی، ہردیال لائبریری، دہلی۔ حسن نظامی کلکشن دہلی، اترپردیش اسٹیٹ

آرکائیوز، لکھنؤ و الہ آباد، مدھیہ پردیش اسٹیٹ آرکائیوز، بھوپال، بہار اسٹیٹ آرکائیوز، پٹنہ، ہسٹوریکل رکارڈس آفس، گوالیار، ہریانہ اسٹیٹ آرکائیوز، چنڈی گڑھ، پنجاب اسٹیٹ آرکائیوز، پٹیالہ، راجستھان اسٹیٹ آرکائیوز، بیکانیر و جے پور نیشنل لائبریری، کلکتہ، مولانا آزاد لائبریری علی گڑھ، سنٹرل انڈیا ایجنسی رکارڈس آفس اندور اور جو اضلاع ۱۸۵۷ سے متاثر رہے ان ضلعوں کے ہیڈ کوارٹرس کے محافظ خانوں میں۔ مثلاً علی گڑھ، اٹاوہ، آگرہ، فتح پور، مرادآباد، میرٹھ، لکھنؤ، بلندشہر، شاہ جہاں پور، ایٹہ، متھرا، بارہ بنکی، سلطان پور، اعظم گڑھ، بدایوں، بریلی، فرخ آباد، غازی پور، جھانسی، جون پور، للت پور، مرزاپور، مظفر نگر، سہارنپور، پٹنہ، کلکتہ، الہ آباد، پانی پت، میوات، سونی پت، روھتک، فرید آباد، اندور، کھیر، دادری، امروہہ، نوگانواں سادات، چاند پور، نجیب آباد، کانپور۔ ہندوستان سے باہر برٹش لائبریری، لندن، آرمی میوزیم، لندن اور کچھ مخطوطات نیشنل لائبریری، تہران، مجلس لائبریری تہران، آستانہ قدس لائبریری، مشہد میں بھی ہیں۔ فرانس کے نیشنل آرکائیوز میں بھی کچھ دستاویزات ہو سکتی ھیں۔ ۱۸۵۷ پر فارسی و اردو میں دستاویزات، روزنامچے، تاریخوں، تذکروں، فارسی و اردو شعرائے کلام اور اس دور کے لوگوں کے خطوط کی شکل میں ملتا ہے۔

مجھے لگتا ہے کہ ۱۸۵۷ سے پہلے جو ہمارا عالم تھا اور پھر ۱۸۵۷ میں شورش عندلیب نے چمن میں روح پھونک دی وہی مستی کا عالم آج بھی ہے۔ ۱۸۵۷ پر پہلی کتاب W. Taylor جو پٹنہ کا کمشنر تھا اس نے Patna Crisis کے عنوان سے لکھی جو لندن سے ۱۸۵۸ میں شائع ہوئی۔ ان حالات سے متاثر ہو کر سر سید احمد خاں نے ۱۸۶۰ میں دو کتابیں لکھیں سرکشی ضلع بجنور اور اسباب بغاوت ہند۔ اس کے بعد شاہجہاں آباد سے متعلق ایک کتاب سید محمد علی موسوی شاہجہاں آبادی نے ''مرغوب

دل'' کے عنوان سے لکھی جو ۱۸۶۷ میں شائع ہوئی اس میں دہلی کا جہاں اور ذکر ہے غدر سے متعلق بھی لکھا ہے۔ ذکاء اللہ نے تاریخ عروج انگلیشیہ لکھی ۱۹۵۷ میں ہم نے ۱۸۵۷ کی سوویں سال گرہ منائی لیکن ۱۸۵۷ سے متعلق فارسی وار دو دستاویزات سے متعلق کچھ طے نہیں کیا۔ آزاد ہندوستان میں مسلم تہذیب وثقافت کے تحفظ واحیاء کی ذمہ داری دوواداروں پر ہے۔ علی گڑھ مسلم یونیورسٹی اور جامعہ ملیہ اسلامیہ۔ اسلیے کہ علی گڑھ مسلم یونیورسٹی اور جامعہ ملیہ اسلامیہ کا قیام ایک تحریک کا نتیجہ تھا نہ کہ پارلیا منٹ کے ایکٹ کا جس طرح جواہر لال نہرو یونیورسٹی وجود میں آئی ۔ ان دونوں یونیورسٹیوں میں شعبہ تاریخ، شعبہ فارسی، شعبہ اردو، اور شعبہ اسلامک اسٹڈیز ہیں ۔ ۱۹۵۷ میں یہ دونوں یونیور سٹیاں اپنے شباب پر تھیں ۔ بڑے بڑے مورخین اور دانشوران دونوں یونیورسٹیوں سے وابستہ تھے تو انھوں نے ان دستاویزات پر ایسا پروجیکٹ کیوں نہیں بنایا۔ علی گڑھ یونیورسٹی کے بانی نے تو ۱۸۵۷ پر تن تنہا دو کتابیں لکھ دیں اور شعبہ تاریخ اسی دانشگاہ کا کوئی کام نہیں کر سکا جبکہ اسکو سینٹر آف ایڈوانس اسٹڈیز کا درجہ بھی مل گیا۔ جامعہ ملیہ اسلامیہ کی تو بنیاد ہی آزادی کی تحریک کا نتیجہ تھی اور علی گڑھ سے علحدہ ہی اسی لیئے ہوئے تھے کہ آزادی کے ساتھ کام کریں گے۔ انگریزوں کے عہد میں تو آزادی سے کام کر نے کا جذبہ تھا اور آزادی کے بعد آزادی کی پہلی تحریک یعنی ۱۸۵۷ پر جامعہ نے کیوں سرد مہری طاری رکھی اور کیوں نہ ۱۸۵۷ کی دستاویزات پر کوئی کام شروع کیا۔ ولیم ڈالرمپل اس بات میں حق بجانب ہیں کہ ۱۸۵۷ کے ۱۵۰ سال گزر جانے کے بعد ایک بھی تحقیقی مقالہ ان دستایزات پر مبنی کسی ہندوستانی یونیورسٹی میں پیش نہیں ہوا۔ جب علی گڑھ مسلم یونیورسٹی اور جامعہ ملیہ اسلامیہ کا یہ عالم ہے تو ہم دہلی یونیورسٹی جواہر لال نہرو یونیورسٹی، کلکتہ یونیورسٹی۔ ممبئی یونیورسٹی، الہ آباد یونیورسٹی، لکھنو یونیورسٹی، پٹنہ

یونیورسٹی، سنٹرل یونیورسٹی حیدر آباد، عثمانیہ یونیوسٹی، علاقائی یونیورسٹیوں اور کالجوں کے اساتذہ سے کیا توقع کرسکتے ہیں اسلیئے کہ ان دانشگاہوں کے مورخین عام طور سے فارسی اور اردو زبان جانتے ہی نہیں۔

۱۸۵۷ تو دور کی بات ہے عہد سلطنت اور مغل عہد کے فارسی ماخذوں پر ہمارے آزاد ہندوستان میں کیا کام ہوا ہے۔ضیاء الدین برنی کی تاریخ فیروز شاہی اور ابوالفضل کی آئین اکبری کی تدوین و اشاعت کا کام سرسید نے ہی کر دیا تھا پھر انگریزوں نے فارسی ماخذوں کی تدوین و تراجم اور اشاعت کا کام کیا جن کی بنیاد پر علی گڑھ مسلم یونیورسٹی، جامعہ ملیہ اسلامیہ، دہلی یونیورسٹی، جواہر لال نہرو یونیورسٹی اور دوسری یونیورسٹیوں اور کالجوں کے اساتذہ اور ریسرچ اسکالرز کام کر رہے ہیں۔ان فارسی ماخذوں کی تدوین و تراجم کا کام تو چند ہی ہندوستانی مورخین نے کیا ہے جن میں جادو ناتھ سرکار، سید حسن عسکری، شیخ عبدالرشید، نجیب اشرف ندوی، ستیش چندرا، ضیاء الدین ڈیسائی، اقتدار حسین صدیقی، جوہری، مظفر عالم عذر انظامی، تسنیم احمد اور عزیز الدین وغیرہ ہیں۔عہد وسطی کے زیادہ تر فارسی ماخذ ابھی بھی مخطوطات کی شکل میں، ہی مختلف آرکائیوز، میوزیم اور لائبریریوں کے شعبہ مخطوطات میں محفوظ ہیں۔اور آج تک ان کی تدوین و اشاعت نہ ہوسکی۔اگر ہم اندازہ لگائیں تو ان فارسی مخطوطات کی تدوین و اشاعت کا کام زیادہ برٹش راج میں ہی ہوا اور آزد ہندوستان میں اسکے مقابلہ میں کم ہوا۔اگر انگریز فارسی ماخذوں کی تدوین، تراجم اور اشاعت نہ کر جاتے تو جو کچھ جدید دور میں عہد وسطی پر کام ہوا ہے یہ بھی نہ ہوتا اسلیئے کہ آزاد ہندوستان کا عہد وسطی کا مورخ جو سلطنت دہلی، گجرات، بنگال، دکن، جونپور، اور مغل بادشاہوں پر کام کر رہا ہے ان میں بڑی تعداد ایسی ہے جو فارسی زبان سے واقف نہیں ہیں۔

۱۹۷۳ میں انڈین کاؤنسل آف ہسٹوریکل ریسرچ قائم ہوئی۔ اسکے قیام کا مقصد اس وقت کے وزیر تعلیم استاد محترم پروفیسر سید نورالحسن، جو خود عہد وسطی کے ممتاز مورخ تھے کا یہ مقصد تھا کہ کاؤنسل جدید اور آزاد ہندوستان میں، ہندوستان کی تاریخ پر کام ان کے ماخذوں کی روشنی میں کرے گی۔ شروع میں ماخذوں کی تدوین وتراجم پر کافی توجہ دی گئی۔ لیکن کاؤنسل جس کے ممبران ملک کے نامور مورخین ہیں، نے ۱۸۵۷ کے فارسی وارد و دستاویزات پر اپنے قیام سے ۲۰۰۶ تک calendering یا listing پر کوئی پروجیکٹ نہیں بنایا۔ یعنی انگریزوں نے تو ۱۸۵۷ کی کچھ دستاویزات کی presslist تیار کرا کے ۱۹۲۱ میں شائع کرادی جب ہم khilafat اور Non cooperation movement چلا رہے تھے۔ حد یہ ہوئی کہ اس presslist میں غلطیاں ہیں تو اس presslist کا بھی دوسرا ایڈیشن ہم شائع نہ کر سکے جس میں ان غلطیوں کا ازالہ کیا جا سکتا۔ اور آج نیشنل آرکائیوز آف انڈیا میں ۸۶ سال گزر جانے کے بعد بھی presslist کی آج بھی وہی کاپی موجود ہے جو انگریز ۱۹۲۱ میں شائع کرا گئے تھے۔ انل نوریہ اور ولیم ڈالرمپل کو یہ خبر تھی کہ ۲۰۰۷ میں ۱۸۵۷ کی ۱۵۰ ویں سالگرہ ہوگی لیکن ICHR کو کوئی خبر ہی نہ تھی اس کو یہ فیصلہ ۱۹۹۰ میں ہی لے لینا چاہیے تھا کہ ۱۸۵۷ پر کوئی پروجیکٹ بنا کر کام شروع کرتے تا کہ اب کچھ چیز سامنے ہوتی۔ ICHR نے ۱۸۵۷ سے متعلق فارسی وارد و دستاویزات پر کام کرنے کا فیصلہ ۲۰۰۶ میں کیا ہے یعنی اب ایک سال بھی نہیں رہا۔ فارسی کی ایک مثل مشہور ہے ''دیر آید درست آید'' دیر میں شروع ہونے والا کام اچھا ہوتا ہے۔ اب کام شروع ہوا ہے تو کب ختم ہوگا اور کب شائع ہوگا۔ ولیم ڈالرمپل کی کتاب تو ۲۰۰۶ میں شائع ہوگئی۔ میں ICHR کے اس فیصلہ کا خیر مقدم کرتا ہوں اسلئے کہ کم از کم کام تو شروع ہوا۔ اور اگر ۲۰۰۷ میں یہ

کام مکمل نہ ہوا تو ہم اس کام کا فائدہ اس وقت اٹھا سکیں گے کہ جب ملک ۲۰۵۷ میں ۱۸۵۷ کی دو سوویں سالگرہ منائے گا۔ لیکن بقول شاعر

کون جیتا ہے تری زلف کے سر ہونے تک

یہ کوئی نئی بات نہیں ہے جب نظام خراب ہوتا ہے تو اسی طرح کے حالات کا سامنا کرنا ہوتا ہے۔ ابوالفضل ماموری عہد اورنگزیب کا مورخ ہے وہ لکھتا ہے کہ ایک امیر اپنے بچے کو اورنگزیب کے دربار میں لایا اور درخواست کی کہ اس بچے کو منصب عطا کر دیجئے تو اورنگزیب نے کہا کہ یہ تو کم سن ہے اسکو منصب کیسے دیا جا سکتا ہے۔ اس نے کہا کہ اس بچے کو منصب آج عطا کر دیجئے لیکن اسکو جاگیر اس وقت مل پائے گی جب یہ داڑھی والا ہو جائے گا۔ کم از کم ۲۰۰۶ میں ICHR نے کمیٹی تو بنا دی ۱۸۵۷ کے فارسی و اردو دستاویزات پر کام کرنے کے لیے انشاء اللہ کبھی نہ کبھی کام تو مکمل ہو ہی جائے گا۔ اور یہ ان لوگوں کے لیے جنھوں نے ۱۸۵۷ میں انگریزوں سے لڑتے لڑتے شہادت پائی ICHR کی طرف سے ایک اچھا خراج عقیدت ہوگا۔

ایک اہم مسئلہ ان دستاویزات کی بقاء کا ہے۔ نہ صرف ان دستاویزات کا بلکہ باقی تمام اس طرح کے ماخذ کا ہی ہے۔ ان دستاویزات کو رکھے رکھے ۱۵۰ سال گذر گئے اور نیشنل آرکائیوز آف انڈیا، نئی دہلی کے علاوہ چاہے وہ یو۔ پی اسٹیٹ آرکائیوز، لکھنؤ الہ آباد، راجستھان اسٹیٹ آرکائیوز، بیکانیر و جے پور اور ہر جگہ کہیں بھی ایر کنڈیشننگ کا انتظام نہیں بلکہ یہ دستاویزات ۴۲ ڈگری اور ۲ ڈگری سینٹی گریڈ میں موسم گرما اور موسم سرما اور برسات کے موسم میں رکھے رہتے ہیں اس سے ان دستاویزات کو سخت نقصان پہنچ رہا ہے۔ اب ان کی حالت یہ ہے کہ اگر آپ کسی دستاویز کا مطالعہ کریں تو اسکا کاغذ ٹوٹنے

لگتا ہے اور کچھ دستاویزات تو ختم ہو چکی ہیں۔اسی طرح نیشنل آرکائیوز آف انڈیا کے علاوہ اب صرف اکا دکا آرکائیوسٹ کے کوئی فارسی نہیں جانتا۔ان آرکائیوز کی فارسی سے متعلق جگہوں کو پر ہی نہیں کیا گیا۔ چاہے وہ نیشنل میوزیم ،نئی دہلی۔اتر پردیش آرکائیوز لکھنؤ،سالار جنگ میوزیم حیدرآباد، راجستھان اسٹیٹ آرکائیوز، جے پور، فارسی محکموں کے شعبوں سے متعلق جگہوں کو پر نہیں کیا گیا۔بیگم حضرت محل نے ۱۸۵۷ میں قیادت کی لیکن اتر پردیش آرکائیوز،لکھنؤ نے ان پر کیا کام کیا ہے۔ان پر موجود ماخذوں کی لسٹنگ تک تیار نہیں کی گئی۔مرکزی اور صوبائی سرکاروں کو توجہ دینی ہوگی تب ہی یہ ماخذ محفوظ رہ سکیں گے اور ان پر کام ہو سکے گا۔

دوسرا اہم مسئلہ اب ان دستاویزات کے مطالعے کا ہے۔یہ دستاویزات زیادہ فارسی وارد وخط شکست میں ہیں ولیم ڈالرمپل نے تو محمود فاروقی کی مدد سے ان دستاویزات کا مطالعہ کیا۔پروفیسر عرفان حبیب نے ولیم ڈالرمپل کی کتاب کے جائزہ میں اس طرف توجہ دلائی کہ اب خط شکست پڑھنے والے بہت کم ہیں۔ان کا کہنا ہے کہ برٹش راج میں فارسی وارد وخط شکست پڑھنے کی تعلیم وتربیت ہوتی تھی لیکن اب نہیں ہوتی۔لیکن اگر آزاد ہندوستان میں ایجوکیشن کمیشن کے ممبران نے فارسی وارد وزبان سے تعصب برتتے ہوئے اس کی تعلیم کو اسکولوں میں ختم کرادیا تو یہ ان کا فیصلہ ہوگا۔لیکن علی گڑھ مسلم یونیورسٹی اور جامعہ ملیہ اسلامیہ میں اعلیٰ تعلیم کے ساتھ ساتھ اسکول ایجوکیشن بھی ہے اور دونوں یونیورسٹیاں اپنے اسکولوں کا سلیبس بنانے میں آزاد ہیں۔تو علی گڑھ اور جامعہ کے ارباب حل وعقد اور مورخین اور دانشوروں نے اپنے اسکولوں کے نصاب میں فارسی وارد وخط شکست کی تعلیم وتربیت کو کیوں نہیں رکھا۔اور علی گڑھ نے نہیں رکھا تو یہ وہ جانیں جامعہ تو قائم ہی اسی لیے ہوئی تھی کہ علی گڑھ پر

حکومت کا اثر ہے اور تعلیم آزادی چاہتی ہے۔ تو جو چیز برٹش راج میں اسکولوں کے نصاب تعلیم کا حصہ تھی اسے نکال دیا گیا جبکہ اس کو اور بہتر کرنے کی ضرورت تھی۔ پھر دونوں یونیورسٹیوں میں شعبہ فارسی و اردو موجود ہیں تو بی۔اے۔ آنرز میں ایک مضمون خط شکست کی تعلیم و تربیت سے متعلق ہو سکتا تھا۔ آج ہم کہہ رہے ہیں کہ خط شکست کے پڑھنے والے ہی نہیں رہے لیکن ہم نے اس کے لیے کچھ نہیں کیا۔ پروفیسر مشیر الحسن کی بات کافی حد تک اثر انداز ہو سکتی ہے کہ ولیم ڈالرمپل کے کام کے بعد بھی کیا ہمارے سست مورخین نہ جاگیں گے۔ لیکن میں مشیر الحسن سے سوال کرتا ہوں کہ اب جاگنے سے فائدہ کیا ہوگا؟ اس لیے کہ جب ہم ۱۸۵۷ سے متعلق دستاویزات جو فارسی و اردو خط شکست میں لکھے ہوئے ہیں ان کو پڑھنے والے ہیں نہیں رہے دستاویز کی ایک لائن پڑھنا دشوار ہے۔ جو اساتذہ شکست پڑھنے کے ماہر تھے انھوں نے دوسروں کو اس لیے نہیں سکھایا تا کہ ان کی اہمیت برقرار رہے۔ اور وہ ہی اس کے استاد رہیں جیسا کہ غالب نے کہا ہے حالانکہ وہ بات دوسری ہے:

ریختہ کے تم ہی استاد نہیں ہو غالبؔ   سنتے ہیں اگلے زمانے میں کوئی میر بھی تھا

یہ تو ۱۸۵۷ کی دستاویزات کا مسئلہ ہے اگر سرسید آئین اکبری کی تدوین و اشاعت اور انگریز اس کا ترجمہ نہ کر دیتے تو آئین اکبری کے پڑھنے والے بھی نہ ملتے۔ جو کچھ کام آئین اکبری پر مورخین نے کیا ہے وہ سرسید اور بلوک مین کا مرہون منت ہے۔ سرسید نے ۱۸۵۷ سے متعلق کچھ دستاویزات کی نقول اپنی کتاب سرکشی ضلع بجنور اور اسباب بغاوت ہند کی تصنیف کے دوران کرائیں تھیں جو مولانا آزاد لائبریری کے شعبہ مخطوطات میں محفوظ ہیں ان کی بھی حالت خستہ ہے۔ ان دستاویزات پر بھی جدید تحقیق کی روشنی میں کوئی کام نہیں ہوا۔ ۲۰۰۶ میں شعبہ تاریخ علی گڑھ مسلم یونیورسٹی نے ایک انٹر

نیشنل سیمنار سرسید پر اپنی تاریخ میں پہلی مرتبہ کرایا اس سیمنار میں بھی کوئی مقالہ ان دستاویزات پر پیش نہیں کیا گیا۔

اس دور میں دہلی سے تین اخبارات شائع ہورہے تھے جن کا ۱۸۵۷ میں بڑا اہم کردار ہا ہے۔ دہلی اردو اخبار یہ دہلی کا پہلا اردو اخبار تھا۔ جو ۳۷۔۱۸۳۶ میں جاری ہوا اس کے ایڈیٹر مولانا محمد باقر تھے۔ پہلے اس کا نام دہلی اخبار تھا بعد میں دہلی اردو اخبار ہوا۔ مولانا محمد باقر کو بھی ان کی تحریروں کو بنیاد بنا کر انگریزوں نے پھانسی دے دی۔ جولائی ۱۸۵۷ میں اس کا نام اخبار الظفر ہوگیا۔ دوسرا صادق الاخبار تھا۔ اس کے ایڈیٹر امداد حسین تھے یہ اخبار ۱۸۵۷ میں ہی بند ہوگیا۔ سراج الاخبار فارسی زبان میں شائع ہوتا تھا اور بہادر شاہ کے روزنامچہ کی حیثیت رکھتا تھا۔ خواجہ حسن نظامی نے ان اخبارات پر کام کیا۔ لیکن بعد میں ان اخبارات پر کام نہیں ہوا۔ جب کہ اس کی بھی کاپیاں نیشنل آرکائیوز آف انڈیا کمشنرز آفس' دہلی' دہلی اسٹیٹ آرکائیوز اور کچھ لوگوں کے اپنے ذاتی ذخیروں میں محفوظ ہیں۔ ان اخبارات پر ایک کام علیحدہ ہوسکتا ہے کہ ۱۸۵۷ سے متعلق یہ اخبارات کن مسائل پر بات کررہے تھے۔

سرسید نے ایک اہم کام یہ کیا کہ انگریزوں کی حکومت قائم ہوجانے سے اب مسلم تہذیب وثقافت کو خطرہ لاحق ہوجائے گا اس لیے کہ نہ صرف انھیں مسلمانوں کے ان کارناموں سے دلچسپی نہیں تھی بلکہ اس کو تباہ و برباد کرنے کی کوشش بھی کریں گے۔ انھوں نے دہلی کے آثار قدیمہ پر ایک کتاب آثار الصنادید ۱۸۴۶ میں لکھی۔ اسی کتاب میں ایک شعر لکھتے ہیں:

از نقش و نگار در و دیوار شکستہ   آثار پدید است صنادید عجم را

ان آثار کو جاٹ اور مرہٹہ پہلے ہی نقصان پہنچا چکے تھے۔ اب انگریزوں کی باری تھی اور ہوا بھی

ایسا ہی کہ شاہجہاں آباد کو ریل سے جوڑنے کے لیے لال قلعہ کا ایک برج، بیگم اورنگ آبادی کی بنائی ہوئی مسجد اور زیب النساء کے مقبرہ کو ۱۸۵۲ میں منہدم کردیا۔ حالانکہ ریل کی پٹری موری گیٹ کے سامنے لاکر اسٹیشن تعمیر کرسکتے تھے جس طرح اجمیری گیٹ کے سامنے نئی دہلی ریلوے اسٹیشن ہے۔ اس سے ان کے دو مقصد تھے ایک تو مسلمانوں کو تکلیف پہنچانی اور دوسرے شاہ جہاں آباد میں انگریزی فوج اور ہتھیاروں کو ریل کے ذریعہ لایا جاسکے۔ شیعی مسلک سے تعلق رکھنے والے مسلمانوں کی ایک مسجد شاہ جہاں آباد میں تھی لیکن ریلوے لائن سامنے سے گذرنے سے شیعۃ الصفا مسجد کا تعلق شاہ جہاں آباد سے منقطع ہوگیا۔ شیعی آبادی شاہ جہاں آباد میں اور مسجد ریلوے لائن کے دوسری طرف۔ یہ صرف مسلمانوں کو اذیت پہنچانے کے لیے کیا تھا۔ ۱۸۵۷ میں انگریزوں نے دہلی پر قبضہ کرنے کے بعد سب سے پہلے کشمیری دروازہ اور کچھ اور دروازوں اور کھڑکیوں کو جگہ جگہ سے شاہ جہاں آباد کی فصیل کو اڑادیا تاکہ آئندہ ۱۸۵۷ جیسی حالت ہو تو شاہ جہاں آباد کے راستے کھلے رہیں۔ اس لیے کہ جن دروازوں کا ذکر خیر المنازل اور آثار الصنادید میں ہے وہ دروازے اور کھڑکیاں آج ہیں ہی نہیں۔ جیسے کیلا گھاٹ دروازہ، کابلی دروازہ، لاہوری دروازہ، خیراتی دروازہ، راجگھاٹ دروازہ، کلکتہ دروازہ وغیرہ۔ جامع مسجد کے سامنے ایک مسجد اکبر آبادی بیگم زوجہ شاہ جہاں نے تعمیر کرائی تھی ۱۸۵۷ میں انگریزوں نے اس مسجد کو بھی مسمار کردیا۔ اس مسجد کے کتبات کو سرسید نے حفاظت سے رکھ لیا، اور جب ایم۔ اے۔ او کالج میں جامع مسجد تعمیر کی تو ان کتبات کو مرکزی محراب پر نصب کرادیا۔ انگریزوں نے جامع مسجد کے سامنے ایڈورڈ کا مجسمہ لگادیا اور اسکا نام، ایڈورڈ پارک رکھا۔ یہ بھی مسلمانوں کو اذیت پہچانے کے لیے کیا۔ اسلام نے بت پرستی کو منع کیا اور ایڈورڈ کا مجسمہ جامع مسجد دہلی کے سامنے لگادیا۔ اور کمال کی بات

یہ ہے کہ آزاد ہندوستان کی حکومت میں کیا فرق رہا۔ تاریخ کا کوئی خیال آزاد ہندوستان کی حکومت نے بھی نہیں کیا۔ اگر پارک بن ہی گیا تھا تو آزاد ہندوستان میں پارک کا نام سبھاش پارک رکھ دیا جب کہ اس پارک کا نام شاہ جہاں پارک ہونا چاہیے تھا۔ یہی زیادتی آگرہ میں بھی کی ہے کہ جو سڑک قلعہ سے تاج محل کو جاتی ہے اسکا نام راجہ جی مارگ رکھ دیا۔ راجہ جی کا قلعہ اور تاج محل سے کیا تعلق۔ اسکا نام ممتاز محل مارگ ہونا چاہیے تھا۔ انگریزوں نے آگرہ کے قلعہ کے دروازے کا نام امر سنگھ گیٹ رکھ دیا۔ اور ۲۰۰۳ میں جب بھارتیہ جنتا پارٹی کی حکومت تھی تو اسنے قلعہ کے دروازہ کے سامنے شیواجی کا مجسمہ کھڑا کردیا۔ چاہے انگریز ہوں یا ہندوستانی حکمراں۔ یہ سب کام ہندوستان کی تاریخ کو مسخ کرنے کے لیے کئے ہیں۔ جامع مسجد اور قلعہ مبارک کے درمیان کوچہ بلاقی بیگم اور خانم بازار تھا وہ سب مسمار کردیے غالب نے اپنے ایک دوست کو لکھا کہ ''جامع مسجد سے راج گھاٹ تک اینٹوں اور پتھروں کے اتنے ڈھیر لگے ہوئے ہیں کہ اگر انھیں ہٹادیا جائے تو ہو کا عالم ہوجائے۔'' غالب کے اس جملہ سے اس مسماری کا اندازہ ہوتا ہے۔ شاہجہاں نے یہ جگہ معماران تاج محل وشاہجہاں آباد کو رہائش کے لیے دی تھی۔ اور شاہ کلیم اللہ کا تعلق اسی خاندان سے تھا۔ اب صرف اس میدان میں شاہ کلیم اللہ کا مزار رہ گیا ہے۔ اور مولانا آزاد کی قبر جو آزاد ہندوستان میں ہی بنی ہے۔ مدرسہ رحیمیہ کو بھی مسمار کردیا گیا۔ اسی طرح کی انہدامی کاروائی قلعہ مبارک میں بھی کی انگوری باغ، مہتاب باغ اور دیگوا باڑی باغ سب تباہ کردیے اور فوجی بارک تعمیر کردی گئیں اور بہت سے مکانات بھی مسمار کردیے گئے۔ قلعہ مبارک کی شکل بھی بدل دی۔ حیات بخش باغ کی عمارت کو انگریز فوجیوں کا اصطبل بنادیا۔ دیوان عام کو برٹش افسروں کے آرام کا کمرہ بنادیا، رنگ محل کو فوجیوں کے کھانے کا کمرہ بنادیا۔ قلعہ کے لاہوری

دروازہ کا نام وکٹوریہ گیٹ رکھدیا۔ میں ولیم ڈالرمپل کی اس بات سے متفق نہیں کہ جب وہ یہ کہتے ہیں کہ قلعہ مبارک میں انگریزوں کی بنائی ہوئی بارکوں کو مسمار کردینا چاہیے۔ قطعی نہیں ان کی مرمت کرا کے درست رکھنا چاہیے تا کہ آنے والی نسلیں دیکھ سکیں کہ انگریزوں نے کیا زیادتیاں قلعہ کے ساتھ کی تھیں۔ لیکن آزاد ہندوستان میں قلعہ مبارک پر کوئی خاص توجہ نہیں دی گئی باوجود اس کے کہ ۱۵/اگست کو یوم آزادی کا پروگرام یہیں منعقد ہوتا ہے۔ قلعہ کے جس حصے پر ۱۵/اگست کا پروگرام ہوتا ہے وہ دیوار اورنگزیب نے تعمیر کرائی تھی۔ شاید اسے یہ پتہ ہو کہ جب ہندوستان آزاد ہوگا تو آزادی کے پروگرام کی ابتداء اس کی تعمیر کردہ دیوار سے ہی ہوا کرے گی لیکن جب اس حصے کو بڑا کرکے بنایا گیا تا کہ لفٹ وغیرہ لگائی جاسکے تو لال قلعہ کی تعمیر اور اسکے پتھروں کا ذرا بھی لحاظ نہیں رکھا گیا اور یہ حصہ اس خوبصورت صحن میں انتہائی بدنما اور بھدے موٹے موٹے پتھروں سے تعمیر کیا گیا ہے جس وقت لال قلعے میں یہ موٹے بدنما پتھروں کی چنائی ہو رہی ہوگی اس وقت شاہ جہاں کی روح ہمارے پھوہڑپن اور گنوارپن پر ہنس رہی ہوگی انگریزوں نے نہ صرف ۱۸۵۷ کے بعد ہندوستانیوں کو ہی پھانسی نہیں دی بلکہ ان کے قلعوں، گڑھیوں اور مکانات کو بھی مسمار کردیا۔ ریواڑی، دادری، جھجھر، میوات، بلبھ گڑھ، فرخ نگر، جہاں گیرآباد، امروہہ، مرادآباد، علی گڑھ وغیرہ کے قلعہ اور مکانات کو منہدم کردیا گیا۔ نجیب آباد میں مسلمانوں کو اذیت پہنچانے کے لیے انگریزوں نے جامع مسجد کے صحن کو نیلام کردیا وہاں آج بھی لوگوں کے گھر بنے ہوئے ہیں اور گھروں کی گندی نالیاں مسجد کے صحن میں بہہ رہی ہیں۔ قلعوں کو اسطرح مسمار کیا گیا تا کہ پھر ان کا استعمال نہ ہو سکے۔ اس تباہی کا نقشہ ایک شاعر نے کیا خوب کھینچا ہے۔

اے فلک! اس سے زیادہ نہ مٹانا ہرگز　　مٹ گئے تیرے مٹانے کے نشاں بھی اب تو

انگریزوں نے دہلی کو کیوں تباہ کیا۔ اسکی وجہ حالی نے بیان کی ہے۔

آں کر لیتے تھے یاں ٹھیکی جہاں کے انتخاب　　تیرا معمور تھا ایک عالم میں مرجع اور ماب

کردیا تھا تیری آبادی نے ملکوں کو خراب　　بستے تھے آ آ کے تجھ میں شیخ و شاب

دستہ تھا گویا تو گلہاے رنگا رنگ　　جھمکٹا تھا تجھ میں ترک وفرس وروم وزنگ کا

ضیاء الدین برنی جو چودھویں صدی کے مورخ ہیں اپنی تاریخ فیروزشاہی میں لکھتے ہیں کہ ۱۲۵۸ میں بغداد کے زوال کے بعد دہلی رشک بغداد بن کرابھری دنیاے اسلام کے جید عالم ہندوستان آئے۔ مسلم دنیا میں دہلی مسلم تہذیب وثقافت کے اہم مراکز میں تھی اوراس کا برباد کرنا انگریزوں کے لیے ضروری تھا۔ ۱۸۵۷ کے بعد انگریزوں نے قلعہ مبارک کی لائبریری کو لوٹا اور لندن لے گئے جس طرح ۲۰۰۳ میں بغداد کے میوزیم کو لوٹا۔ اگر سرسید نے ۱۸۴۶ میں آثارالصنادید نہ لکھدی ہوتی تو ۱۸۵۷ کے بعد دہلی کے آثار کو جونقصان انگریزوں نے پہونچایا اس کا ہم اندازہ نہیں کرسکتے تھے۔ اس لیے کہ فارسی ماخذ ان آثار پر اتنی معلومات نہیں فراہم کرتے۔ میرے خیال سے سرسید کا اہم اور زبردست کارنامہ ’آثارالصنادید‘ ہے اس لیے کہ اس دور کے کسی اور مسلم دانشور میں یہ صلاحیت نہیں تھی۔ ایم۔اے۔او کالج نہیں، اس لیے کہ کالج تو ان کے معاصرین نے بھی قائم کیے۔ لیکن افسوس کہ سرسید نے تو قدیم آثار کی حفاظت کی خاطر بڑی محنت و کاوش کے ساتھ ایک کتاب آثار الصنادید لکھدی۔ لیکن ۲۰۰۳ میں سرسید ہاوس میں ایک پرشکوہ عمارت تعمیر کرکے سرسید ہاوس کی تاریخ اور کریکٹر کو ختم کردیا۔ جب کہ آرکیالوجیکل سروے آف انڈیا کا تو قانون ہے کہ کسی بھی آثار قدیمہ کے

قریب کوئی نئی عمارت تعمیر نہیں کی جائے گی۔ اور یہ اس یونیورسٹی میں ہوا جس کا نام علی گڑھ مسلم یونیورسٹی ہے۔ اور جس یونیورسٹی میں تاریخ کا سینٹر آف ایڈوانس اسٹڈی اور آرکیالوجی کا بھی شعبہ ہے۔ مجھے یاد ہے کہ جب میں علی گڑھ یونیورسٹی کا ۱۹۶۸ میں طالب علم تھا تو ہر سال اسٹوڈینٹس یونین کا یہ پہلا مطالبہ ہوتا تھا کہ سرسید ہاوس کو اسکے نقشے کے مطابق درست کرایا جائے اور جب یہ سب کچھ ہوگیا تو اب یہ ہوا۔ بقول شاعر

اب ہم ہیں اور ماتم یک شہر آرزو

لیکن آزاد ہندوستان میں بھی قلعہ مبارک کی مرمت اور حفاظت پر کوئی خاص توجہ نہیں دی گئی۔ لیکن ۲۰۰۲ میں قلعہ مبارک سابق وزیر ثقافت، جگ موہن کی توجہ کا مرکز رہا جس کے نتیجے میں کافی کام ہوا اور قلعہ میں زندگی کے آثار دوبارہ عیاں ہونے لگے۔ لیکن اب پھر کوئی توجہ نہیں دی جارہی اس لیے کہ ابھی کافی کام باقی ہے۔ باغ کے چشموں کی روش کو دوبارہ ٹھیک کیا گیا تھا اب پھر ٹوٹے ہوئے پتھر پڑے ہیں۔ باغ کے ایک حصے کا پتھر بالکل ٹوٹ گیا اور کوئی دیکھنے والا نہیں۔ قلعہ مبارک کی ۲۱ویں صدی عیسوی میں حالت ہماری بے حسی و بے توجہی کا مرثیہ پڑھ رہی ہے۔

یوں تو دستاویزات ہزاروں ہیں اور ان پر یو جی سی یا آئی سی ایچ آر کو کوئی بڑا پروجیکٹ بنانا چاہیے تب ہی یہ کام مکمل ہوسکتا ہے۔ لیکن میں نے اپنے مطالعہ کے بعد ۱۸۵۷ کی ۱۵۰ویں سالگرہ کی مناسبت سے ۱۵۰ دستاویزات کا انتخاب کیا تاکہ میرا نام بھی اس فہرست میں شامل ہوجائے جن لوگوں نے ۱۸۵۷ کی ۱۵۰ویں سالگرہ پر کوئی کام کیا تھا۔ اور یہ میری طرف سے ان لوگوں کو خراج عقیدت ادا ہونے کا ذریعہ ہوگا جنھوں نے ملک کی حفاظت میں اپنی جانیں دیدیں۔

بہادر شاہ نے ١٨٥٧ میں عیدالاضحیٰ سے قبل کئی حکم جاری کیے کہ جن میں گائے کے ذبیحہ کی سخت ممانعت کی اور باقاعدہ کوتوال اور تھانہ داران شاہ جہاں آباد کو حکم جاری کیا کہ یہ ان کی ذمہ داری ہوگی کہ عیدالاضحیٰ کے موقعہ پر گائے کی قربانی نہ ہو۔ اور جو بھی اس جرم کا مرتکب ہوگا اس کو سخت سزا دی جائے گی۔

ایک دستاویز ٨/اپریل ١٨٥٧ کی جسمیں بہادر شاہ کی طرف سے حکم جاری ہوا ہے کہ محرم میں باجانہ بجایا جائے اس سے ظاہر ہوتا ہے کہ عزاداری امام حسین کی بنیاد جو دہلی میں صوفیا نے ڈالی تھی اس کا پاس ولحاظ مغل بادشاہوں نے رکھا۔ بہادر شاہ دوم بھی اسی بات کا لحاظ رکھتے ہوئے عزاے حسین کے دنوں میں باجا بجانے کی ممانعت کرر ہے ہیں جس کی کاپی کوتوال شہر دہلی اور جملہ تھانہ داران شاہ جہاں آباد کو بھیجی جارہی ہے۔

دستاویز مورخہ ٢٠/مئی ١٨٥٧ امام باڑہ تعمیر کردہ عشرت علی سے متعلق ہے جس کے لیے زمین مغل بادشاہ اکبر دوم نے دی تھی اس امام باڑہ پر حیدر علی نے قبضہ کرلیا۔ ان کا قبضہ ہٹوانے کے سلسلے سے درخواست ہے۔ درخواست سے ثابت ہوتا ہے کہ اس دور میں قانون شکنی کافی بڑھ چکی تھی اور سکنی جائدادوں کے علاوہ لوگ وقف فی سبیل اللہ جائدادوں پر بھی قبضے کررہے تھے۔

دستاویز مورخہ ٢١/مئی ١٨٥٧ سے ظاہر ہوتا ہے کہ کچھ عورتوں اور بچوں کو عیسائی سمجھ کر گرفتار کرلیا گیا۔ کیا انیسویں صدی کے نصف میں مسلم عورتوں کی شناخت ختم ہوگئی تھی اور انھوں نے بھی وہی لباس پہننا شروع کردیا تھا جو عیسائی عورتیں پہنتی تھیں اور اسی وجہ سے انھیں گرفتار کر کے قید کردیا گیا۔

٢٧/مئی ١٨٥٧ ساکنان درگاہ حضرت نظام الدین اولیا جن میں ہندو اور مسلمان دونوں شامل تھے انھوں بہادر شاہ کو درخواست دی کہ گوجر اس قدر چوری اور ڈکیتی کرر ہے ہیں جس کی وجہ سے

ساکنان درگاہ حضرت نظام الدین اولیا، کٹرہ ارادت مند خاں، عرب سرائے، نظام پور سخت پریشان تھے اور رات کی نیند حرام تھی رات بھر جاگ کر گذارتے تھے اب جب سے تھانہ عرب سرائے میں قائم ہوا ہے تب سے امن ہے اور ہم رات کو سو سکتے ہیں۔ اس دور کی افراتفری سے سب سے زیادہ فائدہ گوجروں نے اٹھایا جس کی وجہ سے لوگ عاجز و پریشان ہو گئے۔ راجہ ناہر سنگھ جو بلبھ گڑھ کے حکمراں تھے ان کے خطوط میں بھی گوجروں کی سخت شکایت ہے۔

مورخہ ۱۰ر جون ۱۸۵۷ اصغر علی ولد سید ظہیر علی کے رشتے کے سلسلے میں ہے۔ اس خط سے ظاہر ہوتا ہے کہ لوگ کس طرح حسب و نسب میں دلچسپی رکھتے تھے اور کسی بھی رشتے کے طے کرنے سے پہلے شجرے کے بارے میں معلومات بہم کی جاتی تھیں۔

مورخہ ۱۰ر جولائی ۱۸۵۷ ایک عرضی حافظ عبدالرحمٰن کی ہے کہ دہلی میں کاروبار نہ ہونے کی وجہ سے انھوں نے اپنے ذریعہ معاش کے لیے کباب بیچنے کا کام شروع کر دیا۔ پولس نے کچھ قصائیوں کو گاؤکشی کے الزام میں گرفتار کیا تو ان کو بھی گرفتار کر کے جیل بھیج دیا تو انھوں نے بادشاہ کو عرضی لکھی کہ میں قصائی نہیں۔ کاروبار ختم ہونے کی بناء پر کباب بیچ کر روزی کمانے کا ذریعہ بنایا تاکہ معاش کا انتظام ہو۔ تب بہادر شاہ نے حکم جاری کیا کہ ان کو رہا کیا جائے۔ یہ عرضی دلی میں سب لوگوں کی بدحالی کی غماض ہے کہ لوگ کس طرح پریشان تھے دوسرے بہادر شاہ نے گاؤکشی کو کس سختی سے روکنے کی کوشش کی تھی۔ تیسرے پولس بغیر کسی تفتیش کے لوگوں کو گرفتار کر لیتی تھی۔

مورخہ ۱۲ر جولائی ۱۸۵۷ میں ایک عرضی بہادر شاہ کو شیخ غلام نبی ساکن امروہہ نے لکھی کہ وہ بنارس میں انگریزی فوج کی نوکری چھوڑ کر بہادر شاہ کی نوکری کرنے کے لیے حاضر ہوئے۔ یہ عرضی

ظاہر کرتی ہے کہ ہندوستانی کس جذبے کے ساتھ اپنی نوکریوں کو چھوڑ چھوڑ کر بہادر شاہ کی نوکری کرنے کے لیے آرہے تھے۔ ایسے ہی ایک شخص غلام عباس ہیں جو مظفر نگر کے ساکن تھے انھوں نے بھی برٹش سرکار کی ملازمت چھوڑی اور بہادر شاہ کو عرضی مورخہ ۱۹؍جولائی ۱۸۵۷ کو پیش کردی کہ وہ اب انکی خدمت میں حاضر ہیں۔ اپنی اس عرضی میں یہ بھی لکھ رہے ہیں کہ بزرگ فدوی کے قدیم سے نمک پروردہ حضور رہے ہیں تو یہ جذبہ بھی کام کررہا ہے۔ ۱۲؍ذی الحجہ کی ایک دستاویز ہے جو فہرست ہے ان ۱۳۸ اشخاص کی کہ جو امروہہ سے آکر بہادر شاہ کی نوکری میں شامل ہورہے ہیں۔ جب کہ ان تمام اشخاص کو بہادر شاہ کی حیثیت کا علم ہوگا اور ساتھ ہی جو حالات دہلی کے تھے لیکن ان تمام باتوں کے پیچھے ایک جذبہ ہے کہ انھیں کھینچ کرلا رہا ہے ان تمام اقدامات کا ہم انگریزوں سے چھٹکارا اور اپنی حکومت حاصل کرنے کا جذبہ تھا۔

۲۵؍جولائی ۱۸۵۷ کی دستاویز میں ایک رپورٹ درج ہے کہ مسماۃ دل پسند کو غلام محی الدین بھگا کرلے گیا اس کی تلاش کی جائے اور اس کو واپس کیا جائے۔ اس سے ثابت ہوتا ہے کہ کس طرح کے حالات دہلی میں تھے کہ کس طرح کا سماج بن رہا تھا۔ اس دستاویز پر دہلی کے تمام تھانوں کی مہریں اور تھانہ داروں کے نام لکھے ہیں اور کاروائی کا وقت لکھا ہوا ہے۔ جس سے پولس کے انتظام پر روشنی پڑتی ہے۔ ایسی ہی ایک اور رپورٹ ہے۔ مورخہ ۲؍اگست ۱۸۵۷ جسمیں پریم سکھ حجام ساکن محلّہ بہر کھڑی نے تھانہ میں ایک رپورٹ لکھوائی کہ اسکی بیوی مسماۃ کلالی، چندا خلاصی کے بہکانے پر زیورات وغیرہ لے کر چلی گئی ہے۔ اس کی تلاش کی جاوے۔ اس کا پورا حلیہ لکھا ہوا ہے اور سامان کی فہرست سے جو لے کر گئی ہے اس رپورٹ کو بھی دہلی کے تمام تھانوں میں بھیجا گیا ہے۔ یہ اس دور کے سماجی حالات

کی عکاسی کر رہا ہے۔

۴/اگست ۱۸۵۷ کی دستاویز سے پتہ چلتا ہے کہ کچھ لوگوں نے قطب مینار کے نیچے کھیتی کرنا شروع کردی لہذا ان کی اس زمین کو کہیں اور منتقل کیا گیا تاکہ مینار کو نقصان نہ پہونچے۔ کمال کی بات ہے کہ آزاد ہندوستان میں قطب مینار کی چاردیواری سے ملا کر سڑک نکال دی جس پر دن بھر ڈی ٹی سی کی بسیں چلتی ہیں ان کے وائبریشن اور پولیشن سے قطب مینار کے آثار کو نقصان پہونچ رہا ہے۔ ۱۹۵۲ کے پہلے پلانرس نے سڑک نکال دی جس میں رائے پھتوڑا کے قلعہ کی دیوار کو بھی توڑ ڈالا گیا ایسا لگتا ہے کہ ان آثار سے ۱۹ ویں صدی تک لوگوں کو دلچسپی تھی۔ مرزا سنگین بیگ نے سیر المنازل لکھی اور سرسید نے آثار الصنادید لکھی تاکہ کم از کم ان آثار کو کتابوں میں محفوظ کردیا جائے۔ منسٹری آف کلچر اور آرکیالوجیکل سروے آف انڈیا تماشہ دیکھ رہے ہیں اور انتظار کر رہے ہیں کہ کب یہ عمارتیں گریں۔ انگریزوں نے تو ان آثار کو کھلم کھلا منہدم کرایا اور ہم اپنی لاپروائیوں سے ان آثار کو منہدم کرنے کا کام انجام دے رہے ہیں۔

۲۷/جولائی ۱۸۵۷ کو بادشاہ نے ایک حکم جاری کیا اسمیں لکھا کہ اب تک لوگ جب انھیں خط وغیرہ لکھتے تھے تو حضرت جہاں پناہ کے لقب سے نوازتے تھے لیکن بادشاہ نے اس لقب کو ترک کرکے۔ ''غریب پرور سلامت'' کا لقب اختیار کرلیا ہے۔ اب جو بھی ان سے متعلق لکھے گا اس میں یہی لقب لکھے گا بادشاہ کا اپنے لقب کو تبدیل کرنا بڑا تاریخی اور اہم واقعہ تھا۔ اس لیے کہ مغلوں نے ترک منگول نظریہ بادشاہت کو اپنایا اور اس کے تحت یہ القاب اپنے نام کے ساتھ شامل کیے۔ اب بہادر شاہ کو اپنی حیثیت کا اندازہ ہو رہا تھا اور انھوں نے اپنے القاب کو بدل دیا۔

۲۱؍جولائی ۱۸۵۷ دوسری دستاویزات گاؤکشی کی سختی سے ممانعت کے لیے بہادر شاہ کے حکم نامے جاری ہورہے ہیں اور پوری کوشش اس بات کی ہے کہ عیدالاضحیٰ کو کوئی مسلمان گاؤکشی نہ کرسکے۔ بہادر شاہ نہیں چاہتے تھے کہ ہندوؤں کے جذبات کو ٹھیس پہنچے تو انھوں نے دہلی کے کوتوال اور تھانہ داروں کو ہدایت جاری کی کہ وہ اس پر نظر رکھیں اور ایسے اقدامات کریں کہ کوئی مسلمان گاؤکشی کا مرتکب نہ ہوسکے۔ سرسید نے بھی گاوءکشی کو ترک کرنے کی ہدایت کی۔ ۱۹۷۱ میں ایرانی عالم آقای محسن الحکیم نے ایک فتوی جاری کیا تھا کہ اگر کوئی جانور جس کا ذبیحہ اسلام نے حلال قرار دیا ہے لیکن اگر وہ غیر اسلامی ملک میں کسی دوسرے مذہب میں مقدس جانور ہے تو ایسے جانور کی قربانی کو ترک کرنا بہتر ہے۔ اور اس میں انھوں نے ہندوستان کی مثال دی کہ جیسا کہ ہندوستان میں گائے کو مقدس جانور مانا گیا ہے۔ اور اب تو قومی پرندہ کو بھی مارنا قانونا جرم ہے۔ بہادر شاہ کا یہ قدم قومی یک جہتی کے میدان میں اہم قدم تھا۔

۳۱؍جولائی ۱۸۵۷ کا ایک خط راجہ ناہر سنگھ جو بلبھ گڑھ کے جاٹ راجہ تھے بہادر شاہ کے نام ہے انھوں نے اس خط میں اپنی وفاداری سے متعلق لکھا ہے کہ لوگ میرے خلاف افواہیں پھیلا رہے ہیں کہ میں آپ کا وفادار نہیں بلکہ انگریزوں سے مل گیا ہوں یہ سراسر الزام ہے۔ راجہ نے مزید لکھا ہے کہ مجھ سے پہلے کسی نے اس طرف توجہ نہیں دی کہ بلبھ گڑھ میں ایک بھی مسجد نہیں تھی میں نے ایک مسجد قلعہ میں اور ایک جامع مسجد شہر میں تعمیر کرائی تاکہ لوگ اس میں نماز پڑھ سکیں۔ راجہ ناہر سنگھ نے انگریزوں سے مقابلہ کیا اور پھر انھیں چاندنی چوک میں پھانسی دے دی گئی۔ جاٹوں کا مغل باشاہوں سے تعلق رہا اورنگزیب کے عہد میں ۱۶۷۹ میں گوکلا جاٹ نے بغاوت کی اور پھر بہت عرصے تک تعلقات خراب

رہے آخر میں یہ شکل اتنی بدل گئی کہ بہادر شاہ کا ساتھ دینے پر جاٹ راجہ ناہر سنگھ کو پھانسی دی گئی۔

۹/اگست ۱۸۵۷ بہادر شاہ کا خط ہے جسمیں لکھا ہے کہ تم نے حکیم احسن اللہ خاں جو میرے طبیب ہیں ان کا آنا قلعہ میں بند کر دیا ہے وہی میرا علاج کرتے ہیں اور میرے مزاج سے واقف ہیں۔ دراصل اب جن لوگوں کا قلعہ پر قبضہ تھا انکی سمجھ کے مطابق حکیم احسن اللہ خاں انگریزوں سے ملے ہوئے تھے اور بہادر شاہ کے علاج کے بہانے وہ انگریزوں کو قلعہ کی خبریں مہیا کرتے تھے اس بناء پر ان لوگوں نے حکیم احسن اللہ خاں کے قلعہ میں داخلے پر پابندی لگادی۔ جس کی شکایت بہادر شاہ کر رہے ہیں۔

۱۰/اگست ۱۸۵۷ کو قلعہ میں ایک اور حادثہ پیش آیا اور وہ یہ تھا کہ بادشاہ کے خاص سامان کی چوری ہوگئی جسمیں ان کا وہ صندوقچہ بھی چوری ہوگیا جسمیں بادشاہ کی مہریں تھیں اس پر بہادر شاہ نے سخت احتجاج کیا اور کہا کہ اگر تم لوگوں کو میرے ساتھ اسی طرح کا سلوک کرنا ہے تو میں درگاہ قطب الدین بختیار کاکی چلا جاؤنگا اور مجاوری کروں گا۔ ایک اور خط اس واقعہ سے منقول ہے جو انھوں نے نواب جھجھر کو لکھا تھا کہ میں یہاں کے حالات سے تنگ آگیا ہوں تم مجھ کو کچھ اونٹ اور کچھ سوار ساتھ کردو تو پہلے میں درگاہ قطب الدین بختیار کاکی پر حاضری دوں گا اور پھر وہاں سے مکہ چلا جاؤں گا اور باقی زندگی وہیں گذاروں گا۔ اس کے پیچھے کسی انگریز کی انگریزی زبان میں تحریر ہے جس میں لکھا ہے کہ یہ کاغذ محل میں ملا تھا اور ہم بادشاہ کے اس پلان سے باخبر نہ تھے۔ اس سے دو باتیں ظاہر ہوتی ہیں ایک تو یہ کہ بہادر شاہ دلی کے حالات سے عاجز آچکے تھے اور یہاں سے جانا چاہتے تھے دوسرے خط پر جو تحریر انگریز کی ہے اس سے یہ ظاہر ہوتا ہے کہ اگر ان کو بادشاہ کے اس پلان کا علم ہوتا تو وہ بادشاہ کی مکہ

جانے میں مدد کر دیتے اور جو وقت انھیں بعد میں پیش آئی اس سے بچ جاتے۔

ایک خط مورخہ ۱۹/اگست ۱۸۵۷ کا ہے جس میں لکھا ہے کہ ایک فوجی دستہ دہلی سے لکھنؤ بھی گیا لیکن اس کے پہونچنے کی کوئی اطلاع نہیں ملی۔ اس سے ظاہر ہوتا ہے کہ دہلی کی فوج کو دوسرے علاقوں میں بھی انکی مدد کے لیے بھیجا جا رہا تھا۔

دستاویز مورخہ ۲۱/اگست ۱۸۵۷ میں مسکرات کی دو دکانیں جو جامع مسجد کے نیچے ہیں ان سے افیون کی خریداری کا حوالہ ہے کہ افیون بیچنے والے کی دوکان بند ہے۔ یعنی جو مسجد عبادت کے لیے شاہ جہاں نے بنائی تھی اس کے چاروں طرف دکانیں قائم ہو گئیں اور اس میں مسکرات کی دکانیں بھی قائم ہو گئیں۔ ایسا لگتا ہے کہ یہی دوکانیں تھیں جو بڑھتے بڑھتے پورا بازار بن گئیں اور جامع مسجد کو چاروں طرف سے گھیر لیا۔ سابق وزیر اعظم، اندرا گاندھی نے ۱۹۷۶ میں ان دوکانوں کو ہٹوا دیا اس لیے کہ اس کی وجہ سے مسجد کی تمام عمارت چھپ گئی تھی اور مسجد کو نقصان پہنچ رہا تھا۔

دستاویز مورخہ ۲۲/اگست ۱۸۵۷ اسپتال جرنیلی، دریا گنج، جس کے انچارج امام بخش ڈاکٹر تھے اس میں ان ادویات کی فہرست ہے کہ جس کی اسپتال کو ضرورت تھی۔ اس سے ان دواؤں کا اندازہ ہوتا ہے کہ جو مریضوں کو اس دور میں استعمال کرائی جاتی تھیں۔

دستاویز مورخہ ۲۳/اگست ۱۸۵۷ بہادر شاہ کا حکم نامہ ہے جو افسران سکھان پلٹن کے نام ہے۔ اور سکھوں کی پلٹن کو کافی سراہا گیا ہے۔ اس سے ثابت ہوتا ہے کہ کچھ سکھ بھی بادشاہ کے ساتھ تھے تو اس سے اس بات کی تنسیخ ہو جاتی ہے کہ سکھ صرف انگریزوں کا ساتھ دے رہے تھے۔ کچھ سکھ مغل باشاہ بہادر شاہ کے ساتھ بھی تھے۔

خط مورخہ ۳۰/ اگست ۱۸۵۷ بڑا اہم ہے کہ فوج کے پاس کچھ ذرائع نہ تھے اور نوبت فاقہ کرنے کی پہونچی اور کوئی شخص اتنی مدد نہیں کر رہا تھا کہ ان کو کھانا بھی مل جائے تو اس بات کا انتباہ کر رہے ہیں کہ اگر فوج فاقے سے رہے گی تو چھوڑ کر چلی جائے گی اس لیے کہ انھیں اندازہ ہو رہا ہے کہ تمام شہر دہلی معہ اہل کاران انگریزوں کے ساتھ سازش رکھتے ہیں۔ اس سے ثابت ہوتا ہے کہ شہر دہلی کی بڑی آبادی انگریزوں کے ساتھ تھی لیکن اس سے یہ بات بھی صاف ہوتی ہے کہ دہلی کی ایک بڑی تعداد انگریزوں کے خلاف بھی تھی اس لیے کہ ایک دستاویز کے مطابق کشمیری گیٹ سے قلعے تک پہونچنے میں انگریزی فوج کو پانچ دن لگے۔ اگر عوام میں انگریزوں کے خلاف ایسا جذبہ نہ ہوتا تو اس قدر سخت مقابلہ کیسے ممکن تھا۔

۲۶/ جولائی ۱۸۵۷ کا انگریزوں کا جاری کردہ ایک حکم نامہ ہے جس میں اسی بات کی تفتیش کی جارہی ہے کہ جہانگیر آباد کے قلعہ کو مسمار کرنے کا جو حکم دیا تھا تو اب تک وہ مسمار کیوں نہیں ہوا۔ اس میں اس کی وجہ بتائی گئی ہے کیونکہ سخت بارش ہو رہی ہے۔

ایک فتوی جہاد ہے جو ۱۸۵۷ میں جاری ہوا لیکن تاریخ اور سنہ نہیں لکھا گیا اس میں انگریزوں کو کفار کہا گیا ہے اور ہدایت دی جارہی ہے کہ جہاں جہاں کفار نظر آئیں ان کو قتل کر دیا جائے اور پورے جذبہ سے دین اور ملک کی حفاظت ان انگریزوں سے کی جائے۔ اس پر اکتیس مواہر کے دستخط ہیں۔

اگست ۱۸۵۷ کی دستاویز میں ایک نقشہ مجرمان مفرور کا ہے کہ جنھوں نے بہادر شاہ کی نوکری کی۔ اس میں ہندوستانیوں کی تعداد ۱۱۶۰ ہے۔ ۱۱۶۰ افراد میں زیادہ تر نام مسلمانوں کے ہیں۔ اس فہرست کو گورنمنٹ پریس دہلی سے شائع کرایا گیا۔

حکم نامہ مورخہ ۸رنومبر ۱۸۵۸ کا معافی نامہ ہے جس میں ملکہ وکٹوریہ نے ان ہندوستانیوں کو معاف کیا ہے کہ جو بغاوت، لوٹ مار اور قتل وغیرہ میں شامل نہیں تھے بلکہ صرف نوکری چھوڑ کر خطرہ کی وجہ سے چلے گئے تھے اور پھر گھر بیٹھ گئے اور جب حالات بہتر ہوئے تب حاضر ہو گئے۔ ایسے لوگوں کو معافی دی گئی۔

حکم بتاریخ ۲۹رمارچ ۱۸۶۱ جاری ہوا کہ جنتریوں میں سنہ جلوس یعنی سلطنت شاہنشاہ مغل یا مغل بادشاہ دہلی چھپا تھا۔ جو غلط ہے۔ اب آئندہ سے سنہ ملکہ معظّمہ چھاپا جائے۔ یہ حکم اور اس طرح سنہ جلوس مغل بادشاہ دہلی کا جاری رہنا اس ذہن وفکر کی غمّاضی کرتا ہے کہ مغل بادشاہ کس حد تک لوگوں کے ذہن ودماغ کو متاثر کیے ہوئے تھا کہ ۱۸۵۷ میں بہادر شاہ کو بادشاہت سے علیحدہ کر دیا لیکن ۱۸۶۱ تک جنتریوں وغیرہ میں سنہ جلوس مغل بادشاہ ہی چھپتا رہا۔

دستاویز مورخہ ۶رستمبر سے واضح ہوتا ہے کہ مغل بادشاہوں، شہزادوں وشہزادیوں نے جو باغ لگائے تھے وہ دہلی کی خوبصورتی کو بڑھا رہے تھے دوسری طرف وہ دہلی کو آکسیجن اور گرمی کی شدت سے بچا رہے تھے۔ دہلی میں جو افراتفری ۱۰رمئی ۱۸۵۷ سے شروع ہوئی اس کا اثر انتظام پر بھی پڑا جس کا پورا پورا فائدہ اس دور کے دہلی کے بدمعاش لوگوں نے اٹھایا اس لیے کہ انگریزی انتظام ختم اور بہادر شاہ کا انتظام خراب ہی تھا تو ان لوگوں نے سوچا کہ اس سے فائدہ اٹھایا جائے اور باغون کے درختوں کو کاٹ کر بیچ دیا جائے یہ حکم اسی سے متعلق ہے کہ بہادر شاہ کو خبر ملی کہ لوگ باغ اسد خاں کاٹ رہے ہیں لہذا انھوں نے انتظامیہ کو متنبہ کیا کہ وہ ایسا کرنے سے روکیں۔

۱۳رستمبر ۱۸۵۷ کو مغل شہزادہ محمد خضر نے کوتوال شہر کو حکم دیا کہ وہ ہندو ومسلمانوں کو کشمیری دروازہ

پر بھیجیں۔ ظاہر ہے کہ اسی حکم کی تعمیل دہلی کے ہندو مسلمانوں نے کی جس کی وجہ سے انگریز فوج بڑی مشکل سے کشمیری گیٹ سے داخل ہو سکی اور اس قدر سخت جنگ تھی کہ کشمیری گیٹ سے لال قلعہ تک انگریزی فوج کے پہونچنے میں پانچ دن لگ گئے۔

دستاویز ۱۲ر ستمبر ۱۸۵۷ سے ظاہر ہوتا ہے کہ مسماۃ مبارک النسا نے ایک باغ شاہ جہاں آباد سے دور لگایا تھا اسکی آب پاشی ۲۰۰ روپے سال تھی اس کی وصولیابی کے لیے حکم جاری ہوا ہے۔ اس کا نام باغ مبارک بیگم تھا یہ اکبر دوم کی بیوی تھیں ظاہر ہے کہ دیہات کے لوگ اس نام کو نہ لے کر انھوں جورو کا باغ کہنا شروع کیا ہوگا جورو یعنی بیوی۔ جو آج جور باغ ہو گیا ہے جس کے کوئی معنی نہیں۔ اسی کے نزدیک درگاہ شاہ مرداں ہے اور کربلا، جس کے احاطہ میں نواب مبارک بیگم کا مقبرہ بھی ہے۔

حکم نامہ نمبر ۴۸۵/۱ کے مطابق باغی جودہ پور اور چتوڑ بھاگ گئے اور وہیں پناہ لے لی۔ کپتان فریڈرک نے حکم جاری کیا کہ انھیں گرفتار کیا جائے کچھ تو وہ علاقہ ایسا تھا اور دوسرے راجستھان کے عوام انگریزوں کے خلاف تھے۔ لہذا انگریز ان لوگوں کو گرفتار کرنے میں کامیاب نہ ہو سکے اس لیے کہ انگریزوں نے کئی حکم نامہ اس سے متعلق جاری کیے۔

دستاویز نمبر ۱۰۲۔B اس دور میں مختلف کاروائیاں ہو رہی تھیں ایک یہ کیا کہ بہادر شاہ کو سنی مسلمانوں میں unpopular کرنے کے لیے ایک افواہ یہ اڑا دی گئی کہ بہادر شاہ نے شیعی مذہب اختیار کر لیا ہے۔ تا کہ سنی شیعی اختلافات بڑھ سکیں جس کا فائدہ انگریزوں کو حاصل ہوگا لہذا بہادر شاہ نے شاہ جہاں آباد کے اہم سنی افراد کی طرف سے ایک اعلان جاری کرایا کہ بہادر شاہ سنی مذہب ہی کے پابند ہیں اور یہ افواہ قطعی بے بنیاد ہے۔ سنی شیعی اختلافات کا فائدہ انگریز ۱۸۵۷ کے بعد بھی اٹھاتے

ہے جس کی زندہ مثال اکیسویں صدی کا عراق ہے جو کچھ انھوں نے ۱۸۵۷ کے ہندوستان اور دہلی بیں کیا وہی آج عراق اور بغداد میں کر رہے ہیں۔

مورخہ ۲۳ر مارچ ۱۸۵۷ کا بادشاہ ایران کی طرف سے ایک اعلان جامع مسجد شاہ جہاں آباد پر گادیا گیا کہ وہ عنقریب ہی ہندوستان پر حملہ کریں گے اور اس وقت تک ہندوستانی اپنے آپ کو نگریزوں کی حمایت سے دور رکھیں اور پھر وہ ہندوستان کی حکومت شیعوں کے سپرد کر دیں گے۔ یہ سب نگریزوں کی سیاسی چالیں تھیں۔

ایک دستاویز مورخہ ار دسمبر ۱۸۵۷ کی جارج کوپر کی جانب سے ہے۔ جس میں پچاس ہزار وپے برٹش سرکار نے اس بات پر صرف کرنے کے لیے دیئے کہ بریلی کی ہندو آبادی کو مسلم باغیوں کے خلاف آمادہ پیکار کیا جائے۔ لیکن انگریز اس کوشش میں کامیاب نہ ہو سکے۔ اس سے اندازہ ہوتا ہے کہ جن ہندوستانی دانشوروں کا خیال تھا کہ ہمیں انگریزوں کی مخالفت نہیں کرنی چاہیے اور یہ ندوستان کی فلاح و بہبود میں بڑا کام انجام دیں گے تو اگر انگریزوں کی یہ مثالیں سامنے رکھی جائیں کہ ہ کس قدر گرے ہوئے انگریز حکمراں تھے کہ اس حد تک جا سکتے تھے ان ہندوستانی دانشوروں کی سمجھ نطعی غلط اور بے بنیاد تھی۔

مورخہ ۲۵ر مئی کا فتویٰ جہاد ہے جس میں انگریزوں کے خلاف جہاد کی ترغیب دی گئی ہے اس پر ۱۲۰ افراد کے دستخط ہیں کہ یہ مسلمانوں کا فرض ہے کہ وہ انگریزوں کے خلاف جدوجہد کریں۔

۲ر محرم کے اخبار الظفر میں رسالہ جہاد کے سلسلہ سے ایک خبر ہے کہ رسالہ جہاد کی قیمت ۴ آنہ مقرر کی گئی ہے اور مالدار حضرات سے یہ اپیل کی گئی ہے کہ وہ اس کے سوا اور دو سو روپیہ بھی ادا کر سکتے

ہیں جس سے بڑی مدد ہوگی لیکن اسی کے ساتھ افسوس کے ساتھ یہ خبر بھی شائع کی گئی کہ زیادہ قیمت پر خریدنے والا کوئی خریدار نہیں ملا۔ ایسا محسوس ہوتا ہے کہ مالدار لوگوں کی توجہ کہیں اور تھی اور ان کے یہاں رسالہ جہاد کی کوئی اہمیت نہ تھی۔

ایک دستاویز ہے جس پر تاریخ نہیں اس میں لکھا ہے کہ نواب جھجر کی طرف بہادر شاہ کو بڑا یقین تھا کہ وہ انگریزوں کے خلاف بہادر شاہ کا ساتھ دے گا لیکن تمام اندازے اور تمام وفاداری کے وعدے سب بے کار ثابت ہوئے نواب جھجر نے نہ تو بہادر شاہ کا ساتھ دیا اور نہ ہی پورے طریقے سے انگریزوں کی مدد کی جس کا نتیجہ غدر کے بعد یہ نکلا کہ انگریزوں نے نواب جھجر کو بھی قتل کر دیا۔ ان نوابوں اور راجاؤں میں سب سے بہتر رویہ بلبھ گڑھ کے راجہ ناہر سنگھ کا رہا کہ وہ بہادر شاہ کا حامی رہا اور انگریزوں کے خلاف لڑا اور آخر میں انگریزوں نے اس کو بھی پھانسی دے دی۔

دستاویز مورخہ ۸/نومبر ۱۸۵۸ سے واضح ہوتا ہے کہ کمشنر پانی پت نے ملکہ وکٹوریہ کے ہدایت نامہ کے مطابق ۱۲ لوگوں کو معافی دیدی۔ ان لوگوں نے ان حالات کو بیان کیا جس کی وجہ سے وہ نوکری پر نہیں جا سکے ورنہ ان کا کوئی مقصد غدر میں شامل ہونا تھا۔ نہ صرف یہ بلکہ ہزاروں دستاویزات ہیں جن کے مطالعہ کے بعد ہی ہم ۱۸۵۷ کی تاریخ لکھ سکیں گے۔

جہاں تک ۱۸۵۷ کے غدر کی وجوہات ہیں اس پر ہمارے مورخین نے کافی لکھا ہے اور اب نئے کاموں کے آنے کے بعد خاص طور سے نئے ماخذ سامنے آنے کے بعد اب ہمیں دوبارہ ان وجوہات پر کام کرنا ہوگا۔ میرے جد سید شاہ خیرات علی کو نواب آصف الدولہ نے پانچ گاؤں عزاداری محرم کے لیے دیئے۔ ان کا امام باڑہ قصبہ جلالی ضلع علی گڑھ میں واقع ہے جہاں شجاع الدولہ نے ۱۷۷۴ میں

عزاداری محرم بھی کی تھی۔ ۱۸۰۴میں برٹش سرکار نے وہ گاؤں ضبط کر لیے۔ جب میں اتر پردیش آرکائیوز، لکھنؤ میں ۱۸۵۷پر کام کر رہا تھا تو یہ فائل وہیں مل گئی۔ یہ فائل مجھے ۲/اگست ۲۰۰۶ کو تر پردیش آرکائیوز واقع مہانگر میں دو پہر ۱۲ بجکر ۱۵ منٹ پر ملی۔ اس فائل کے ملنے سے مجھے خوشی ہوئی ور صدمہ بھی۔ خوشی اس بات کی کہ میرے خاندان سے متعلق ایک فائل مجھے مل گئی جو ہمارے خاندان کے تاریخی کارنامہ پر روشنی ڈالتی ہے اور ایک اہم ثبوت ہے۔ اور صدمہ اس بات کا ہے کہ میرے والد روفیسر حکیم سید محمد کمال الدین حسین مرحوم نے خاندان کی تاریخ پر بہت کام کیا۔ کاش کہ یہ فائل ان کی ندگی میں مل جاتی تو وہ کتنا خوش ہوتے اور خاندان کی تاریخ پر مزید لکھتے۔ جس طرح ابوالفضل کی خواہش تھی کہ وہ اپنے خاندان کی تاریخ لکھتا لیکن وقت نہ ہونے کی وجہ سے آئین اکبری کے اختتام پر پنے خاندان کا تذکرہ لکھ دیا۔ اسی طرح میں نے بھی اپنے خاندان کا مختصر تعارف کرا دیا۔ میں نے اس ئل کے کچھ اہم فیصلوں کی زیروکس کاپی کرائی اور جب جلالی گیا تو ان کی قبر پر رکھدی۔ یہ ایک چھوٹی ی مثال ہے۔ انگریزوں کے ظلم وزیادتی کی کہ کس طرح سے انھوں نے ہندوستانیوں کے بنیادی حقوق کو پامال کیا۔ برٹش سرکار کی ان ظلم وزیادتیوں کے خلاف ۱۸۵۷میں ہندوستانی اٹھ کھڑے وئے اور انگریزوں کی جانیں لے لیں اور اپنی جانیں دے دیں۔

بہادر شاہ کو رنگون میں قید کر دیا گیا اور جب انکو یہ احساس ہو گیا کہ اب ان کو ہندوستان جانا صیب نہیں ہوگا اور ان کو قبر بھی ہندوستان میں نصیب نہ ہوگی تو شاعر ہونے کی وجہ سے اپنے احساسات کو ان الفاظ میں بیان کیا ہے۔

کتنا ہے بد نصیب ظفؔر دفن کے لیے
دو گرز زمیں بھی مل نہ سکی کوے یار میں

لیکن جب ہم ۱۸۵۷ کی ۱۵۰ ویں سالگرہ منا رہے ہیں تو کتنا فرق آ گیا کہ ایک شاعر نے کہدیا۔

دہلی میں آ کے رہنے کی خواہش کریں نہ اب
رنگون میں پڑے رہیں اپنے مزار میں
کہدو ظفر سے دلی کے اس کوے یار میں
دو گز زمین ملتی ہے ستر ہزار میں

(1)

National Archives of India,Documet No. B - 139 F.1

dated 16th April, 1857

یادداشت آنکہ دوبندی تال

مبلغ چہار صد روپیہ کہ نصف آن دوصد روپیہ می شود برین اسباب مفصلہ ذیل از نزد لالہ شیوراج معرفت مظفر الدولہ قرض گرفتہ بجہت وتصرف خود آوردم اوازو کہ مبلغ مذکور ہنگام وصول شدن تنخواہ بلاغہ رحمت خواہم دادو اگر تا عرصہ یک سال تنخواہ وصول نشود مرسس آراضیِ راست کہ مال را قروضہ زر خود بگیرد بنابراں این چند کلمہ بطریقِ نمک نوشتہ داشتہ شد۔

....

(2)

NAI D.No. 130 - 185 18th April. 1857.

Bearing seal (not readable)

بخدمت جمیع تھانہ دار صاحبان مہربان دوستان تھانہ داران شہر دہلی۔ بعد سلام آنکہ اس وقت جرنیل طالع یار خاں صاحب کوتوالی میں تشریف فرما ہوئے کہ تم تاکیداً رقعہ کسے بنام تھانہ داران شہر لکھ دو کہ محرم میں باجا بجنے نہ پاوے وجہ اس کے یہ ہے کہ بگل کے آواز نہ بند ہو جاوے اور غنیم سر پر گرامی کسی طرح کے مسودہ وقت پیدا نہو کیواسطہ بہر سہ حک مذہب کے قطع نظر حکم سے سب کو لحاظ اس بات کا دل سے رکھنا چاہیے سوای اس کے اور بھی رولہ غل

کے نہج سے نہو اس کا انتظام رکھیں کہ ایک آدمی کو اس اپنے علاقہ کو محفوظیں سے اور تاکیداً مجالس کر دیویں اور نیز سیاہہ دارای اور جمعدار کسب اپنا بدستور سابق جاری رکھیں فقط لہٰذا بخدمت الصاحبان مصدعہ ہوں کہ بذات خود مصروف بندوبست بہ تعمیل الحکہ کے رکھو گے اور کاربند رہیں اور وقت شام تو ادراتپ ہرہ دار مردم محتاط رہیں تم اسی طرح بندوبست کرو کہ ناگواری نہ معلوم ہو اور سب کو نقش تہہ دل سے پیش کریں اور جلد جلد نقل اس کے لے کر دوسری تھانہ کو جلدی سے بھیجو ٹھہر ٹھہر کے عرصہ میں تعمیل اس کے ہو جاوی فقط

صد بخش خاں نائب کوتوال و بنیاد سنگھ نائب کوتوال

محررہ ذی الحجہ سہ محررہ ۳ محرم ۲۱

العبد	العبد	العبد	العبد
سجدیا سنگھ تھانہ دار	بادل خاں تھانہ دار	محمد نظام الدین تھانہ دار	محمد مرزا انای گلزار
دریبہ۔ مہر،	مہر، فیض بازار۔		کوتوال شہر
راج گھاٹ۔			مہر، کوتوال شہر۔

العبد	العبد	
محمد رضا اللہ خاں	میر بخش تھانہ دار	۲/محرم ۱۲۷۴ھ کو تعمیل
تھانہ دار ترکمان، مہر	چاندنی چوک، مہر	۳/بجے روز کے آیا فوراً
		روانہ آمدہ کیا۔

امیر امانت علی خاں تھانہ دار گورالہ باد۔ مہر/ ۳/محرم ۱۲۷۴ھ بعمل ۳/بجے روز کے

روانہ تھانہ آیندہ کیا۔ مرزا محمد خاں بیگ ولد یکہ کار قاسم خاں

سوم محرم الحرام ۴ے ھ۔

علی جان تھانہ دار بدر پور۔ غلام حسین تھانہ دار راج گھاٹ محمد اکرام اللہ

خاں تھانہ دار کشمیری دروازہ

سیوم محرم ۲۱ معلی وقت سرسر کے پہونچا فوراً روانہ کیا

العبد۔ محمد امیر علی تھانہ دار نگم بود۔ مہر

....

(3)

NAI Document No. 6 dated 29 th Ramazan, 21 Julus.

dated 14 April, 1857 Bearing Seal

میر محمد سلطان ظہیر الدین سپہ سالار ۱۲۷۳

حکم نامہ

حوالدار میجر اسری انڈیا

آنکہ کمپنی نے برقلم ترجمان بھوانی دبی و دریں شناساں را برای حفاظت مکان و

اسباب و بندوبست دیگر وفساد بر مکان موسس الدولہ مرزا فاضل بیگ بہادر تعینات

کردہ دہند اندریں باب تاکید شناسند تحریر بتاریخ ۲۹ ر ماہ رمضان ۲۱ سنہ

عالیجاہا

دوروپیہ اپنے پاس سے دے کر دریچہ خرید نے اسباب کے برقنداز ساتھ کر دیا۔ ۱۰

ذی قعدہ ۲۱ ھ کوتوال شہر

....

(4)

NAI document no. B193 F. 1 dated 16th May, 1857

اخبار ڈیوڈی خاصہ دربار معلّٰی مرقوم بتاریخ بست و یکم شہر رمضان ۲۱ ھ معلّٰی براز سبز و بسبب حضور والا خاصہ یوس فرمودہ آرام کردند ڈیوڈی خاصہ بخدمت معموری صحن بخیریت و اگشت چوکی خواصان آبدار بار برداران ملکی نہ جولاران وغیرہ درچوکی شب حاضر بودند۔ حضرت قدر قدرت از خواب استراحت بیدار گشتہ از امورات موری انواع یافتہ نماز وظیفہ ادا کردند۔ صحت حکم احترام الدولہ بہادر برای ملاحظہ نمودن نبض حضور والا از ڈیوری خاصہ درایید برآمد شدند۔

حضور والا اندرون دیوان خاص دربار فرمودند چہل و نونفر انگریز ہار اقید بودند برار کشتہ کردن انگریزان را فوج طلب نمودہ بودند۔ حضور والا دادند فوج را اخبار است ۔ اور اقرار ساز تصرف شمشیر و طبل کردہ واز جمع از ڈیوڑی خاصہ دارند براند شدند۔ جمیع سرداران ایران اہلکاران متصدیان بدربار حاضر شدہ بہر باب مجرا گردیدند۔

خوانہائے نعمت خاصہ دراز شدہ حضور والا خاصہ نوش فرمودہ مہیا کشتی کردہ استراحت

نمودند۔ ہنگام سیر بیدار گشتہ نماز عصر ادا کردند۔

امراز بہ ڈیوڑی خاصہ چوک تحسین خواجہ سرای مرزا الہی بخش کلاں بہ لوری پائیں چوک مرزا الٰہی بخش خورد خواہد ماند۔

پانزدہ عدد دو شالہ شالے از دست جھولے الہی خانم امیر بیگم باز مداری لوسکما مہ دانی حوالہ احمد قدیر بیگ توشک خانہ والہ محہ کری تحسین خواجہ سوای مرزا الٰہی بخش کلاں براند شدند۔

قریب دو گھڑی روز باقی ماندہ حضور راند اندرون تسبیح خانہ دربار فرمودند۔ جمیع سرداران فوج ہا طلب فرمودہ۔ مرزا مغل بہادر ہمراہ گرفتہ حاضر شدند۔ جمیع سرداران امیران حاضر بودند سرداران فوج ہای از حکم ادام شود۔ حضور والا تضمین مران واز حاصلی صفائی کرایدہ دار داز ڈیوڑی خاصہ درامد براید شدند۔

....

(5)

NAI- Document No. 73 - F.1 Dated 20th May , 1857

حضرت جہاں پناہ سلامت۔

یہ امام باڑہ معہ آراضی سکنی وحویلی واقعہ کونچہ بولاقی بیگم۔ عرصہ تخمیناً پنج ماہ راست سے شیخ فیض دخیل محنہ کر حسینی بیگم زوجہ صادق علی اور سرفراز علی متولی کے ہے اور مرار از چپ نکیلو بر عالیہ بیگم متوفہ دختر محمد کر کا بکرایہ تین روپیہ ماہواری کے رہتا ہے اور جریران پان پارچہ کرتا ہے حد یہ ہے عشرت علی خاں ناظر نے یہ زمین امام باڑہ کے حضرت محمد اکبر شاہ بادشاہ سے

۶ـہ جلوس میں لی اور امام باڑہ باہتمام سید عبدالرحیم شاہ تعمیر کرایا اور انجم النسا بیگم ہمشیرہ ای مودت کر کے سید عبدالرحیم شاہ کو متولی امام باڑہ کا کیا۔ دوسرے سید ممدوح بارود تعمیر امام باڑہ کے مورخہ ۲۴ ذی الحجہ ۱۸۴۵ـہ آید کے اپنیکے بوقت برای مجلس بابت سال یہ سب کرتا رہا روز انتقال عبدالرحیم شاہ کے حیدر علی معہ برہ سپاہی بادشاہ امام باڑہ میں آپلٹا سو ۲۶ر جنوری ۱۸۴۶ء کو حیدر علی اور برہ سپاہی بادشاہ بحکم عدالت برخاست ہوئے فیض دخل سرفراز علی وعالیہ بیگم اور حسینی بیگم بدستور سابقِ قدیم کے کرا دیا تیسرے یہ سید حیدر علی مدعی عدالت دیوانی ہو کے پاس آ کر سو ۲۹ نومبر ۱۸۵۰ء کو طالبہ بیگم متوفہ اور حسینی بیگم عدالت واقعہ کر کے مقدمہ ما باز ور حیدر علی مدعی نادم ہوا۔ چوتھے اب یہ مکان حویلی اور آراضی سکنی متعلقہ امام باڑہ اسی بکرار مغلِ بصیغہ سوکا ضبط ہوا اور راہدے کرایہ کے مکانات متعلقہ امام باڑہ لوکا ایجی میں جاتا ہے اور میں روپیہ دریا یہ اندے کرایہ سے دوح کو امام باڑہ بہلی تو کی برس تک سرفراز علی متوفی کو ملا اور ور سے غالب چون سرفراز علی متوفی کے روز انتقال عالیہ بیگم ہمشیرہ اس کے مسمی کو حال شاہی سرکار سے مقرری ملتا ہے اور کچھ واسطہ حیدر علی خواہ حیدر حسن کا نہیں ہے۔ پانچویں یہ آراضی امام باڑہ وقف پر ملکیت کسی کی نہیں اور یہ حیدر حسن کو چاہیے تھا کہ جس روز انتقال عبدالرحیم شاہ متوفی بحکم عدالت کیونکہ مکان کو صدر کر دعوی عدالت دیوانی میں نادم ہوا اور فیض دخیل حسینی بیگم اور سرفہ عرصہ پنجاہ برس سرکار ست ہوئے اور حضور والا ان کو دلا ویں برخاست ہوئی زیرا کہ اور یہی اس مکانات میں۔ واجب بود عرض نمود اسباب دو پسر بکروچ۔

(6)

NAI D. No 73 F.1 Dated 20th May,1857

سند تحقیقات مقدمہ عرضی دعویٰ حیدر حسین

بیان مسمی میر عزیز الدین ملازم میر حیدر حسین ساکن قلعہ مبارک سے معلوم ہوا کہ یہ امام باڑہ تعمیر کیا ہوا نواب عشرت علی خاں خواجہ سرای بادشاہی مرور پچاس برس کے ہے انہوں نے اپنی ہمشیرہ انجم النسا بیگم واسطہ سکونت کے بطور مالکیت کے دیدیا ہے یجدود انہو نکے عبدالرحیم خاں خاوند انجمن النسا اور بعد وفات انہوں نے میر حیدر حسین کو ہزار روپیہ انجمن النسا کو ملا بعد اوسکے غدر البار غہسر کاری سے ضبط ہوا۔ چہار پانچ برس ہوئے پھر مرزا رجب علی بہادر کلکڑی میں یعنی لوکل ایجنسی مبلغ ۳ روپیہ کرایہ دیتے رہے اور وہ کرایہ سرکار سے ہم کو ملتا رہا کو داس باب کے این جملہ ہیں۔

العبد قاضی عزیز الدین

مسمیان نور الدین خواجہ غلام علی و محمد بخش پسر حیدر حسین سے متن الفقہاں کہا یہ امام باڑہ عشرت علی خاں خواجہ سرای بادشاہی کا ہے غالباً حیات اپنے کے وہ قابض رہا بعد وفات انہوں کے عبدالرحیم، انجمن النسا بیگم رہے بعد وفات انکے عبدالرحیم لاولد تھا صادق علی برادر زادہ اپنے کو بیٹا گردان رکھا تھا صادق علی کے اولاد میں یعنی بیٹی بیٹا ہیں اور میر حیدر علی ہیں تنازعہ پیش ہوا ضبط سرکار میں ہوگیا صادق علی کی اولاد یعنی مسمی سرفراز علی پسر اوسکے کو متولی گری ہوئے۔ مبلغ تین روپیہ سرکار سے بابت متولی گری سرفراز علی حاضر مدار کو ملتا رہا

اور یہ مجنون ہو گیا پھر اس کو بباعث جنوں کے دریا نہ موقوف کر دیا اور حیدر حسین کو متولی کیا آج تک ملتا ہے اب اس امام باڑہ کے حضور والا مالک ہیں سرفراز علی نے ہمشیرہ سے نکاح صاحب عالم بہادر سے ہوا تھا سو وہ اب اس مکان میں والدہ سرفراز علی اور صاحب عالم بہادر سکونت پذیر ہیں

العبد	العبد	العبد	العبد
نورالدین بقلم خود	خواجہ غلام علی	محمد بخش معمار	سید حیدر حسین

(7)

NAI document no. B. 109 F .01 dated 21st May, 1857

حضرت صاحب عالم وعالمیان سلامت

بموجب حکم حضور انور مسماۃ امیر بیگم و بادشاہ بیگم معہ بچہ شیر خورہ اونکی کے جو بہ علت اشتباہ کرشنان نے کی مقید حوالات کوتوالی تھے بحراست بجی خواص حضور کہ نام غاں بخت کے روانہ حضور کیا گیا اور اظہار ان کے مومن کے ہوتی کوتوالی میں قلم بند نہیں ہوئی لیکن از روی گواہی ایک کس موتوں نامعلوم الاسم کے معلوم ہوا کہ یہ مسلمان ہیں از اذن اور خلاصی ان کے از روی شریعت کے اونے لہذا او اسطہ ملاحظہ کے روانہ کیا۔ انجہ کہ رای عالے ہوئی کار بند دادیں الی دیہات دومت حامایاں۔

محررہ

قاضی فیض اللہ کوتوال شہر دہلی ۲۶ رمضان المبارک ۱۲۷۳ء

مہر ابوالمظفر سراج الدین محمد بہادر شاہ بادشاہ غازی

....

(8)

NAI Document No. B-100.F.12,Dated 25th May, 1856

مہر دفتر کرنل سلطان مرزا محمد خضر بہادر ۱۲۷۳ھ

متکفلات مہمات سلطانی یعنی تھانہ داران وکوتوالان شہر دہلی وسرولی بدانند کہ چوں مسماتان محمدی خانم (۱) و وزیرن (۲) وسکینہ خانم (۳) ومنی (۴) ونوربی (۵) و ابرن (٦) ورحیمی (۷) وبخشی خانم (۸) وحسینی خانم (۹) باطفلان مفصلہ الذیل حسین مرزا پسر محمدی خانم مصطفیٰ بیگ و (فضل حق) پسر فضہ خانم کریم بخش پسر رحیمن علی جان پسر منی بہادر پسر دیگر منی علی بخش پسر منی قادر محسن پسر منی غلام رحمان پسر وزیرن، پیر بخش پسر رحیمن جملگی ہژدہ اسامی کہ دراشتباہ کرسٹانیان اسیر شدہ بودند، پس از دریافت بے قصوری وثبوت اسلام حکم رہائی انان از صادر شدہ لازم کہ احدی از آنہا متعرض ومراحم شود۔ قدغن بلیغ پنداشتہ حسب الحکم بہ عمل آرند۔ فقط/المرقوم یکم ماہ شوال ۱۲۷۳ھ.

....

(9)

NAI Document No. B - 100 F.12 dated 25th May, 1856

مہر سلطان مرزا محمد خضر بہادر۔ مہر دفتر کرنیل ۱۲۷۳ھ

متکفلان مہمات سلطانی تھانہ داران وکوتوالان شہر درونی و بیرونی بدانند کہ چوں مسمیان خدا بخش وخدا بخش دوم وآغا مرزا وعبداللہ در اشتباہ کرستانیان بی قصور اسیر شدہ بودند پس از دریافت بی قصوری ونبوت اسلام حکم رہائی انان از صادر شدہ لازم کہ احدی از ناظمان وبکفنان متعرض ومزاحم انان شود۔ مدعی بلیغ می داشتہ حسب الحکم بعمل آرند

تحریر فی التاریخ یکم ماہ شوال ۱۲۷۳ھ

....

(10)

NAI Document No: B-68 F-5 Dated 27th May, 1857

مانایاں کہ ساکنان رئیسان درگاہ حضرت نظام الدین اولیاء اہل اسلام واہل ہنود و کٹرہ ارادت مند خاں ایم۔

جس روز سے کہ یہ عملہ تھانہ بدرپور عرب سرائے میں متعین ہوا ہے اس طرح آسائش اورامن رہا ہے کہ ہیچ گونہ تکلیف کے اعلیٰ اوراوتا کو ہی پہونچتے بلکہ قبل از تھانہ کی تمام شب بیداری اور ہوشیاری بخوف قوم گوجر اور رہ زنان رہتے تھے اور اب از وقت تقرری تھانہ ہر

کوئی ہر سہ بستی یعنی درگاہ حضرت نظام الدین اور عرب سرائے اور کٹرہ میں بہ آرام اپنے اپنے گھر میں سوتے ہیں اور بوجہ مواضعات میں لوٹ مار موقوف ہوگئی ہے کہ تھانہ دار صاحب نے اپنے علاقے کے گوجروں کو بلوا کر مچلکہ لئے اور ذمہ داری کرائیے اور ہم لوگوں نے ابتدائے تقرری تھانہ سے اب تک کسی طرح کی شکایت عملہ تھانہ کی کسی رعایا کی زبان سے نہیں سنی اور اگر کوئی کری تو یہی کہی اس واسطہ یہ چند کلمہ بطریق محضر کے لکھ دئے ہیں کہ سند ہوویں اور عندالحاجت بکار آویں تحریر تاریخ ۳ رشوال ۲۱ھ معلّی

العبد	العبد	العبد	العبد
میر خورشید علی ساکن	سنگھ رام نمبردار	ٹیکارام ساکن کٹرہ	ٹھاکر جی
درگاہ	کٹرہ ارادت	کٹرہ ارادت	زمیندار کٹرہ رادت
	مندخاں	مندخاں	مندخاں
العبد	العبد	العبد	العبد
سید قمر الدین	سید شرف الدین	سید ظہور الحسن	سید بدیع الدین
ساکن درگاہ	ساکن درگاہ	ساکن درگاہ	ساکن درگا
مہر	مہر	مہر	مہر

العبد	العبد	العبد	العبد
میر علی	گوری مل	گلاب سنگھ	بھگوان داس
ساکن درگاہ	زمیندار نظام پور	ساکن درگاہ	ساکن درگاہ
مہر	مال گذار بادشاہی	مہر (ہندی)	
العبد	العبد		
جگن ناتھ	رام پرشاد برہم		
ساکن درگاہ	ساکن عرب سرائے		

مہریں اردو میں ہیں

(11)

NAI Document No: B110 F.171 Dated 6th June, 1857

شجاعت نشان کوتوال شہر معلوم نماید بکرار باین مدکری کہ وبلدار وزخمی شدن محبت علی بجیر دوشدہ است بہ جمیت دوشدہ است والمصدقہ تعلقہ سپاہی گزر قاسم خاں است لازم کہ نفوذ و افزود شقہ خاص تحقیقات جملہ مراں ملیکہ و بیلدار و بخت نمودہ دیسمو کہ صدر الصدور برد برای دادرسی مطلوبان فریاد دید۔

مرقوم ۱۳؍شوال ۲۱ سنہ معلّی

مہر ہے لیکن پڑھی نہیں جا سکی

صفحہ۲

بنام تھانہ دار دفعہ واسطہ کاتب متحاس کے لکھا گیا۔ فقط

تحریر ۱۴ ارشوال ۱۲۷۳ ہجری

....

(12)

NAI Document No. B-192- F-2 Dated 10th June, 1857.

بہ جناب فیض مآب قبلہ وکعبہ مخدومی ومکرمی دام ظلہم

بعد پا آوری عجز ونیاز اور تمنای حصول ملازمت اکثر معاوضت کے التماس کرتا ہوں کہ عنایت نامہ سامی مملو بہ ہزاراں عنایت احقر پاس معہ رقعہ خادم حسین خاں پہونچا بڑی خوشی خورمی ہوئی۔ حق تعالٰی آپ کو معہ فرزندان باین شفقت وعافیت سلامت رکھے۔ بندہ پھر سر مو مشکور اور ممنون آپ کی عنایت کا ہے بلکہ درم ناخریدہ بندہ ہے زبان آپ کی خوبیوں کے شکر سے قاصر ہے اگر بہر سر مو زبان ہوں تو بھی عشر عشیرہ اوس شکر کا ادا ہو نہیں سکتا۔ قبلہ من جو کچھ کہ از شفقت بزرگانہ اب کے تجویز میں آیا وہ مناسب ہے اور بہتر ہے اور موجب آپ کی صلاح اور رضامندی کے راضی ہوں مگر اتنی باتوں کا حال مجھ کو عنایت نامہ سے دریافت نہیں ہوا۔ حال لڑکے کے نانا کا معلوم ہوا کہ سید ہیں مگر حال طفل معلوم نہیں کہ سید ہیں یا مغل ہیں یا پٹھان ہیں کہ تاخیر لفظ خان کے بعد مراسم کے موجود ہے اور تقدیم لفظ سید یا

لفظ میر یا مرزا کے نام پر نہیں۔ بایں حسب معلوم نہیں کہ سید ہیں یا امتی ہیں مگر ماں کی طرف سے شریف النسب معلوم ہوتے ہیں اور یہ معلوم نہیں کہ بھائیوں میں شامل ہیں یا علیحدہ ہیں اور حال عمر ہمیں معلوم کہ کتنی ہے اور حال سکونت معلوم نہیں کہ کس محلّہ میں ہیں اور حال ریاست معلوم نہیں کہ حویلی گھر کی ہے یا بہ کرایہ سکونت رکھتے ہیں وعمدہ بات یہ ہے کہ والہ اعلم کچھ نام علم رکھتی ہیں یا نہیں کچھ شوق علم کا ہے یا نہیں اور سوا اس مشاہری قلعہ کے کچھ اور ملک حویلی یا کرایہ دکاکیں یا آمدنی ملک وغیرہ کچھ ہے یا نہیں اور وجاہت میں کیسے ہیں گوری ہیں یا گندم گون ہیں یا سانولے ہیں۔ تن توش کیسا ہے ریش بردت آغاز ہے یا نکل چکی ہے۔ بہ ہمہ جہت دریافت حال فرمائی ان باتوں کا جواب دیجئے۔ مجھ کو سب طرح قبول ہے۔ مگر دو تین بات کا بہت خیال ہے۔ ایک تو علم کا اور دوسرے مذہب کا کہ غیر مذہب نہ ہوں۔ تیسرے یہ کہ مقبوح نہ ہوں اگرچہ حسین نہ ہوں مگر معیوب وقبیح نہ ہوں روئے کم ہے۔ مگر خیال اس بات کا نہیں جو قابلیت رکھتے ہوں تو معیت مزاج بھی ہو سکتی ہے غرض بعد رفع ان شکوک کے بچوں وقوۃ الٰہی اب کی مرتبہ رسم ورسوم کچھ نشان وغیرہ کے ہو جاوی گی لازم ہے کہ ان حالات کو دریافت کر کے اطلاع فرمائی والسلام فقط

....

(13)

NAI Document No. 192 F1/4 Dated 10th June, 1857.

بجناب فیض ماب قبلہ وکعبہ ام دام عنایتہم

بعد آداب بندگی کے التماس کرتا ہوں کہ عنایت نامہ حضور کا معہ نقشہ کیفیت حالات طرف مالی بدست رحیم بخش پہونچا۔ یہ بات نزدیک احقر کی بچند وجوہ نامناسب ہے۔ معلوم ہوتا ہے کہ یہ شخص اغلب شریف القوم نہیں کیونکہ بندی فی بعض دوستان رئیس شاہ جہاں آباد سے اس کا حال دریافت کیا تو معلوم ہوا کہ گوہر اس کا صدف شرافت سے ہراہی قلب ہے۔ معلوم ہوا کہ تحقیق ازقوم کے حجام تھے مگر شاہ عالم کے وقت میں داروغہ ہو گئے تھے اور ورای اس کی اور کوئی بات کی تحقیقات کے حاجت بھی نہ رہی۔ اب ان کا حال قرائن سے بھی معلوم ہوتا ہے۔ کہ لعل ان کا کان شرافت سے پرون ہی چاہتے ہیں کہ کھوٹا تامڑا اپنا کسی احمق خوری کے ہاتھ بہ گراں لعل ابدار کے قیمت کو بیچ ڈالیں سو یہ کب ہوسکتا ہے کہ جوہری قدرشناس جواہر کوٹھی گھر کی امتیاز نہ کریں شرافت تو اونکی اسی بات سے معلوم ہوگئی کہ ایک بہن تو مصاحب الدولہ کو یعنی بھائی کو انیس الدولہ کے بیاہی گئی اور دوسری ہمشیرہ اونکی کسی اپنے دوست نہالی کے ساتھ بھاگ گئی اور بڑے بھائی نے اوسکی میاں جان کنجن کے پٹی جو صاحب رام کا سالا تھا اسی کے حبالہ نکاح میں لائے شرافت کا حال جن کے یہ ہوتو وای اوس شریف نسب پر جو اونکھ شریف سمجھے تابسر شتہ چہ رسد اب رہ گئی۔ عنایت سے توقع یہی ہے کہ ازراہ بندہ نوازی کے اب کی مرتبہ جو رشتہ آوی تو پہلے ان کے سب مدارج دریافت فرمائیں احقر کو مطلع فرمادیں مرزا صادق صاحب میرے بڑے دوست ہیں اور حال مردم شہر سے خوب واقف ہیں۔ لوگوں کے حسب نسب سے خوب واقف ہیں۔ پہلے اون کو بھی اطلاع فرما کے تب ہی مجھ کو اطلاع فرمادیں تو بہتر ہے اور آپ کی تو شفقت

میں کچھ شک نہیں مگر قسمت میری کو کیا کروگے میں آپ کی عنایت کا بڑا ممنون و مشکور ہوں۔ اگر کچھ بخشی جی کے گھر تحریک کے ہو تو بدست میر عاشور علی اطلاع فرمادیں اور قبلہ من اب میری پاہتی پر کمان رکھتے ہیں مگر خوب ہوا کہ آپ پر بھی میری خوش قسمتی کا حال روشن ہوگیا۔ بخدمت صاحبزادہا سلام نیاز برسر، بموجب میر عاشور علی صاحب بندگی و نیاز۔ از زیادحد ادب فقط

....

(14)

NAI- Document No. B192 F-03 Dated 10th June, 1857.

خان صاحب مشفق مہربان مظہر الطاف بیکران محبّ علی خان صاحب زاد الطافتہ از سادات بدست بعد از سلام مسنون الاسلام و اشتیاق سامی مواصلت مکشوف فرمای لطف انتمای باد درین ولا از تحریر میر کبیر علی صاحب معلوم شدہ کہ آں صاحب بہ مقدمہ تقرر نسبت پیوند۔ میر عاشور علی ہمشیرہ زادہ حقیقی میر کبیر علی دریافت و تحقیقات حسب و نسب اور منظور خاطر داشتہ ترسیل خطوط برای تفحص حال یک دو جای نمودہ اند۔ چنانچہ خطی بہ دریافت این حال در موضع فرید پور کہ ازین جا بہ فاصلہ یک کروہ واقع است فرستادہ بودند۔ صاحبان فرید پور بہ جوابش زبانی گفتہ فرستاد کہ آں صاحب پیوند ہمشیرہ زادی خود درین جا موقوف دارند و از حسب و نسب آنچہ کہ خلاف واقعہ بود و اصلا حقیقی نداشت۔ پیش آں صاحب گفتہ

فرستادند مہربان من حقیقت حال برین منوال است کہ دیہہ مسکن مایان آبادی شش صد شصت سال و سوائی سادات قوم دیگر دراین جا ساکن نسبت و از سادات باہرہ مشہور و معروف اند وقریب دوصد خانہ سادات سکونت دارند و با یک دیگر خود قرابت و پیوند۔ اکثر واقع می شوند و جای دیگر رشتہ رابطہ کم می شود و یک دو جائے در قصبہ کوتانہ نیز اتفاق پیوند شدہ و کنیر ہے در قصبہ پنڈولی کہ از سادات باہرہ اند۔ رشتہ پیوندی شود۔ اگر آں صاحب را دریافت کردن منظور خاطر بود خطوط بنام رؤسائے سادات پنڈولی و بانام سادات این جا نوشتن مناسب بود دریافت ایں حال از چنیں کسانی کہ برائے مطلب خود خوردہ گیری دیگری می نمایند مناسب بود شابان نبود۔ کلام مختصر اگر آں صاحب راتقرر نسبت از ہمشیرہ زادہ میر کبیر علی صاحب شخصی بدریافت قومیت وحسب ونسب باشد میر کبیر علی صاحب و نیز ہمشیرہ زادہ میر موصوف درحسب ونسب وقومیت مثل تمامی سادات وتاہذالیوم از اقوام غیر کفو سوای سادات کسی جانے باہم پیوند وآمیزش نشدہ واز سادات بنی عم و یک حدی سادات پرست اند ہر کسی کہ شک انداز خاطر شریف شدہ محل اعتماد ندارد و قابل سماعت نیست۔ آں صاحب از طرف حسب ونسب خاطر مطمئن دارند و شک وشبہہ کدام نوع بخاطر نیارند زیادہ والسلام الراقم

عبدہ اصغر علی ولد سید ظہیر علی مضمون خطوط آں فدویست بے جنگ درترنگ وشبہہ نیست فقط

مہرین۔ سید محفوظ علی۔ سید اسد علی۔ امداد علی۔ علی حسین۔ میر ساجد علی۔ ۵ رمہریں

پڑھی نہیں جا سکیں۔ قد ثبت و حق صادر فی هذا القرطاس من شرافت نسب سید عاشور علی السرسی

خبر احق عباد الزمن مدرس مدرسہ لکھنو۔ مہر سید نثار حسین حسینی۔ غفرہ الرب ذوالمتن بالحسین والحسن۔

(15)

NAI Document No. B-192-F.1 Dated 10th June, 1857.

بجناب فیض ماب قبلہ و کعبہ مخدومی دام عنایتکم

خادم ولی حسین علی بعد تشریح نیاز مندی اور توضیح مراتب بندگی عرض شاہی کہ کمترین تا تحریر خط ہذا تحریر ہے۔ اور نوید اعتدال مزاج عالی کی شافی مطلق سے چاہتا ہے۔ عرصہ چند روز کا گذرتا ہے کہ جز انحراف مزاج سامی کی جادہ اعتدال سے میں نے سنی طبیعت بہت فکر مند ہے۔ یقین واثق ہے کہ شافی برحق فی شفای کلی بتصدق بیمار کربلا علی ابن الحسین علیہ السلام کی سی عطا فرمائی ہوگی اور بندہ یہی بدعای صحت مزاج عالی شبانہ روز مصروف ہے ابروے معایگی از صد قبول فرمادی شایان عنایت یہ ہے کہ مژدہ اعتدال مزاج اقدس سے کمترین کو خوشنود فرمادیں کہ طبیعت میری بہت فکر مند ہے بنابر آں آدم ملازم کو واسطے معائنہ صحت مزاج سامی کی معہ عریضہ نیاز روانہ کیا ہے اور ضمناً کچھ حال سابق یہی دریافت کرنا منظور تھا اور وہ حقیقت یہ ہے کہ آپ نے از راہ عنایت کے نوازش نامہ سابق میں تحریر فرمایا تھا کہ نانی صاحبہ مہدی حسن کی بقضای الٰہی رحلت کرگئی ہیں ابھی دو چار روز جواب میں توقف

ہے سو اپنی اس تحریر پر عرصہ بیس پچیس روز کا گذرتا ہے شاید حضور نے بہ حالت صحت کچھ تحریک اس مقدمہ میں فرما کر جواب حصول کیا ہوگا یا این کہ شاید نور عین فراولیں اور ان کی طبیعت دشمنان کسل مند ہوئی ہوگی تو کچھ خیال اس باب کا پیش نہاد خاطر شریف نہ رہا ہوگا اب گستاخانہ التماس ہے کہ جو طبیعت آپ کی بہ فضل ایزدی بحال ہو قدم رنجہ فرما کر اور طاقت نہ ہو تو ان کو بلا کر جواب اس مقدمہ کا لینا ضرور ہے یا از راہ مہربانی کی بڑی صاحب زادی کو بھیج کر باقر حسن کو بلا کر جواب حصول کرنا مناسب ہے بلکہ میں نے سابق کا عذر میر عبداللہ صاحب کا حضور کی خدمت میں بیان کیا تھا واللہ اعلم کہ ان کی بناوٹ تھی یا راست تھا اوس کلام پر میری حضور نے فرمایا تھا کہ میں باقر حسین اور مہدی کو بلکہ زیادہ تر ان کی والدہ کو رضامند کرلونگا میرا ذمہ ہے مگر اب معلوم نہیں کہ آپ ان کو رضامند فرمانے میں کیوں عاجز ہیں اور وہ جواب کیوں نہیں دیتے بلکہ آپ نے فرمایا تھا کہ اور بھی جگہ ہے اور ذکر محسی می کے بھی گھر کا فرماتے ہیں مگر نہیں فقط اپنی عزت کے باعث وہاں کا انکار کرتا ہوں اور ایک داغ بھی ان میں ہے وہ جو فدوی نی بیاں کیا تھا اس واسطے البتہ کو یہ کراہت نا ہے الا نہ وہ امر ہیں ہمیں انہیں کیا نسبت فقط ایسے احتیاط کے سبب کے فقیروں کو اپنے حال کے مناسب جان کر اور لڑکی کی اہلیت تم مفتون ہیں اور آپ نے یہی فرمایا تھا کہ یہ لڑکا از بس حلم زیادہ اندرسی رکھتا ہے اس واسطے میری پسند نہیں میں چاہتا ہوں کہ کوئی ایسا ہو کہ ہوشیار چالاک چار پیسے کمانے والا ہو تو بہتر ہے بنا برآں متصدعہ خدمت ہوں کہ آپ ساری باتیں وہاں جا کر فراموش کر گئے اور کہیں تلاش حضور نے نہ کی اور نہ ان سے جواب حاصل ہوا اور میں اس انتظار

میں مرکر تمام ہو گیا اور مقروض زیر بار اتنا ہوا کہ بیان نہیں کر سکتا کہ شاید محمول بخلاف کوئی ہوگا۔ مگر خدای علیم بہتر دانا ہے میری راستی اور دروغ گوئی پر اور ذکر میر ناصر علی کا بالکل پھر نہ آیا کہ وہ کون شخص ہیں اور کیا معاش اور کیا حسب ونسب رکھتے ہیں۔

....

(16)

Document No. B-60. F-64 Dated 18th June, 1857.

روزنامچہ نذر اور چاندنی چوک تعلقہ کوتوالی مرقوم ۲۵رشوال ۷۳ھ

عنایت الٰہی سے صرف ہے

موجودات علیہ سامہ

نمبر	نام غلہ	وجہ	کیفیت	نمبر	نام غلہ	وجہ	کیفیت
۱۔	حافظ امین الدین تھانہ دار	=	برائے سرکار	۲۔	درگاہ برج سرر	=	برائے سرکار
۳۔	میر شمشیر علی جمعدار	=	=	۴۔	محمد خاں برقندار	=	ہراول
۵۔	رضی الدین برقنداز	=	دوم	۶۔	محمد خاں برقنداز	=	سیوم
۷۔	حیدر علی برقنداز	=	چہارم	۸۔	صوب خاں برقنداز	=	سرادہ
۹۔	مع ائمہ برقنداز	=	سرادہ	۱۰۔	رام برقنداز	=	سرادہ

۱۱۔ غلام حسین برقنداز	= درسر	۱۲۔ غلام حسین برقنداز	= ڈرسر
۱۳۔ عبدالرحیم	= سیوم	۱۴۔ شیخ سرائے برقنداز	= سیوم
۱۵۔ رحیم جاٹ برقنداز	= سیوم	۱۶۔ گلاب جاٹ برقنداز	= سیوم

مدت درراز

روزنامچہ پنج دیروزہ سرشت محمد خاں برقنداز بردام کوتوالے

بردوم اور سیوم و چہارم روز

کسب روز صبح سے دوسری تک کلامی سہ صدر اور دس بجے سے دو بجے تک جمعدار رحیم جاٹ صوی برتندوزری اور دو پہر سے شام تک

شیخ سرائے غلام صدے رحہ زدری واسطے نگرانی حال درعیان و معار باراں کے علاقہ بدر پور معروف کسب رویدا پر ایک کست نائب کوتوال صاحب کا علاقہ

برادہ سب سے ہر چہارم سب یک ضرب رہی

کسب سب شام سے گذرہ تحریک غلام حسین برقنداز مفرور تھا وہ اسے دوم یک پورنیہ غلام صدے برقنداز ازاں روز دوی سے

....

(17)

NAI Document No. 111B. F. 20 Dated 3rd July, 1857.

کوتوال صاحب مشفق مہربان زاد اقبالہ

از طرف صوبہ دار فیض اللہ سلام نیاز آنکہ و روز اک ماء الماسات گردیدہ سبیل در دروازہ اندہ مرمت است وکیل سنگ شدہ دروازہ لاہوری مسدود بمسقر و چند انگاشتہ شود مگر نصرت خاں یک طرف بیکراری نیازی ورد خود مذکور نفر ستندہ بود و بچہ عجز شود کام دروازہ خراب است حکم سرکار است کہ دروازہ لاہوری شدہ و باز از صبح کشادہ شود

....

(18)

NAI Document No. B111b- F.20 Dated 3rd July, 1857.

اللہ-- مہر محمد بخت خاں سپہ سالار افواج ۱۲۵۳--اکبر

کوتوال شہر دہلی حفظہ

مستری سرکار نزد ایشاں آنچہ کہ سالہ وغیرہ از آں عزیز القدر طلب نماید ظاہر از کدہ جوالہ اش نمودہ و بندہ تحصیل فائز بذریعہ حسب الحکم بغرت آرند فقط

دھم ذی قعدہ ۳ ۷ے مرا کری

....

(19)

NAI Document No. B-199 F-121 Dated 8th July, 1857.

قلم سے موصولہ ۲۱/ذی قعدہ ۱۲۷۳ھ

برخوردار نامدار کامگار مرزا ظہیر الدین عرف مرزا لعل بہادر معلوم نمایند برآں نور چشم واضح است کہ اکنوں در خزانہ زر قلیل ماندہ و آمدنی ہیچ جا معلوم نمی گردد و آنچہ بقدر اندک باقی ماندہ بہ عرصہ قریب صرف خواہد شد لہذا اغیر ارقام می رود کہ امروز باعث جمیع افسران پلاٹن سابق را برای مشورہ بنای تجویز وسرانجام زر کہ بہ ضرورت یومیہ بکار آید و برہان سیاہ آنرا کوٹ می گویند تاکید باید کرد در آنچہ بعد مشاورت در ہمہ گر کدام تدبیر مناسب قرار پذیرد آں را در عرضی آنہا نویسانیدہ فردا بحضور بگذرانند زیرا کہ قبل از صرف تمام وکمال در باقی تجویز این اثر از لوازم احتیاط وواجبات است چہ در سرکار والا از قدیم خزانہ نبودہ وچوں بہ حاصل در پیش کش نرسیدہ جمیع ملازمان قدیم وجدید در تکلیف اند وآنچہ در زمان گذشتہ از ساہوکاران شہر مبلغ یک لکھ بست ہزار روپیہ قرض سود سے برای صرف خاص طلب شدہ بود تمام وکمال بمعرض ایصال در نیامدہ پس درین حالت از کجا خبر گیری دیگراں خواہد شد این جملہ امور مفصلاً ومشروحاً کہرک افسر باید فہمانید و فردا جواب نویسانیدہ ضرور بحضور پرنور باید گزرانید مرقوم ۱۵/ذیقعدہ ۲۱ء معلّیٰ۔

(20)

NAI Document No. B- 101- F-132 Dated10th July, 1857.

بہ عز عرض بندگان عالی ومتعالی حضرت ظل سبحانی خلیفہ الرحمٰن فی دامہ سلطنتہ

خداوندا یہ فدوی ذات کا قصائی نہیں ہے اور پیشہ قصائی کا کرتا ہے بلکہ پیشہ گاوَ دیکھنے کا کرتا تھا اب کہ بیچ ان دنوں کے تمام کاروبار شاہ جہاں آباد کے بند ہیں یہ فدوی نان شبینہ سے تنگ ہوا لاچار پیشہ کباب فروشی کہ گونہ مداخلت بیچ اوسکے رکھتا تھا اختیار کیا۔کل کے دن کہ چند قصائی بہ علت گاوکشی گرفتا ہوکر اس فدوی کی دوکان کے آگے سے گذرے اس وقت فدوی درستی گوشت واسطے کبابوں کے کر رہا تھا۔سپاہیان جنگی نے باشتباہ قصاب کے مجھ فدوی کو بھی گرفتار کرلیا چنانچہ ہمراہ قصابوں کے مقید کوتوالی ہوں جوکہ میری حالت اور پیشہ سے تمامی محلّہ لعل چاہ واقف ہیں اون سب کے شہادت سے اظہر کےاوس۔ سے بے جرمی اس فدوی کے ثابت ہے ہمراہ عرضی ہذا کے حضور میں گذران کر امید رکھتا ہوں کہ جان بخشی اور رہائی اس خانزاد کے ہور ہے واجب تھا عرض کیا۔الٰہی آفتاب دولت اور معدلت وانصاف کا ہمیشہ چمکتا رہے۔

عرضی فدوی حافظ عبدالرحمٰن امیدوار رہائی ص

۸۳ ۱۲۷۳ھ حکم ہوا کہ سائل کو رہائی دی جاوی

حکم ہوا کہ سائل نے محض یہ مفصل کہی ہے کہ سائل قصاب نہیں ہے پروانہ بنام کوتوال

شہر جاری ہوئی کہ مسائل کو واسطے لکھنے اظہار کے اس محکمہ میں بھیج دو اور یہ بھی لکھو کہ کون کون شخص گرفتار قید ہیں اون کا نام و نشان لکھو ۱۷/ ذیقعدہ ۲۱ سنہ موصولہ دفتر ۲۲/ ذی قعدہ سنہ ۲۱

....

(21)

NAI Document No. B-99 F-1 Dated 12th July, 1857.

بسم اللہ الرحمٰن الرحیم

عزت پرور سلامت حضرت ظل سبحانی خلیفہ الرحمانی خلد اللہ ملکہ

جناب عالی خانہ زاد رحمت سپردیم۔ سواران ہندوستانی سے بذریعہ چٹھی مقام عدل پور متصل بنارس سے آیا۔ دو تین روز اوپر مکان اپنی بیچ امروہہ کے مقیم رہا اور اب کمترین در دولت حضور مصلح گنجور پر حاضر ہے اور خانہ زاد فقط میں اپنی ذات سے یہاں ہے دوسرا میرے رجمنٹ کا کوئی شخص نہیں ہے واسطہ اطلاع کے گذارش ہے۔

عرضی

فدوی خانہ زاد شیخ غلام نبی سوار

....

(22)

NAI Document No.B-71- F-119 Dated 18th July, 1857.

مبلغ پنج روپیہ بابت بجز یکصد امیر خاں ولد نور خاں کو بعد از وصول ہے۔

تحریر ۲۵/ ذی الحجہ ۱۲۷۳ھ

العبد

مرزا لال

مہر۔ (جو پڑھی نہیں جاسکی)

....

(23)

NAI Document No. B-139 F-8 Dated 19th July, 1857.

بغرض قدم بوساں حضرت جہاں پناہ سلامت   برساند

جناب عالی فدوی ترمرہ سواران رجمنٹ چہارم بہ عہدہ دفعہ داری ہی فیصلہ انگریزوں کا مقام مظفر نگر سے کر کر تاریخ ۲۹/ عید الفطر کو حضور میں حاضر ہوا اب بیچ جنگ و جدل اور جاں فشانی کار سرکار میں مستعد ہوں اور بزرگ فدوی کے قدیم سے نمک پروردہ حضور کے تھے اس واسطے امیدوار ہوں کہ اب فدوی پرورش حضور کے بعد فیصلہ پہارٹی کے بہ عہدہ معززی سرفراز ہووے اور مراد اپنی پہونچ کر دعای دولت حضور میں مشغول رہے واجب تھا۔ الٰہی آفتاب دولت چمکتا رہے۔ فقط

فدوی نمک پروردۂ قدیم غلام عباس دفعدار ملازم

رجمنٹ چہارم ترپ اوہ امد مظفر نگر

معروضہ ۷/ذی الحجہ ۲۱ سنہ جلوس

مہر غلام عباس

....

(24)

NAI Document Dated 21st July, 1857.

مہر دار الامان خاص حضور والا

حکم

کوتوال شہر بوقت جمیع تھانہ داران شہر فہرست اسم نویسی آں کس اہل اسلام کہ بخانہ اسرمادہ گاو باز مرتب کردہ مچلکہ واقرار نامہ عدم گاؤکشی خفیہ وعلانیہ بکردو در آں مکان کہ نیل گاو پسندی بدستور سپہ باز و دانہ چارہ ایں باسہ رود موعودہ دہالے بخانہ خود خوراینده باشد برای خرائے مطلق نکشاند و بسیار تقید دارد کہ اگر بعد سہ روز بموجب فہرست و مملکہ اگر موجودات کار بدستور نخواہد شد باخفیہ ذبح کشی خواہد کی سرا خواہد یافت واز حال کشتہ خواہد شد و معنی داردو سینی گاؤ در کولوائے باطلب این در مکانے باتقرر مکان علحدہ برای دوشی آنہا ضرورت ندارد۔ فقط ہفتم ماہ ذالحجہ ۲۱ سنہ معلیٰ

رقعہ ہای بنام جمیع تھانہ داران نوشتہ شد

۸/ذالحجہ

نقل گرمرشد

(25)

NAI Document No.38 Collection No.43 Dated July 23, 1857.

حکم اشتہار آنکہ

نسبت جمیع رعایای قصبہ رھتک حکم عام محا گردد کہ احدی دست تعدی براحدی درازنکند و دراطاعت برداران دولت خواہ سرکار معلیٰ حاضر باشند۔ عنقریب جملہ انتظام وفوج شائستہ برای بندوبست فرستادہ خواہد شد بہر صورت آسائش ورفاہ رعایا نظر سرکار روالا است و ہرکس کہ تمردی وعدل حکمی خواہند کرد سزای سنگین خواہد یافت۔ لہٰذا برای اطلاع خاص وعام اشتہار ہذا اجراء یافتہ

المرقوم غرہ ذی الحجہ ۲۱ جلوس معلیٰ

....

(26)

NAI Document No. B115 F.50 . 12th Zilhijja, year is not mentioned

یادداشت

فرد سپاہی آمد امروہہ در شاہ جہاں آباد

(۱)علی داد خاں (۲)علی بخش (۳)محمد حسین (۴)دائم علی (۵)الٰہی بخش

(۶)وصل خاں (۷)حسین بخش (۸)محمد بخش (۹) مہربان علی (۱۰) نجف علی

(۱۱) بنیاد علی (۱۲) الٰہی بخش ثانی (۱۳) نجیب اللہ (۱۴)منیر علی (۱۵) کریم بخش

(۱۶)منیر خاں (۱۷) کریم بخش (۱۸)عظیم اللہ (۱۹)داؤد خاں (۲۰) شیخ عبدو

(۲۱)غلام علی (۲۲)شہاب خاں (۲۳)خدا بخش (۲۴)محبّ اللہ خاں

(۲۵)پیر (۲۶)شجاعت خاں (۲۷)میر ٹیپو (۲۸)علی بخش (۲۹)علی حسی

(۳۰)ظہور علی (۳۱) محمد خاں ثانی (۳۲)کریم خاں (۳۳)فضل حسین

(۳۴)محمد خاں (۳۵)منور خاں (۳۶)نعیم اللہ (۳۷)پیر بخش (۳۸) کریم خاں ثانی

....

(27)

NAI Document No. B120 - F-137 25th July , 1857

مہر تھانہ فیض بازار، خاص دارالخلافہ شاہجہاں آباد ۱۲۷۱ھ معلّٰی

بخدمت سیف علی کرار خاں وغیرہ فرمان مخلصاحب تھانہ داران سہ سعد سلام و نیاز

شب گذشتہ کو مسماۃ دلپسند گیر امامی ملازم سابق غلام محی الدین حسین خاں پدر فرمانی بہ تحدیح

سازش کے بھگا لے گیا اور ساپدر مذکور نے بتاریخ سرام نواب خاں قصوری تلاش کرتے

ہوئے لہٰذا التماس ہے کہ اپنی اسی علاقہ میں مرتب کاردیاں وگومیدارں تلاش کر۔۔۔امامی

مذکور کے حسب حلہ دہلی کے فراں اور بصورت دستابی پاس راقم کے بھیج دئے۔ ۳؍ذی الحجہ

۱۲۷۱ھ معلّٰی مسماۃ دلپسند کررا ایک اوسط قد مرم اندام جدا صاحب بلندی موسہ ابروح کلاں

کانوں میں بالیاں عمر ۲۵ تمت سال امامی سیاہ رنگ معد مسماۃ آنکہ اوسکی حتی الوجودہ صحت

رو بملاعی سر پرہل

العبد محمد مرزا امامی تپہ بھوجلا پہاڑی

مہر تھانہ بھوجلا پہاڑی خاص دارالخلافہ

شاہجہاں آباد ۲۱ ؁ معلیٰ

۴ رذی قعدہ ۲۱ ؁ معلیٰ وقت شام کے آیا

العبد محمد امیر علی تھانہ دار نگم بود

مہر پڑھی نہیں جاسکی

واقع ۴ رذی الحجہ وقت چہار گڑی دن رہی

روانہ کی گئی

العبد محمد اکرام اللہ تھانہ دار کور کشمیری دروازہ

مہر، پڑھی نہیں جاسکی

العبد محمد صدق بلید دار لاہوری دروازہ

مہر۔ محمد صدق

چہارم ذی الحجہ ۷۳ ؁ وقت تین بجے آیا۔

العبد محمد رضا اللہ خاں تھانہ دار ترکمان

مہر پڑھی نہیں جاسکی

۴ رذی الحجہ ۱۲۷۳ ھ کو بعمل دو بجے دن

کے فوراً روانہ آیندہ کیا گیا

العبد میر امانت علی خاں تھانہ دار کورالہ باد

مہر پڑھی نہیں جاسکی

العبد میر امانت علی خاں تھانہ دار کورالہ باد

مہر پڑھی نہیں جاسکی۔

العبد مرزا مجید خاں بیگ داروغہ کور قاسم

خاں ۴ رذی الحجہ مہر، تھانہ قاسم خاں خاص

دارالخلافہ شاہجہاں آباد ۲۱ ؁ معلیٰ

العبد فیض طلب خاں تھانہ دار کور الملک

مہر پڑھی نہیں جاسکی۔

(28)

NAI. Document No-B84 F.22 26th July, 1857.

مہر کچہری سالار بہادر سنہ ۲۱ معلیٰ

مکرم دروازہ۔۔۔

بنام افسران پلٹن حسینی شقدار حکم ہوتا ہے کہ ایک افسر کلاں پلٹن کا کل وقت الیہ کہیں بجے کے حضور میں حاضر ہوتا تاکید جانو

مرقوم ۴؍ ذی الحجہ سنہ ۲۱ معلیٰ

....

(29)

NAI -Document No. B.120 F.142 Dated 27th July, 1857.

مشفق فدویان جمیع تھانہ داران شہر دہلی سلامت رہو

جو کہ تم سب تھانہ داران حضور والا میں عرائض اپنے بھیجتے ہو اون عرضیوں کے حاشیہ پر حضرت جہاں پناہ سلامت لکھتے ہو اس واسطہ لکھا جاتا ہے کہ از تاریخ ہذا عرضی کے شروع پر غریب پرور سلامت لکھا کرو حضرت جہاں پناہ سلامت مت لکھا کرو تصدیع بلیغ جاننا۔ راقم خدا بخش خاں بابت کوتوال پنجم ماہ ذی الحجہ سنہ ۲۱ معلیٰ

واقع ۶؍ ماہ ذی الحجہ سنہ ۲۱ جلوس وقت چہار گھڑی دن سے آیا اور گیا

العبد محمد اکرام اللہ خاں تھانہ دار کشمیری دروازہ

واقع شش ذی الحجہ ۲۱ سنہ جلوس معلیٰ وقت پانچ گھڑی دن حضور کے پہونچا

العبد محمد امیر علی تھانہ دار نگم بود

دو مہریں ثبت ہیں (لیکن پڑھی نہیں جا سکیں۔ غالباً دونوں تھانہ داروں کی ہونگی)

....

(30)

NAI - Document No. B.122 F.17 Dated 28th July 1857.

مہر تھانہ دار بھوجلا پہاڑی خاص دار الخلافہ شاہجہاں آباد ۲۱ سنہ معلیٰ

عزت پرور سلامت

جناب عالی آج سہ پہر پھر دن چڑھے مینڈھو خاکروبہ کوچہ میر عاشق نے خبر پہونچائی کہ مسمی لچھر فقیر نابینا قوم کہار لاوارث دس پندرہ دن سے بہ عارضہ بخار و اسہال بیمار ہو کر مر گیا ہے۔ فوراً کرنل کوچہ مذکور میں گیا تو زبانی ایک محلّہ کے بیمار ہونا لاوارث مذکور کا واضح ہوا۔ سوا دو روپیہ او سکے برآمد ہوئے چنانچہ بعد تحریر صورت حال لاش کو سپرد ایک محلّہ کے کیا گیا کہ مسمن کہار وغیرہ ایک محلّہ نے تصرف از مذکور اور کچھ اپنے پاس سے لگا کر لاش او سکی موافق مذہب ہندوان اوٹھادی۔ اطلاعاً عرض کر کے فرد صورت حال کوائف عرض ہذا ابلاغ کیا زیادہ حد ادب الٰہی آفتاب معدلت چمکتا رہے۔

عفت

نمک خوار معدوتی　　　　تپہ بھوجلا پہاڑی

معروضہ ٦/ذی الحجہ ۱۲۷۳ھ ہجری نبوی

....

(31)

NAI - Document No.1 Bearing Seal of Hafiz Aminuddin- undated

صبح تک جمعدار معہ نصیر الدین برقنداز امی غلسیفہ براس معروف کے روندامی ہو ۵/ذالحجہ ۱۲۷۳ھ مضمون معہ بداسر الجلا نامی اور لعل لے کن اور لعل دس بحث ان کے آیا فوراً بمعہ رامدی برقنداز کے روانہ اس کو کیا۔

العبد	العبد
میر امانت علی خاں تھانہ دار بدر پور	محمد مرزا
العبد	العبد
محمد احسان اللہ تھانہ دار ترکمان	مرزا محمد خاں بیگ تھانہ دار کررہاسہ

(سات مہریں جن میں سے صرف محمد احسان اللہ کی پڑھی جا سکی)

....

(32)

NAI Ducument No. B.103 F.134 Dated 29th July 1857.

مرشد بقعہ آفاق صاحب عالم وعالمیان سلامت

بعز عرض رساند۔ جناب عالی شقہ حضور کا بہ طلب کیفیت اس باب کے کہ جو کبابی تمہاری کوتوالی میں گرفتار ہے کیفیت لکھو۔ کس شخص نے اس کو گرفتار کرایا معہ نام ونشان ان لوگوں کے اطلاع دو۔ حقیقت یہ ہے کہ مسمی عبدالرحمان ولد محمد پناہ شیخ پیشہ کبابی ساکن چاہ شیریں کٹرہ غلام محمد خاں وممن ولد عظیم اللہ ساکن قدم شریف کو دیبی پرشاد سکسینہ حوالدار کمپنی اول نے کہ بہ عنایت لاہوری دروازہ کے ہے بہ علت گاؤکشی اس عبارت سے کہ انگریزوں نے سازش کر کے پانصد روپیہ کر کے ہمارے گارد کے سامنے بہ مراد تنازعہ ہو جائے۔ ہندو مسلمانان میں گاؤکشی کری اس علت میں گرفتار کوتوالی ہوئے کیفیت یہ تھی سو عرض کری۔ الٰہی آفتاب دولت واقبال پایاں باد۔

عرض فدوی سید مبارک شاہ خاں کوتوال شہر

معروضہ ۱۸رذی قعدہ ۲۱

مہر (مہر پڑھی نہیں جاسکی)

....

(33)

NAI Document No.B.111c. F.44 Dated 29th July, 1857.

حضرت جہاں پناہ سلامت

بعد عرض میرساند۔

حضرت اقدس درباب احتیاط گاؤکشی گذارش پرداز ہوں کہ جواہل اسلام سکنائے شہرسے جس کسی کے ہاں گائے پرورده ہوں منگا کر کوتوالی میں مرورایام عیدالضحیٰ اگر باندی جاویں تو کوتوالی میں اس قدر جگہ نہیں کہ پچاس چالیس بھی راسیں کھڑی ہوں اور یہ تمام شہر میں جس اہل اسلام کے گای ہوہیں وہ منگائی جاوینگی قریب جانا اس رائے کے ہونگے اس کے واسطے ایک جگہ وسیع یا احاطہ ہونا چاہیے کہ جب اور وہاں محصور راس تو بداست نمک خوار کوئی ایسی جگہ نہیں ہے اور اگرچہ منگایا جاویگا غیر مستحسن اور مفید واسطہ مالکان مادہ گاوان کے ہے چونکہ سب طرح کے بشر دور اندیش اور کوتہ اندیش ہیں۔ مبادا اس میں نارضامندی مالکان کے ہو کہ اوس میں نوع دیگر ظہور نہ کرے اس واسطہ اگر حکم ہو تو تھانہ داران اپنے اپنے علاقے کے کہ جن کے یہاں گاے ہیں وہ اہل اسلام سے ہیں مچلکہ لے لیویں نا جیسا حکم ہو وہ محامد تا حاوی الٰہی احباب امال پایاں

فدوی سید مبارک شاہ خاں کوتوال

معروضہ ۷/ذی الحجہ ۲۱ ــــہ

مہر

(پڑھی نہیں جا سکی)

....

(34)

NAI - Document No.8 F.38 Dated 30th July. 1857

حضرت جہاں پناہ سلامت

بعز عرض کہ امروز بوقت شب از قضای میر ساند۔ الہی جناب والد مغفور مرزا محمد بہادر بخت انتقال نمود۔ امیدوار تفصلات اندازم کہ بہ محافظان مقبرہ ہمایوں حکم عالی صادر شود کہ در مدفون کرد۔ نسازندے ای جلوس جنازہ چہار زنجیر فیل و چہار تمن مرحمت شود۔ واجب بود عرض نمود الہی آفتاب اقبال تاباں و درخشاں باد

عرضی

فدوی دلاور بخت عرف خدا بخش

۸/ذی الحجہ ۲۱ سنہ معلیٰ

....

(35)

NAI - Document No.43 Dated 9th Zilhijja 21st Year.31st July , 1857.

آفتاب عالمتاب سلطنت و اقبال آسمان خورشید جہاں تاب برج ابہت و اجلال حضرت ظل سبحانی خلیفہ الرحمانی دام اقبالہ۔

فدوی ذرہ مقدار حلقہ بندگی راز یور گوش و گردن ساختہ ہم نقوش سجود جبہہ برافروختہ بعز عرض بازیان آستان زمین آسمان و حاضران عتبہ عرش نشان می رساند۔ برآئینہ ضمیر خورشید نظیر اظہر من الشمس و ابین من الامس است کہ اہلکاران سابق کار این فدویت شعار بر عہدہ ھا معلومہ مقرر بودند کلید اختیار چہ گونہ امور در پنجہ تصرف ایشان تفویض بود بامردگاں از کوتہ فہمی ہای دراز دست خیانت درامانت دید غبن در نقود و اجناس و اموال لکھا روپیہ بکشادند۔ ہرگاہ کہ این راز مخفی ظاہر گشت و از این جانب تجویز محاسبہ و مطالبہ برروی کار آمد ہریکی بہ حیلہ و بہانہ ازیں جا برخاستہ در دہلی بہ خانہ خود ہا نشستند و خوف باز پرس کارپردازاں و کارکنان خلافت در دل بے خوف خود نیاوردند و از سست رای کمر نمک حرامی چست بستہ در ہر مقدمہ متعلقہ این ریاست و مرجوعہ سلطنت رخنہ انداز خرابی و ابتری گردیدند و می گردند چنانچہ اکثر سخنان ناراست و دروغ بد مسامع انصاف مجامع حضور پرنور رسانیدہ مزاج اقدس و اعلیٰ و طبع معلیٰ را کہ از قدیم زیادہ متوجہ حال این کمترین بود برجلال زدند یعنی برگشتہ و آشفتہ کردند کہ راجہ بلب گڑھ در ظاہر ا اہالیان خسروانی و در باطن با اعالیان انگلستانی موافقت دارد و شیشہ و باروت بہ ارادہ فاسد ذخیرہ می نماید و راہ کشادہ آمد و شد بر تجار و بیوپاری و مسافر بند ساختہ و ہم چناں نظر مرحمت بنگاہِ عتاب و خطاب و زحمت مبدل گشت کہ مولوی احمد علی وکیل و معتمد این خاکسار بی اعتبار کہ ہمیشہ حاضر باشِ دربار فیض بار می ماندہ بہ خیال بی آبروی خود دستار آبرو

رادردست گرفتہ دراین جا آمدہ وقلندر بخش خاں رسالہ داررا کہ حسب الارشاد فیض بنیاددر خدمت مبارک حاضر بود حکم برخاستگی دہانیدند فقط جناب عالی آنچہ کہ معاندان کلمات ناموافق بگوش نصفت نیوش آں عادل دوراں رسانیدہ اند محض دروغ بے فروغ است ومی خواہند کہ درہم چو پیرانہ نقش خیرخواہی خود بر صفحہ ضمیر معدلت تصویر آن افسر خدیو دوراں دام ملکھم بہر رنگ منقوش ساختہ زرکثیر اندوختۂ این ریاست راازباز پرس اہلکاران بادشاہی بازداشتہ ہضم نمایند۔ احقر عبودیت آگین وبزرگان این عقیدت گزین خان زاد موروثی و خیراندیش صمیمی آں خاندان والاشان وآں دودمان عظیم الامتنان ہستند وگاہی خیال نافرمانی آں فرمانروای شش جہت وہفت کشور دردل نگذشتہ،۔

زر کامل عیارم در و مادر رسی خالص گرم صدبار بگد ازی نیفتم از عیار خود

ومصداق این مقال مصدق این حال آنست کہ درایامی کہ غبار این فتنہ وفساد برخاستہ

رنگ منقوش ساختہ زرکثیر اندوختہ این ریاست راازباز پرس اہلکاران بادشاہی بازداشتہ ہضم نمایند۔ احقر عبودیت آگہن وبزرگان عقیدت گزین خانزادِ موروثی وخیراندیش صمیمی آں خاندان والاشان وآں دودمان عظیم ہستند وگاہی خیال نافرمان آں فرمانروای شش جہت و ہفت کشور دردل نگذشتہ۔

زر کامل عیارم در و قادر رسی خالص گرم صدبار بگد ازی نیفتم ار عیار خود

ومصداق این مقال ومصدق این حال آنست کہ درایامی کہ غبار این فتنہ وفساد برخاستہ

نشستہ بود این حلقہ بگوش دردہلی بضرورت قیام می داشت۔ اگر نقوش معانی ارادت دلی وصور

عقیدت اصلی دردل انکسار منزل منقوش و مصور نمی داشت۔ معرفت میر فتح علی صاحب داروغہ چرا پیغام حصول ملازمت کثیر الافادات آں زیب اورنگ سلطنت می ساخت۔ چوں بہر رنگ صورتہای اعتقاد و انقیاد برلوح خاطر نیاز ماثر مصور نمی بود پس چگونہ صورت این از روی مخفی و دیرینہ و این تمنای مکنون وکہنہ رنگ ظہور و بیان می گرفت۔ این معتقد قدیمی بہر وجہ دولت خواہ آں والا جاہ زاد اللہ اجلالہم است گو دشمنان ناموافق ہرچہ خواہند بتراشند

دردیدہ من نیست بجز نقش تو محرم   آئینہ من صورت بیگانہ نگیرد

واگرچہ این عبودیت پناہ صمیمی مذہب ہندوانی دارد مگر نظر بر طریقہ ہمہ اوست گویاں کردہ تابع پیشروان دین محمدی و مطاع پیروان ملت احمدی است حتی کہ اندرون قلعہ خاص بلب گڑھ کہ از ابتدائی آبادی اندرون قلعہ مذکور چہ بلکہ بیرون آں در آبادی گنج کدام مسجد نبود، مسجد جامع کہ بلند و سنگین و پایدار ست بنا کردہ و نیز مکان عیدگاہ بہ وسعت و فراخی دل مومنان متصل باغ دلکشانی خود بنا گردانیدہ و این دولت خواہ ازلی و ترقی خواہ ابدی ہموارہ ارتفاع اعلام دین محمدی می خواہد فقط حضور مکرمت ظہور نظر عتاب را بدیدۂ رحمت بدل فرمایند و بدستور سابق نگاہ عنایت و التفات از سرِ نو شامل حال این مترصد العنایت دارند و بریاوہ گوئی و بے ہودہ بیانی مخالفانہ و ناموافقان اعتماد ندارند

زابنای جنس خود بحذر باش زانکہ آب   با آن سرشت پاک آئینۂ دشمن است

واز راہ مراحم کثیر و مکارم وفیر بہ بندگان کار پردازان شہنشاہی و کار پردازان شاہنشاہی نفاذ حکم قضا شیم فرمایند کہ معاندان و مخالفان مسبوق الذکر را گرفتار ساختہ حوالہ این مطیع و منقاد

جاودانی فرمایند تا گرد فتنه و فساد فرونشیند و غبار خوفگی و نامهربانی از گوشه دامن ضمیر صفویت پذیر دور شود و این ارادت گزین محاسبه غبن لکھا روپیه خود گرفته جبر نقصان نماید و آنکه مسمی رستم علی باشنده کراولی عرضی خود بدین مضمون در سر رشته دفتر لاٹ صاحب بهادر گذرانیده که مسمی گینڈا وغیره یازده کس دو عرابه محموله گندم و آرد گندم از موضع کراولی برای رسد رسانی به دهلی می بردند تھانه دار راجه بلب گڑھ آنهارا از اثنای راه گرفتار ساخته در بلب گڑھ رسانیده و اجناس محموله عرابها ضبط گردیده فقط۔ عالیجاها معروضه عرضی دهنده محض نادرست و خلاف واقع است و حقیقت راست، راست ولی کم و کاست این مقدمه آنست که مسمیٰ گینڈا سرخیل بدمعاشان و رهزنان معه دیگر بدمعاشان باشندگان دیه خود اولاً موضع نگلی علاقه بدرپور را بغاوت بردند و مال و اسباب مفروته بدیه خود و دیگر دیهات قرب و جوار رسانیدند و بعده اراده غارت گری موضع مگروله معموله بلب گڑھ معه جم غفیر و جمع کثیر غارت گران۔ بموضع مذکور حمله آوردند۔ اتفاقاً تھانه دار و تحصیل دار فرید آباد گشت کنان بر سرحد مگروله رسیدند و این هنگامه برپا دیدند۔ غارت گراں ڈاکوان بمجرد رسیدن ایشاں قرار برفرار نهادند و تحصیل دار جرات را کاربسته این چند اسامی را گرفتار ساخته و مشک بسته چالان عدالت فوجداری به نمود۔ مثل این مقدمه موجود است برای صداقت معروضه اگر ارشاد شود اصل یا نقل آں بنا بر ملاحظهٔ انور حضور عدالت ظهور روانه سازد تا از سماعت آں حال قرار واقعی این مقدمه دریافت بندگان والا گردد فقط۔ و هم چنیں است حال بگھی و نبی بخش سوداگر۔ تشریح این مقدمه چناں است که بگھی ماخوذه ملازمان این بنده درگاه از صوبه دار قومی برهمن پلٹن زن سیٹ به قیمت خریده نبی بخش سوداگر

درآں سوار کردہ روانہ بلب گڑھ کردہ بودند۔ حضور فیض گنجور بالضرور تحقیقات این مقدمہ فرمایند فقط۔ وآنکہ یک دو چٹھی انگریزی از بگھی برآمد و ماشاء اللہ کہ فدوی راد ہم مردمان فدوی را ازین حال اطلاعی نیست کہ کاتب ومکتوب الیہ آن کیست و مضمون آن چیست و کدام است۔ پس صاف ظاہر است کہ دشمن راج چٹھیات را بطور جعل از کسی انگریزی خواں نویسانیدہ در بگھی مذکور خفیہ نہادہ است وصداقت این ہمہ معروضہ از مولانا محمد شاہ نظام الدین صاحب دامت برکاتہم فرمایند واز جواب باصواب ہذا بعرضی مشرف وکامیاب گردد۔ الٰہی آفتاب دولت واقبال وخورشید، فتح وفیروزی ہموارہ تاباں ودرخشاں باد

عرضی

معروضہ سانوں سودی دوج ۱۹۱۴   فدوی راجہ ناہر سنگھ بہادر والی بلب گڑھ

مہر ''راجہ ناہر سنگھ بہادر''

(36)

NAI - Document No. B.20 F.161 Dated 2nd Agust 1857

مہر پڑھی نہیں جاسکی

بخدمت شریف جناب کوتوال صاحب وجمیع تھانہ دار صاحبان اندرون شہر دہلی بعد سلام ونیاز واضح باد۔ آج بوقت تین بجے دن کے مسمی پریم سکھ حجام ساکن محلہ بہر کھڑلی بہ حاضری تھانہ ہوکر کہا کہ مسماۃ کلالی زوجہ میری کل شام سے بہکانے پر چند اخلاصی ساکن محلہ

مذکور سے اسباب مفصلہ ذیل لے کر چلی گئی ہے اور حلیہ اوسکا ذیل میں درج ہے چھپایا ہوی
کہ تلاش اوسکی ہو جاوے لہذا جب درخواست سائل بخدمت صاحبوں کے متکلف ہوئے
براہ مہربانی اپنے اپنے علاقہ میں معرفت خاکروبان وچوکیداران تلاش مسمات مذکور کے معہ
مال کے فرمائیں بصورت دستابے پاس راقم کے بھیج دیجئے۔ فقط ۱۱/ذی الحجہ ۲۱ء معلیٰ

نقد سونہ برنجی تھالی بڑی ھوبرگر کرن پھول نقرعی درگوش ہیں یک جوڑی
حلیہ ۵ یک یک پہونچی نقری دردست بالیں

مسمات کلایی۔ قوم نائن۔ بعمر جوان۔ گندم رنگ۔ فراخ پیشانی۔ کلام خم۔ پیوستہ۔
ابروا۔ اوسط بدن کبری سودائی سے ہوں فقط

الراقم۔ محمد امیر علی تھانہ دار نگم بود

واقع ۱۱/ذی الحجہ ۲۱ء وقت شام تھانہ میں آیا نقل گرفتہ روانہ کیا

العبد محمد اکرام اللہ تھانہ دار کشمیری دروازہ ۱۱/ذی الحجہ ۷۳ء

مہر پڑھی نہیں جاسکی محمد فیض بخت خاں تھانہ دار

العبد مہر پڑھی نہیں جاسکی

میر نظر علی تھانہ دار چاندنی چوک ۱۱/ذی الحجہ کی رات کو لفافہ لئے

مہر پڑھی نہیں جاسکی العبد مرزا احمد بیگ محرر تھانہ گذر قاسم

۱۲/ذی الحجہ ۷۳ء ۱۲ھ کو تعمیل چھ بجے دن کے آیا فوراً روانہ اندر کیا گیا

العبد۔ مرزا محمد خاں بیگ تھانہ دار

العبد۔ میر امانت علی خاں تھانہ دار گذر الہ باد   مہر پڑھی نہیں جاسکی

....

(37)

NAI document No. 13 dated 3rd April, 1858.13 Cavalry

رسالہ سیزدہم

تاریخ ۳ راگست ۵۸ء کو تین دنوں کا مہر و دستخط ہو چکا ہے کہ ہوگیا۔ بموجب حکم صاحب اسٹنٹ کمشنر بہادر شامل حال کی گئی۔

....

(38)

NAI - Document No. B11d F.17 Dated August, 1857.

مہر ۱۲۳۴ء   ۲۱ جلوس

شجاعت نشان کوتوال شہر محفوظ باشند

ایک کوٹھہ سرکاری واقع بازار چاندنی چوک واقع ہے اور اوس پر مسماۃ فیض بخش طوائف بطور کرایہ مسکن مدری اور جس وقت محصل واسطے مانگنے کرایہ مانگنے اوسکے جاتا ہے تبادھوں پیش اگر ادای کرایہ نہیں کرتے لہذا حکم ہے حسب نشاندہی لالہ رنگین لال ملازم

سرکار کے تم محصل کوٹھہ کرایہ دار مذکور کا لکھ کر حساب اوسکا ہواوسکا بعلت از باقی کرایہ فرق کرکر بہ تعمیل حکم رپورٹ کرو۔ تحریر بتاریخ تیرویں ماہ محرم ۲۱ سنہ معلیٰ

تھانہ دار چاندنی چوک رابرای رعایت نوشتہ کہ عرضی ارسال داشت

....

(39)

NAI - Document No. B-102 F.40 Dated 4th August, 1857.

باینکہ ایزدبخش اللہ ساکن دہبادکہ امام بخش ساکن رولہ لالو ومجدالدین ساکن صاحب لوے دوکہ آراضی پای مینار واقعہ خواجہ صاحب ہیں بعد حکم سرکار والا قلعدارے کری تھی۔ اب حکم والا واسطہ اتباع اس کے چادر ہی برار آنچہ سے پکڑنی اپنی اولا کوساس کہ عصر جازاد میں مختصر ساکام مہرولی دادار بی وغیرہ کا وجہ ہجرت آراضی مذکور میں کہ کشتکاری اس کے ہر کرتے ہیں سرکار میں گذارنے گے اور ناگذران سے ذمہ بنوت کے آراضی مذکور کوتھی جوتیں گے اور بالکل ہات میں لگائی کے مزرعہ سرحد کچھ فطری اور یا کہ یکہ دی کہ مبداء ادم بضرورت صوت اس کے جوسرکار شری دیوموجب آفتاب مہرپرور۔

۱۳۔ ذلحجہ ۲۱ سنہ

....

(40)

NAI - Document No. B139 F.10 Dated 7th August, 1857.

عقیدت شعار راول رنجیت سنگھ رئیس جیسلمیر مورد عنایات شاہی بودہ بدانند گردھاری سنگھ صوبہ دار کمپنی گرانڈیل رحمت ۱۶ بمبئی بوساطت مشیر الدولہ ممتاز الملک فدوی خاص محمد بخت خاں گورنر جنرل بہادر بحضور حاضر آمدہ مظہر شد کہ آں عقیدت شعار جملہ کفاران راتہہ تیغ نمودہ علاقجات خود را از وجود ناپاک و مصفی نمودہ برای نام احدی را بہ علاقہ خود نگذاشتہ بنا برایت خاطر اقدس از استماع این معنی از طرف آں عقیدت شعار نہایت خشنود گردیدہ۔ لہذا بنام ایشاں غرار تام می آید کہ بہ علاقہ خود خیال انتظام نمایندہ کہ احدی از مخلوق خدا متاذی نشود واگر جمعیت کفاران از راہ دریا بہ علاقہ ایشاں رسد آنہارا قتل نمایند این معنی موجب استرضای تمام خاطر حضور اقدس خواہد شد و ہر گونہ تمنا و درخواست کہ از حضور انور خواہی خواست حلمہ پذیرائی خواہد یافت زیادہ تفصلات شناسند۔

مرقوم بستم ۲۰ ماہ ذی الحجہ ۱۲۷۳ ہجری مطابق ۲۱ جلوس معلیٰ۔

Saved Page. Issued

The king 20th August 1857 Zilhijjah

....

(41)

NAI - Documnet No. 139 - 9 Dated 7th August, 1857.

Translated

عقیدت شعار راؤ بہار ارئیس کچھ بجھ مورد تفصلات شاہی بودہ بدانند گردہاری سنگھ صوبہ دار کمپنی گڑاندیل رحمت ۱۶ ارنمی خاطر بوساطت مشیر الدولہ ممتاز الملک فدوی خاص محمد بختِ خاں گورنر جنرل بہادر بحضور حاضر آمدہ مظہر شد کہ آں عقیدت شعار جملہ کفاران راتہہ تیغ نمودہ علاقجات خودراز وجود ناپاک آنہا پاک و مصفی نمودہ برای نام احدی را بہ علاقہ خودنگذاشتہ بنابراین خاطر اقدس از استماع این معنی ازطرف آں عقیدت شعار نہایت خشنود گردیدہ لہذا بنام ایشاں غرار تام می آید کہ بہ علاقہ خود خیال انتظام نمایندہ کہ احدی از مخلوق خدامتاذی نشود واگر جمعیت کفاران ازراہ دریا بہ علاقہ ایشاں رسد آنہاراقتل نمایند این معنی موجب استرضاء تمام خاطر اقدس خواہد شد وہر گونہ تمناودرخواست کہ ازحضور انور خواہی خواست ہمہ درجہ پذیرائی خواہد یافت زیادہ تفصلات شناسند۔

مرقوم ۱۶ر ذی الحجہ ۱۲۷۳ ہجری مطابق ۲۱ سنہ جلوس معلیٰ۔

....

(42)

NAI - Document No. 43/50 dated 9th August, 1857

لغایت

شقہ بنام راجہ ناہر سنگھ

فدوی خاص لائق العنایت والاحسان راجہ ناہر سنگھ بہادر مورد تفصلات بادشاہی بودہ بد انداز ارسال ہشت اشرفی نذر گذرانیدہ بہ تقریب عیدالضحی مطلق رفع ملال خاطر نگردیدہ چوں استہزاد نذر مرسوم سرکار دولت مدار شود لہذا نذر مقبول شدہ لازم است کہ برویترہ آباءو اجداد خود از تہ دل مصروف دولت سگالی و خیرخواہی باید شود زیادہ تفصلات شناستہ۔ مرقوم ۱۸ ذی الحجہ ۲۱ سنہ معلیٰ۔

....

(43)

NAI Document No. B135 F.167 Dated 9th August 1857.

حکم نامہ

حکم حضور والا کا یہ ہے ایک تو یہ امر ہے جس طور سے سپاہی کی خوشی ہوئی اس طور پر ہم نے خوشی کی اور اپنی جان کا دریغ نہیں کیا اس واسطہ کہ یہ فوج سے میں نے اقرار کیا تھا کہ تم میری بیٹا بیٹی کی جای ہو خواہ بچہ ہوتا اور ضد کرتا ہے تو اس کی ضد اٹھائی جاتی ہے اس واسطے

میں نے تمہاری ضد اٹھائی اور جس طرح تمہاری خوشی دیکھی اس سے دریغ نہ کیا اور اس ضعیفی کی طرف خیال نہ کیا جس کا خیال کرنا جائز و میرا کیا حال۔ میرا مزاج حکیم احسن اللہ خاں کے ہاتھ رہتا ہے اب میرے فیصلے کا کیا ہے۔

....

(44)

NAI - Document No. B.135 F.167-170 Dated 9-11th August 1857.

حکم نامہ بنام کل افسران افواج شاہی حکم حضور والا کا یہ ہے۔ایک تو امر یہ ہے کہ جس واسطہ سپاہی کے خوشی ہوئی اوس طور پر میں نے خوشی کی اور اپنی جان کا دریغ نہ کیا۔اس واسطہ کہ یہ جو فوج سے میں نے اقرار کیا کہ میرے بیٹا بیٹی کی جائے ہو۔خواہ بچہ ہوتا ہے اور ضد کرتا ہے تو اس کی ضد از حد ہوتی ہے۔اس واسطہ میں نے تمہاری ضد اٹھائی اور جس طرح تم نے کہا وہ کیا مگر افسوس ہے کہ تم نے میری جان کا ذرا خیال نہ کیا۔جس طرف خیال نہ کیا تو چاہتے۔اب ہی کہ میری جو حالت ہے اور جو کرنا چاہتے کہ میرا کیا حال ہوا جاتا ہے ایک ایک لحہ لحہ میں اکثر خراب ہوتا ہے کہ میرا مزاج حکیم احسن اللہ خاں کے ہاتھ میں ہے اور وہ ہی میرے مزاج کی خبر لیتا رہتا تھا۔تو اب میرے بیٹے بجز خدا کی ذات کے اور کوئی نہیں ہے لحہ لحہ میں عجب حال ہوا جاتا ہے اب بیست صاحبوں کے سردار کہ جس طرح میں نے تمہاری خوشی کی ہے اسی کو کرو۔حکیم جی کے اوپر سے گارڈ اٹھا لینا چاہیے اور نبض میری دیکھ جایا کرے۔یہ ایک وقت اور جو تم لوگوں کو دشمن بہکاتے

ہیں ناحق تو اس نے خیال اور جو شخص کہے کہ یہ شخص ایسا ہے تو اس سے کہو کہ اس کی میری جیسی مکرر بیماری باس جس میں ہم کو یہی معلوم ہو کہ یہ دشمن ہمارا بھی اس بموجب سزا ہم اب دیں گے اور یہ مال اسباب جو لٹا ہے سو بادشاہی تھا جائی کہ تحقیق کر کے سب اسباب حضور میں داخل ہو اور جن کی شرارت سے لٹا ہے ان کے مطابق گناہ کی کورٹ کی تجویز سے سزا ملی۔ اگر یہ منظور نہیں ہے تو مجھ کو خواجہ صاحب میں پہونچا دو ساتھ حفاظت کے میں وہاں پہونچ کر مجاوری کروں گا اور بیٹھا رہوں گا اور یہ بھی نہ ہو سکے تو میں یہاں سے اٹھ کھڑا ہونگا جس سے روکا جائے وہ مجھے روک لے کس واسطہ ان کے ہاتھ سے قتل نہ ہوا تمہارے ہاتھ سے ہوا اور رعیت پر جو ظلم ہو رہا ہے یہ رعیت پر نہیں ہے میرے اوپر ہے چاہے سن کر کہ اس کا بندوبست کریں اور نہیں تو مجھ کو جواب دیں۔ میں بھی ہیرا کھا کر سور ہونگا اور ایک صندوقچہ مہر حضور والا کا بروز غارت اسباب حکیم احسن اللہ خاں کے جاتا رہا ہے جو کوئی تاریخ ۱۶/ ذلحجہ سے کاغذ لکھا ہوا اس مد کا ہوگا خانہ قبول ۲۰/ ذی الحجہ ۲۱ سنہ معلی

بقلم مرداس

(45)

NAI Document No. B15 F-4 Dated 10th August 1857.

میرا عجب حال ہے اب مزاج کی خوشی بکی یہ اوسی طرح لینا چاہی اور رہائی دینا چاہی اور یہ اور تم لوگوں کو دشمن بہکاتا ہے۔ تو باقی کہ یہ شخص ایسا ہے تو اس سے کہو کہ اک چٹھی جس میں ہم کہ یہ معلوم ہو کہ یہ شخص ہمارا دشمن ہے اس بموجب سزا اور یہ مال اسباب جو تھا ہی

سو بادشاہی تھا جاری کہ تحقیق کر کے سب اسباب حضور میں سا داخل ہوا اور جن کی شریعت سے تھا ہی ان کو مطابق گناہ کے کوٹ کے تحریر سے سزا ملی اگر یہ منظور نہیں ہے تو مجھے خواجہ صاحب پہونچا دو ساتھ حفاظت کے میں وہاں پہونچ کر مجاوری کروں گا اور تنہا رہوں گا اور یہ نہ ہو کے تو میں یہاں سے اٹھ کھڑا رہونگا۔ جس سے روکا جاوے وہ مجھے روک لے کس واسطہ ان کے ہاتھ سے قتل نہ ہوں۔ تمہاری ہاتھ سے ہوا اور رعیت پر جو ظلم ہو رہا ہے۔ یہ رعیت پر نہیں ہے میرے اوپر ہے چاہیے سب کو کہ اس کا بندوبست کریں اور نہیں تو مجھ کو صورت دیگر میں ہیرا کھا کے سور ہونگا اور ایک صندوقچہ بد حضور والا کا بر در غارت اسباب کلھم حضور کے جاتا رہا جو کوئی تاریخ ۱۶ سے لکھا ہوا اس بد کا ہوا وہ جابر ہوگا۔

۱۸ ؍ ذی الحجہ سے معلیٰ

بقلم کہرمل

....

(46)

NAI Document No. B-135 F.170 Dated 11th August, 1857.

حکم نامہ بنام کل افسران افواج بقلم ہردیوداس

حکم حضور والا کا یہ ہے ایک تو امر یہ ہے کہ جس واسطہ سپاہی کے خوشی ہوئی اس طور پر خوشی سے میں نے کی اور اپنی جان کا دریغ نہ کیا اس واسطے کہ جو فوج سے میں اقرار کیا کہ تم

میرے بیٹا اور بیٹی کی جای ہو۔ بچہ ہوتا ہے اور ضد کرتا ہے تو اس کی ضد اٹھائی جاتی ہے اس میں تو تمہاری ضد اٹھائی اور جس طرح تمہاری خوشی مگر افسوس ہے یعنی میری جان کا دریغ نہ کیا اور اس ضعیف کی طرف خیال نہ کیا تو چاہیے اب یہ ہی کہ میری ضعیفی کی طرف خیال کیا کہ میرا حال کیا ہوا جاتا ہے ایک ایک لمحہ کے واسطے میرا مزاج حکیم احسن اللہ خاں کرتا سید حسن ہے اور تھا یہ ہے۔ میرے مزاج کی خبر ملتی رہتی تھی تو اب میرے مزاج کی خبر کے اسباب حکیم احسن جو کوئی تاریخ ۱۶/ذی الحجہ سے کاغذ لکھا ہوا اس مہر کا ہوگا حابر۔

۱۸/ذی الحجہ ۲۱ سنہ معلٰی

مگر افسوس ہے تم نے میری جان کا دریغ نہ کیا اور اس ضعیف کی طرف خیال نہ کیا تو چاہے اب یہ ہی کی میری ضعیفی کی طرف خیال کر کے میرا خیال کیا ہوتا جاتا ہے ایک ایک لمحہ لمحہ کے واسطے میرا مزاج حکیم احسن اللہ خاں کرتا سید حسین ہے اور تھا یہ میری مزاج کی خبر لیتا رہتا تھا تو اب میرے مزاج کی خبر غیر خدا کے اور کوئی نہیں ہے لمحہ لمحہ میں میرے مزاج کا عجب حال ہوا جاتا ہے۔ اب سب صاحبوں کو سرداران و سپاہیان کو چاہیے جس طرح سے تمہاری خوشی کی ہے اسی طرح پر تم میری خوشی کرو او پر سے گارد اٹھالینا چاہو یہی اور رہائی دینا چاہے اور نبض میری دیکھ جایا کرے۔ ایک وقت اور چلا جایا کرے اور جو ہم لوگوں کے دشمن بہکاتے ہیں باقی تو اسے خیال نہ کرنا چاہیے اور جو شخص کہے کہ یہ ویسا ہے تو اس سے کہو کہ میری چٹھی نہ کر کی لاؤ ہمارے پاس جس میں ہم کو یہ معلوم ہو کہ یہ دشمن ہمارا ہے اس بموجب سزا ہم اب دیں گے اور یہ مال اسباب جو لٹا ہے سو بادشاہی تھا چاہیے کہ تحقیق کر کے سب

اسباب حضور میں داخل کرواور جن کے سراریت سے بھائی ان کے مطابق کرو کہ کوں کے تجویز سے سران کی اگر یہہ منظور نہیں ہے تو مجھ کو خواجہ صاحب میں پہونچا دو سات حفاظت کے میں وہاں پہونچ کر مجاوری کرونگا اور بیٹھا رہونگا اور بیگا ہوگی تو میں وہاں سے اٹھ کھڑا ہونگا۔ جس سے روکا جائے وہ مجھے روک لے کس واسطی کہ ان کے ہاتھ سے قتل نہ ہوا۔ تمہارے ہاتھ سے ہوا اور رعیت پر جو ظلم ہو رہا ہے یہ رعیت پر نہیں ہے یہ میرے اوپر ہے چاہیے سب کو کہ اس کا بندوبست کریں اور نہیں تو مجھ کو جواب دیں۔ میں زہر کھا کے سور ہونگا اور ایک صندوقچہ مہر حضور والا کا بردرغارت اسباب حکیم احسن اللہ خان کا بار ہے جو کوئی تاریخ ۱۶رذی الحجہ سے لکھا ہوا اس مہر کا ہوگا جائز نہیں ہوگا۔

۱۸رذی الحجہ ۲۱ سنہ معلی

....

(47)

NAI - Document No. B60 F-55 Dated 12th August, 12nd 1857.

تقسیم شتر خانہ مرقوم ۱۲ذی الحجہ ۲۱ سنہ جلوس معلی

اصالت خان

دانہ	بھوسہ
۳۳	۱۰

یوم	غلات	لہ عسکا	للعر
٨	/٣	فی روپیہ دوم	/٦

٢٠

....

(48)

NAI - Documemt No. B-139 F-12 Dated 17th August, 1857.

عقیدت شعار رنجیت سنگھ رئیس جیسلمیر مورد مراحم سلطانی بوده بدانند چمن سنگھ ٹھاکر برادر رئیس جے پور بہ وساطت مشیر الدولہ ممتاز الملک فدوی خاص محمد بخت خاں لاٹ گورنر جنرل بہادر ناظم افواج جنگی وامور ملکی شرف ملازمت بندگان عالی حاصل نموده مظہر شد ومقر شد کہ آں عقیدت نشان از روی تمنای قدم بوسی حضور بشرط اصدار شقہ بنام خود بدرجہ اتم می دارد۔ لہذا زیب ارقام می یابد وبر خاطر انور بخوبی اظہر است کہ نام ونشان کفار فرنگ بد اہنگ در علاقہ آں فدوی نمانده باشد اگر بالفرض والتقدیر احدی از آں بفراری وروپوش شده مانده باشد اولاً آن ہا را قتل نمایند وبعده انتظام علاقہ خود نموده معہ جمعیت خود حاضر حضور شود۔ بوقت حضوری ایشاں ہزار گونہ رعایت وشفقت بہ نسبت آں فدوی فرموده بہ منصبی کہ ومریکہ در حوصلہ ایشاں نخواہد گنجند زیاده آں سرفرازی فرموده خواہد شد زیاده تفضلات شناسد۔ فقط

٢٠ ذالحجہ ٢١ سنہ معلیٰ

On Second Page

یہ کاغذ اصل بذریعہ چٹھی بہ مقدمہ جیما جیو روانہ کیا گیا۔ بتاریخ ہفتم ماہ فروری

۱۸۵۹ء اور یہ نقل اسکی شامل کاغذات مثل بادشاہی حسب الحکم رکھی گئی۔

(49)

NAI - Document No. B 130 F. 167 Dated 19th August, 1857.

مہر (پڑھی نہیں جا سکتی)

تھانہ دار صاحب سکر رالہ بادسلم بتاریخ نسخ حرسر ٹھہرا بیٹھا وہ متعلقہ رسالہ ہفتم لکھنو کے

کرادو کہ اسے سولہ روز ہوگئی ادوند خاں اٹبارہ کے لا بواسطہ لیکر جائے۔

ا ء دوم ۲۹ ی/ذالحجہ ۱۲۷۳ھ۔ خدا بخش خاں نائب کوتوال شہر دہلی۔

....

(50)

NAI - Document No. Bundle. 15 F of 9 dated 20th August, 1857

افسروں کو اختیار ہے اگر تمہاری رسائی وہاں کے افسروں سے ہے تو اتنا اختیار پیدا کرو

وزیر علی خاں واکبر کہ جو آگرہ میں پیادہ یہاں آیا ہوا ہے۔ قریب ایک ہفتہ سے اوسکی فوج

میں رسائی ہے ہدایت میں بمقام آگرہ۔۔۔ اسکی خبر کچھ فوج لے کر متھرا جانے کے واسطے

تحصیل زر ہے کہ کس سوار منجملہ سواران کے جو ہانسی کو گئے تھے وہ یہاں آئے اونکے یہاں سے وہاں جا کر اس طور سے معلوم ہوا کہ بارہ ہزار روپیہ گورگانوہ سے فوج ہانسی والی کو ہاتھ آیا یہ روپیہ وہ تھا کہ جو ستیلا کی نذر کا فراہم ہوا تھا وہ تمام و کمال فوج نے تقسیم کرلیا۔ پورب کے رہنے والے روپیہ لے کر کچھ یہاں آگئے ہریانہ کے رہنے والے سوار و پیادہ اپنے گھروں کو چلے گئے نوکر پلٹن کے ہر سر سے و سہ ہزار محمد عظیم چار ضرب توپ بھوانی میں ہیں اور بلکہ اونکی ساتھ ہے اور اونکی خبر تو شام میں آنے کی تھی آیندگان بریلی سے دریافت ہوا ہے کہ وہاں بلوہ عظیم سے خان بہادر رئیس بریلی بھی دس بارہ پلٹن المشہور بہ گندائن پلٹن ولاٹھی پلٹن ٹھہرنے کی ہیں اور کچھ توپ بھی بہم پہونچائی ہیں اور نینی تال کے پہاڑ کی تہلٹی میں زولوب بھیجی ہیں کہ کوئی صاحب لوگ اوترنے نہ پاوی مگر نواب رام پور کے یہاں سے صاحب لوگوں کو معاونت رسد کی ہوئی ہے آج ہنگامی دی روز ہیرا سنگھ برکٹ میجر بادشاہ کے پاس گیا اور بادشاہ نے اوسکی بڑی تسلی کی اور کہا کہ تم اپنے کمپنیوں کو درست سر نوکر لو اور اتواپ اگرچہ ویسے ٹوپی دار نہیں ہے مگر ہم تم کو توپ دیویں گے چنانچہ جتنی توپ کے دینے کا اقرار کیا ہے اور دو ہزار روپیہ۔

ہیرا سنگھ کو دیئے اور شام کمپنی شمح کی موجودات ہے جس سے معلوم ہوا کہ پلٹن نمبر ہفت ہیں۔

چار سپر نوسیا ہے اور ستر میں ہیں تین سو اور بہترین ہیں۔ پانسو نفر اور کوٹہ کٹن جٹ ہیں۔ دو سو نفر باجی رہے ہیں چنانچہ ان پر سہ پلٹن ہیں۔ اکیسو نفر پیادگان ہیں ساتھ سو نفر

سپاہی بہ حساب کشتگان آتا اور سواری فوج اس میں مارے نہیں گئے جس قدر بھاگ گئے ہے چودہ سو سوار اس کمپنی میں تھا اس میں سے پانسو نفر کے قریب بھاگ گیا گولہ انداز پچاس نفر مارے گئے باقی جملہ زندہ آگئے پندرہ گولہ انداز زندہ رہے اور ملازم جدید مارے گئے نسبت اسکی کہ پرانی گولہ انداز عہدہ دار ہوگئی ہیں گوالیار کی فوج کٹن جٹ ہیں کوئی نواب ہے کہ نام اوسکی معلوم نہیں ہوا اوسکی عرضی بحضور بادشاہ آئی کہ اگر مجھ کو افسر فوج قرار دیا جاوے تو آگرہ کے قلعے میں جس قدر گورہ لوگ ہیں اونکا کام تمام کر کر حاضر ہوں۔ آج اوسی کا جواب گیا کہ ہم اوس فوج میں مداخلت نہیں ہے اوسکی اب امیدوار ہیں کہ اگر تم کو سند عنایت کریں کہ تا کہ استقلال ابا ست ہماری کا ہو جاوے چنانچہ آج اوسکی نذر گذری ہے بغیر آدمی کے جیسا کہ دریاب ہوگا۔

....

(51)

NAI- Document No. B IIId F. 243 dated 21st August 1857.

مہر (پڑھی نہیں جاسکی)

شجاعت نشان مبارک شاہ خاں کوتوال شہر حفظہ۔

فرد اسباب مطلوبہ سرکار شریف پروانہ ہذا پہونچ کر تم کو اصدار حکم ہوتا ہے کہ یہ اشیاء دکان داران کلاں سکنائے کھاری باولی سے اچھی قسم اور بک سکتے ہیں۔ تم قیمت اشیا سے

مندرجہ فرد دکاندار مذکورین سے دریافت کر کے وہ قیمت اس کی تہدر اور شیخ قطب الدین واسطے دیکھنے حرم اذن اور سر کے ہمراہ پروانہ تمہارے پاس پہونچے ہیں جلد سزاوار لباس زیب کر کے تاکید حامد بھیج دو۔

۴ ذی الحجہ ۲۱

تعمیل کی گئی

۵ ذی الحجہ ۲۱

....

(52)

NAI Document No. B IIId .F. 243 dated 21st August, 1857

مہر (پڑھی نہیں جاسکی)

شجاعت نشان مبارک شاہ خاں کوتوال شہر حفظہ فرد اسباب مطلوبہ سرکار کا پروانہ میرا پہونچ کر تم کو اصدار ہے حکم ہوتا کہ یہ اشیاء دکانداران کلاں سکنائے کھاری باولی سے اجرم اول مال سکے ہے تم قیمت اشیائے مندرجہ فرد دکاندار مذکور میں سے دریافت کر کے فرد قیمت اوسکے تہدر اور شیخ قطب الدین واسطے دیکھنے چیز اول اور شہر کے ہمراد پروانہ بہ مہاری باسمی بھیے میں صد برادر سرکار اس کا کر کے تاکید جانو بھجدو۔

۴ ذی الحجہ ۲۱

(صفحہ دوپر) تعمیل کی گئی

۵ ذی الحجہ ۱۲۷۳ھ

....

(53)

NAI Document No. 2 dated 1st Muharram 1247, (22nd August ,1857)

گذارش کیا کہ بروقت وسہا نے دوکان دار واہونے دوکان کے تلاش افیون کے دوکان مذکور ہیں لیکن دوکاندار منظور امت ہوگا۔

میر محمد تک کو چلا گیا۔ یکم محرم الحرام ۱۲۷۴ ہجری

....

(54)

NAI - Document No. B - 74 F . 51 22nd August 1857

یادداشت فرد مصارف ادویات اسپتال جرنیلے واقع دریا گنج

باہتمام امام بخش ڈاکٹر تعلقہ بیگ رہے۔ مرقعہ ۱۳ ذی الحجہ ۱۲۷۳ھ

امانت واحد اللہ

ہفت روزہ

موم اصلی پارچہ ملاحسین تارپن تیل سکنجبین سادہ بنو عرق گلاب

۱۰/ یک عدد یک بوتل یک شیشی

پودینہ خشک الائچی خورد کڑ نوصادر لکڑی میدا برای پلٹس

دو من ۱۱۶/

عرق بادیان سناکلی چرائتہ برنجبن روغن السی

یک بوتل ۱۷/ ۱۱/ ۱۱/ ستہ مار

۴/ ۷/ ۸/ ۸/ ۸/

پھٹکری۔ جونک تازہ جونک باسی نحسہ ہوائی دال سن چربی لحک پای

۳/ ۴/ ۴/ ۱۴/ ۲./ برای دوخت

۱۰/ ۴/

فہرست شیخ امام بخش ڈاکٹر اسپتال جرنیلی بھیج دیں

تحریر تاریخ

....

(55)

NAI documnet No. B - 121 F. 114 dated 22nd August, 1857

جناب کولون صاحب مکرم بندہ سلامت

بعداز سلام و نیاز کے التماس یہ ہے کہ حسب الارقام آپ کی جو دوکان مسکرات زیر جامع مسجد پر بطلب دوکاندار ہذا سے استفسار حال افیون کے مسمی صوبے خاں برقنداز کو بھیجا تو دوکاندار مذکور دستیاب نہ ہوا دوکان بند کر کے کہیں چلا گیا ہے ہنوز دوکان نہیں کھولی۔فقط

جو حکم رقعہ موصوف میں جلدی کا تھا نظر بر آں

....

(56)

NAI - Document No. 1 dated 23 August .1857

مہر (پڑھی نہیں جا سکی)

حکم نامہ۔بنام افسران سکھان پلٹن۔

جو قید سب مابدولت کو حضرت جہاں پناہ دوم طلب کم نے فرما کر فرمایا کہ مابدولت کو یقین کامل ہے کہ پلٹن سکھان بخوبی انجام داد شجاعت دے گی اور ازراہ غربا نوازی بہت تعریف تمہارے فرمائے اس واسطہ تم کو لکھا جاتا ہے کہ بغور مطالعہ کل یہ پانچ عدد کے ظہار ہو کر مورچہ شام گر یہ جاویں۔

Second Page

جناب عالی ازراہ پروانہ حضور لامع النور کے اطلاع پائی۔

عرض یہ ہے کہ پلاٹن ہم لوگوں کی بوقت چار بجے دن کے مورچہ تیل واڑہ میں

گئی ہے فقط۔

....

(57)

NAI - Document No. B.111 d. F. 15 dated 24th August 1857.

مہر کرنل صاحب۔۔۔دفتر کچہری۔ ۲۱ ۔

بتاریخ سوم محرم ۲۱ معلّی۔ یک خط محض در باب ارسال معہ سے چرس ہوا۔ جواب محمد حسن خاں یہاں پہونچے اور چرس پر پہونچا۔

سوم محرم ۲۱ معلّی

....

(58)

NAI - Document No. B-70 F.243 dated 30th August, 1857.

بعز عرض بلکا لے تعالی متعالی خداوند نعمت جنابہ خانم دوران درنوسرل جناب بادشاہ بہادرشاہ صاحب دام اقدمہ جناب عالی سے گذارش یہ ہے کہ جس روز سے ہم فدویان قدم بوس حضور فیض گنجور کے ہوا ہوں مگر نامور کچھ پرورش حضور کے ہم فدویان کے نہیں ہوئی اور جو کچھ پاس ہم لوگوں کے موجود تھا تصرف ہوگیا اور اب نوبت فاقہ کے گذرتی ہے۔ اگر

حضور عالی کو پرورش ہم فدویان کے منظور قبول ہوئے از ہم بہتر ورنہ حضور والا ہم خادمان کو صاف جواب ہوجاوے تا کہ ہم لوگ برای راہ پاک پروردگار کے اور قدم بوسی حضور کے جان کر بہ مقام دہلی باہر ہوئے اور توقع وقت حضور کے کمال تھی مگر اولظہور میں نہیں پائی جاتے ہیں اگر اسی قدر رفاقہ کے رہیں گے تو قدم حضور کے ہم لوگ چھوڑ کر برائی کی طرف ہوجاویگی اور بجز ذات حضور عالی کے تمام شہر دہلی معہ اہلکاران طرف انگریزوں کے سازش رکھتے ہیں۔ آئندہ اخبار حضور کو واجب جان کر عرض کیا۔ رہی آفتاب دولت اقبال کا پایاں درخشاں رہے۔ فقط

فدویان ہم سرداران برکت بمقام دلی

مورخہ ۹ ماہ محرم ۱۸۷۳ء

....

(59)

NAI - Document No. B111d F8. 109 Dated 1st September, 1857.

مرشدزادہ آفاق صاحب عالم وعالمیان دام اقبالہ

بعزعرض　　　　　میر ساند

بموجب حکم حضور پرنالہ مکان میرن جان طوائف کا کہ جو مکان مرزا غیاث الدین بہادر کے میں آتا تھا بہ ماموری تھانہ دار نگم بود کے بند کرادیا اور عرض داشت ہذا اطلاعاً

ارسال حضور کو برادر خط تعمیلی تھانہ دار منسلک عرض ہذا ہے زیادہ حداقت احباب سلطنت درخشاں باد۔

عرضی فدوی سید مبارک شاہ خاں کوتوال دہلی

معروضہ ۱۴ محرم ۲۱ سنہ معلیٰ

....

(60)

NAI - Document No.B 111d-122 Dated 15 Muharram, 21:6th September, 1857.

شجاعت نشان کوتوال شہر بہ عافیت باشند باسماع رسید کہ درباغ اسد خاں ملکیت بدرالدین علی خاں از دست بدمعاشاں بربادی شود و درختہارا قطع می کنند باید کہ فی الفور درآنجا رسیدہ بندوبست قرار واقعی نمایند کہ از دست بدمعاشان محفوظ ماند و حقیقت این معروض دارد و آیندہ راچناں تدبیری نمایند کہ ہمہ درختان قطع نشوند فقط

تحریر فی التاریخ ۱۵ ر ماہ محرم ۲۱ سنہ جلوس

نقل شدہ　　　　عرضی ارسال شوی داخل دفتر

....

(61)

NAI - Document No. 15 F. 23 Dated 8th September, 1857.

جناب عالی حال انیست کہ ہر چہ و بر ولہ بہ منصور صاحب و مرزا صاحب مقابلہ کیا پندم مفتی صاحب فرمودند کہ از طرف من نوشتہ دہند کہ رعایاء شہر بچند قسم آباد است ۔ یکی مزدور دویم دستکار سویم مہاجن و تجارت پیشہ چہارم امیر واہم دو قسم اند۔ یکی جاگیردار و زمیندار دویم صاحب جائداد۔ پس این ہنگامہ ہمہ ہارا ناچار کردہ کلیہ چہ پیشہ و چہ تجارت و چہ پیش و جاگیر و چہ زر کرایہ ہمہ ہا مسدود و مریدی پران لوٹ و مرید قبہ باداں و حالا شدن انتظام سرکاری در دین مردمان در احاطہ وہم ہم نمی گذر دیگر ہر یک نوبت بجاں و کارد باستخواں ہست و شب و روز دست بہ دعا ہستند کہ خدا روزی کند کہ انتظام سرکاری گردد مگر در ہم چو موقع گفتگو این قسم نمودن خود را دیوانہ قرار دادن است مگر وقتست تسلط سرکاری خواہد شد کسی را از حاجت و مال ہر گز ہر گز و راج رعیت شما از سعی خود باز نماند فقط

۸ سمت نمبر ملمع ۱۸

طور این کہ در بلند قلعہ میں سے ہیں۔

....

(62)

NAI Document No. B111d F.173 Dated 13th

September , 1857.

مہر

تعلیقہ خاص قلعہ معلیٰ

(بیچ کی لائن پڑھی نہیں جاسکی)

مہر عدالت فوجداری

شجاعت نشان محمد قاضی فیض اللہ خاں کوتوال شہر معلوم نماید۔ اصدار احکام معجز نظام می شود کہ انسان در شہر بہ جمیع پولداران حکم دہد کم ہنود و اہل اسلام جمیع رعایای حضور اند۔ احدی باہم مصدر فساد آنکہ نشوند بلکہ عین وقت یک یک کس برقنداز کوتوالی در آستانہ گرفرستاد منادی باعلام عام کسایندہ دید۔ دریں باب تاکید مزید وقدغن بلیغ دانستہ حسب الحکم اقدس واعلیٰ بجا آردناصر سازد

المرقوم ۲۷ ماہ رمضان المبارک ۲۱ سنہ جلوس معلیٰ

دوسرا صفحہ ۲۔

مہر۔ پڑھی نہیں جاسکی

خداوندا

بموجب حکم حضور کے تعمیل اور بندوبست بموجب منشاء سرکار کے کری گئی کے حد ادب

معروضہ ۲۷ رمضان ۲۱ ھ

قاضی فیض اللہ خان کوتوال

تیسرا صفحہ

Paiad Kotwal Qazi Faiz Ullah

کاغذات دستخطی قاضی فیض اللہ کو بودہ شہر دہلی وغیرہ پروانہ قلعہ کہ

....

(63)

NAI- Documnet No. B 111d F. No. 137 Dated 13th September, 1857.

مہر

دفتر کرنیل محمد خضر سلطان بہادر

شجاعت شعار کوتوال شہر قبلہ حفظہ

جس وقت تم ہر دوی تمام منادی کراو کہ وردمباس بہادر وہاں کرتے ہیں جس ہندو اور مسلمان کو یہ سراسر مذہب کا ہو تو وہ پروای تمام حاضر کشمیری دروازہ ہو جس واسطہ کہ صاحب عالم بہادر وہاں کر گئے اس امر میں ہوا کہ یہ کہ

فقط تحریر ۲۳ محرم الحرام ۲۱ ھ معلیٰ

....

(64)

NAI - Document Dated 13th September, 1857,

Bundle No. 15 Fol.19 Battle of Qudsiya Bagh

دی شب بڑا جنگ عظیم ہوا قدسیہ باغ کی طرف جو مورچہ ہے اس پر بڑا شور رہا تمام رات گولہ اور باڑی چلتی رہی تلنگہ وسنوار قریب بالیو آدمی کے کم وزیادہ مارے گئے اور زخمی ہوئے راقم علی الصباح آج فوج میں گیا تھا ڈولی پر ڈولی آتی ہوئی زخمیوں کے دیکھی اور یہ بھی دریافت ہوا کہ تین ضرب توپ سرکار کے فوج کے ہاتھ لگے۔ فوج میں بے دلی اور ہراس پایا گیا تلنگہ لوگ سنوار ولد کہ گالیاں دیتے ہیں اور سنوار تلنگے کو نامزد کہتے ہیں غرض کہ یہ بحث میں نے بہت جگہ پایا اور سوار و پیادہ نے یہ رات کا حال دیکھ کر اکثر لوگ یہاں سے چلے گئے بلکہ سوار زیادہ گیا اور افسر جو ہیں ان کی بھی کمر ہمت شکست ہوگئی۔ رات کو قبل از سرای کے ایک صوبہ دار سکھوں کی پلٹن کا کہ نام اس کا معلوم نہیں ہوا بلا سلاح و براق سرکاری فوج سے مورچہ اس طرف میں آیا اور کچھ کچھ وہ مشورہ کر کے چلا گیا یہ حال اچھی طرح ظاہر نہیں ہوا مگر ایک معمہ کے۔۔۔ مورچہ میں تھا معلوم ہوا ہے بلکہ وہ آج تحریر چلا گیا ہے کہ ایک سرادہ ہے مریر صاحب کی کوٹھی کو ہو کر اس راہ پر توپ خانہ سرکاری کا کم دخل ہے اوس راہ پر لڑائی ڈالنی چاہیے اور بغیر اس کی وہ صوبہ دار لشکر میں چلا گیا اس کی احتیاط واجب ہے۔ گوجر لوگوں نے اکثر خبر دی ہے کہ تین کمپنی گوراہ مرادنگر کی طرف معہ دو ضرب توپ آگئے ہیں اور کچھ مشنر اون کے گرفتار کر کے یہاں لے آئے ان کے خبر پر کچھ فوج کی روانگی کی خبر

ہے سدھاراسنگھ کے کموی کے یہ خبر علی پور سے مشہور ہوئی ہے بلکہ تحقیق سے ہے کہ علی پور جاویں گے چنانچہ کہار وقلی وغیرہ اوسکی واسطے پکڑے گئے ہیں۔ راؤ تلارام کی عرضی ریواڑی سے آئی ہے کہ میں نے تین لاکھ روپیہ فراہم کیا ہے شبو بخش رسالہ دار کو بھیج دیں کہ وہ آکر لے جاوئیں۔ چنانچہ یہ ہی تحریر ہورہی ہے۔ دی روز بوقت شام سواروں کے مرتب اجمیری دروازہ کے باہر ہوئے تھے۔ مرزا مغل موجود تھے اور انہوں نے سواروں کو بعد پر مٹ مورچال پر روانہ کیا تھا۔

....

(65)

NAI Document No. B-130 F. 248 Dated 12th September, 1857.

تھانہ دار صاحب تھانہ دار دریبہ

عدالت سلطانی درباب وصول مبلغ دوسو روپیہ مسماۃ مبارک النسا بیگم مالک مبارک باغ ساکن کابلی دروازہ بابت آب پاشی نہر جمن فصل ربیع ۵۷ سے ورود ہوا اس لئے ان کو لکھا جاتا ہے کہ مبلغ دوسو روپیہ مسماۃ مذکور سے وصول کرو۔ درصورت توقف جواب دہی ذمہ ان کے ہے۔ قرار۔

خدا بخش خاں نائب کوتوال شہر دہلی

....

(66)

NAI - Document No. 35/2 Dated 4th November, 1857.

نواب صاحب مشفق ومہربان مظہر لطف وکرم فرمائی مخلصان سلمہ اللہ تعالیٰ

بعد تمنائی حصول سامی نمود صلت وافر المسرت کہ متجاوز التحریر است مشہور ضمیر منیر محبت مذ خبری گرداند شامی صحیفہ عطوفت طراز مورخہ دوئیم ماہ اکتوبر سے حال بہ جواب رقیمہ نیاز بایماء این کہ نسبت بہ امور واقع ایام بانسبتی اکثر بہ مخلص چیزی عذر یا جواب بہانہ اظہار در آوردن منظور باشد تحیر تسطیر در آرد وصول اشفاق آوردہ مشکور یاد فرمائی ساخت مسقعا مخلص بہر حال ساختہ و نواختہ و مطیع و فرمان بردار قدیم ونمک خوار موروثی سرکار ابد پایدار است ۔ واز جان ومال حاضرو دائما از تہہ دل بہ خیر خواہی و جانفشانی بہ کار سرکار بہ ہمہ تن مصروف ومستعد بناء علیہ مراتب حسن عقیدت سرکار وحفظ حال خود آں چہ از مخلص ہم دراین ایام بہ ظہور آمدہ دفعات آں در فارسی معہ ترجمہ انگریزی بری توضیح حال تحریر کردہ است رقیمہ ہذا ارسال خدمت درشتہ می شود از ملاحظہ آں حال مفصل منکشف برای ازیں خواہد بود درین صورت از اشفاق والطاف اہالیان سرکار دولت مدار امیدوارم کہ دائما نظر عنایت وتوجہ نسبت بہ حال بنار اشمال مرعی ومبذول باشد کہ سود و بہبود مخلص در ضمن آن متصور است ونقول خطوط وغیرہ کو اغذات نسبت باید از دفتر در جھجھر شامل کردن نتوانستم فقط زیادہ بہجت باد

تحریر چہارم ماہ نوامبر ۱۸۵۷ء

مہر۔اسدالدولہ ممتازالملک عبدالرحمٰن خاں بہادر ہنر بر جنگ

....

(67)

Rajasthaan State Archieves - No.1 Pad No.2 - M-06-1(Parts) Major Head Military Record No.1 Part 5-3 Mutiny Papers.(Bikaner)

Document No.484/1Dated 5th November, 1857.

۱۰ انو امبر ۱۸۵۷ء ۱۲۶۵ھ ۴۸۴/۱

کیفت کپتان ولیم فریڈرک ایڈی صاحب بہادر بحسب مزاج می بور راج موصوف مرقوم ۵رنومبر ۱۸۵۷ء جو فوج چھاؤنی ایری پور کے معہ عنایت اور علاقہ راج جودہ پور بہ صیغہ شیخاواٹی کے آئی ہے ہر دوسری تاریخ اس مہینے تک تو تم کو اس کی خبر ملے کہ پچھمی گڑھ علاقہ سیکر سے دس کوس اور وہاں سے بگالہ گاؤں تک بجی ایک طرف اہالیان راج سے کچھ خبر نہ تھی یہ بھی دریافت ہوا کہ سہ صد آدمی اور دو توپ سیکر سے تعینات مدافعت بہ اغیار مذکور کے ہوتے اہالیان جودہ پور سے کہ دیر فوج اونکہا کادر ند بود خبر آتی ہے سرسرا کہ جس کے طرف کچھ نہیں آتی اور حامی یہ ہے کہ روز روز کے خبر مفصل ہماری پاس انا کری سو راج اس کا بندوبست پختہ اور جلد کر دیں۔

(دستخط انگریزی میں ہیں)

جواب نوشتہ شود

پر چہ خرچ در بابت مراکہ سے ہیں ۳ کوی میں دیں فوج کو رسکتاء لیا اور مقرر صوبوں جو فوج کے اس ۳ یا ۴ کوس کے دیں کیا تھا اور دونوابوں باکد کردی کے پرگنہ روز بروز بردحر کا آیا کرے گا اور اصلاح اس کے معرفت راج وکیلوں سے ہوا کرے گی۔

۷ر نومبر ۱۸۵۷ء

....

(68)

RSA - Document No. 484 -2 ۴۸۴/۲

کیفت راجہ سوای چتوڑ کی طرف سے بنام کپتان ولیم فریڈرک ایڈ یصاحب بہادر اجنٹ راج موصوف مرقوم نومبر ۱۸۵۷ء کیفیت راج مکتوبہ سلو مرشد حال بدین مضمون کا جوفوج چھاؤنی ایرن پور کے معہ باغیان وہ علاقہ جودہ پور تعلقہ شیخاواٹی کے آسری دوسری تاریخ اس سرتک تو اس کی حرلحھن کدہ علاقہ سیکر سے آٹھ کوس اور وہاں سے بکالہ گاؤں تک پہنچنے کے اثر اور ان کی اہالیان کی طرف سے کچھ خبر نہ ملی سو بندوبست اس کا پختہ ہوجاوے یا ہر روز خبر مفصل آیا کرے موصول مطالعہ ہوے سو جواب اس کا یہ ہوگا پرچہ خبر سے دریافت مود کا میں بن کر بری نیر کوڈ برہ فوج مذکور کا سیکھانہ تھا اور منصرم چوکیوں معہ فوج کے قریب میں کوس پر ڈیرہ کہا تھا اور خبر والوں کو تاکید کردی گئی تھی ہر روز پرچہ جر کا انا کرے گا اور اطلاع اس کی وکیلان راج ہراج کو دیا کریں گے۔

(69)

RSA. Document No. 485 -1

۵۸۴/۱

کیفیت کپتان ولیم فریڈرک ایڈیصاحب بہادر را بحسب راج سوای جے پور نام راج موصوف مرقوم ۳رنوامبر ۱۸۵۷ء اصل کیفیت بھوپال سنگھ ناظم سوای رام گڑھ وشیخاواٹی بہ مقدمہ جمعیت باغیان او علاقہ جودہ پور وغیرہ بادیگر مراتب ہم در مخصوص جو آئی تھی بطور اطلاع کے اس محکمہ میں باس راج کی لف ہذا ارسال ہے کہ ایر بنات وہاں سے تجویز ہوگا۔

فقط

(انگریز افسر نے انگریزی میں دستخط کئے ہیں)

(اس پر اوپر نوٹ ہے جو بعد میں لکھا گیا ہے۔اس کی عبارت حسب ذیل ہے۔)

اطلاع ۷رنومبر ۱۸۵۷ء

کہ فوج بخشی وکومی دما کر بخشی کیفیت را حادے کہ سب جمعیت سرکاری کوئی مالک کردیویں کہ نوکری راج کسہر دریغ مکر منشی بملاحظہ کسی ناظم کے چاکری راج کریں

۷رنومبر ۱۸۵۷ء

تحریر ۵رنوامبر ۱۸۵۷ء نمبر ۱۷۰

....

(70)

RSA - Document No. 491 -1 ۴۹۱/۱

کیفیت کپتان ولیم فریڈرک ایڈی صاحب بہادر اجینٹ

راج سوائے جی پور نام راج موصوف کے جو واقع تاریخ ۳۰ ر اکتوبر ۱۸۵۷ء کیفیت وکیل ریاست ٹونک حاضر باش سررشتہ ہذا مشعر بر مقیم ہونا اکثر مفسدان مفرور از دہلی در دیہات علاقہ چتوڑ یعنی بہ موضع لانیہ و منمولہ تعلقہ او نیارہ دنتواڑہ علاقہ راج نظر سے گذری لہذا نقل اس کی رشتہ دور کیفیت ہذا مرسل ہو کر نوکر برقلم ہے کہ مناسب ہے طرف راج سے معتمد طرف او نپارہ وغیرہ میں جاکر بہ تندہی و تلاش تمام گرفتاری باغیان و مفسدان کریں کہ موجب نیک نامی راج کا ہے فقط

(انگریز افسر کے دستخط انگریزی زبان میں ہیں)

(اس پر نوٹ اوپر لکھا ہے)

۲۶ ر خلاصہ ۳ نوامبر ۵۷ء ۱۵۹۱

بنام ضلع دار ضلع و نام رادیہ او نیارہ واسطہ انتظام مفسدان دہلی تحریر ہووی دوم نومبر ۱۸۵۷ء

....

(71)

RSA - Cocument No. 494 -2

کیفیت راج سوای چتور کی طرف سے بنام کپتان ولیم فریڈرک ایڈی صاحب بہادر اجنیٹ راج موصوف المرقوم نوامبر ۷ سنہ ۱۸۵ء ہر طبق وصول کیفیت راج رقم زدہ ۱۶ر اکتوبر سنہ حال درباب سروری مسمی عبداللہ بیگ توپ خانہ کوٹہ کہ حسب معہ بکراس است مقام پذیری اوسکی بمقام ہنڈون بمراد گرفتاری اوسکی بنام فوجدار و ضلع دار ہنڈوں لکھا گیا تھا۔ اگر درکیفیت ضلع دار ہنڈون حوالہ رپوٹ کوتوال ہنڈوں کے بدین مضمون وصول ہونے کا ہر چند تلاش عبداللہ خاں کا شہر میں کیا مگر کسی جگہ پتہ ونشان اوسط نہیں ملا اگر کوئی نشانہ بندہ آجاوی تو گرفتاری اوسکی ہوسکیں پرورنہ تلاش درس میں ہر وقت گرفتاری کے سالار کیا خادم کا فقط لہذا یہ حال کلو اطلاعاً کلکٹر میں ایاوہ۔

....

(72)

NAI - Document No. B.100 F.167 undated.

منکہ فرزند ابوبکر اندو پسر فتح الملک مرحوم ام اقراری کنم ونوشتہ می دہم کہ گاہی از زوجہ خود حرکات ناشائستہ نکنم اگر کنم حاکم دفتری را اختیار است وورثہ بیگم موصولہ، ہیچ سزای خطای من باشد از حضور حاکم تجویز کنانید۔ اکنوں مرا ہمیں منظور است کہ خوشنودی حضور اقدس و ورثہ بیگم موصوفہ شود لہذا این اقرارنامہ نوشتہ دادم تا خاطر جمعی ورثہ بیگم موصوف شود

(73)

NAI - Document No. 43 - 62 un dated

مہر (پڑھی نہیں جاسکی)

فدوی خاص لائق العنایات والاحسان اسد الدولہ مختار الملک محمد عبدالرحمٰن خاں بہادر هنر بر جنگ مورد تفضلات شاہی بودہ بداند چوں از ظہور اکثر امور نا ملایم و بہ سبب کبر سن مبارک وضعف قواہوش ملک و مال نماندہ چنانچہ در موقب غیر از اکتساب سعادت رضای خالق کائنات وصرف بقیہ حیات در عبادات تمنای نسبت ۔ لہذا ارداہ مصمم است کہ عنقریب بہ لباس درویشی درین رنج و دل ریشی اولامعہ کل خاندان تیموریہ بہ درگاہ خواجہ قطب الدین قدس سرہ العزیز رسیدہ بعد انسرام سامان سفر حرمین شریفین زادہما اللہ سرفاً تعظیماً روانگی آں صوب باصواب بہ عمل آید زیرا کہ دنیاء ما فیہا در پیش ہمت والا تہمت اعتباری واقعی نمی دارد۔ لہذا زیب ارقام می رود کہ آن فدوی بہر نوی کہ ممکن باشد ہمرہان رفقائی معتبر خود از سوار و پیادہ زودتر حاضر حضور فیض گنجور گردد وہم رکاب سعادت تابہ درگاہ موصوف بودہ بہ حفاظت جملہ اسباب واثاث البیت ہمہ سلاطینان در آنجا رساند و نیز بقیہ اسباب گران کہ دراین وقت ہمراہ بردن نتوانند و در قلعہ مبارک بہ مساکن خود ہا بگذارند بنا بر حراست این بعض از سپاہ خود ہمراہ ملازمان شاہی متعین ساز دوہم بنا بر استحاط بندگان قدسی تازمان انتہاض دائرہ دولت بہ سوی بیت اللہ شریف بہ مقام درگاہ موصوف بنا بر چندروز جمعیت مناسب گذاشتہ بہ جاگیر خود معاودت نماید کہ دراین صورت غایت استرضا وخوشنودی خاطر

مقدس متصور است و علم نیک نامی آں زبدہ خیر اندیشاں در آفاق عالم مشتہر خواہد شد کہ درچنیں وقت بہ لحاظ توسل قدیم آں گونہ خیرخواہی نمودہ کہ ہیچک از متوسلان قدیم راہم چنیں توفیق نیک رفیق نگر دیدہ۔ پس ہر قدر عجلت در باب رود مستحسن و بجا خواہد بود زیادہ تفصلات شناسد مکرر آں کہ درینجا بار برداری مطلق نیست۔ چہار صد یا پانصد عرابہ و پانصد یا شش صد شتر ہمراہ خود ضرور باید آورد فقط۔

(On the next page it is recorded.)

My dear Colonal ,the enclosed note I picked up from the floor of the palace affords some information about the King's intentions.

21.9.1857 Noting David.

....

(74)

NAI - Document No. B - 100. F. 177 un dated

مرزا چھوٹے صاحب

معلوم نمایند بعد از سلام سنت الاسلام معلوم باشد کہ شما نزا برای اطلاع این امر نگاشتہ ام کہ شما گفتہ بودند کہ من بروز سہ شنبہ درینجا خواہم آمد برای این امر نگارش می رود کہ در آں روز

عرس حضرت جناب عالیہ است شمار ادر آن روز تکلیف خواہد شد باید کہ اگر نزد من ماندن منظور باشد بیایند بتاریخ ہشت دھم بوقت سپہر بیایند چراکہ در ہر دو مکان سہ حرمان جدامجد بروز عرس می مانند برای این امر نوشتہ ام کہ اوشاں این امر رابسیار برخود ناگوار دانند چراکہ ہر سال اوشاں آمدہ می مانند۔ فقط

....

(75)

NAI - Document No. B 102 F. 103 un dated

حقائق آگاہان معارف دستگاہ سالکان حقیقت ناہجان مناہج طریقت حضرت غلام نظام الدین وسید عبداللہ ومولوی محمد سالم وعلاء الدولہ ولد سید محی الدین خاں وسید حسن عسکری ومیاں نیاز احمد صاحبان معلوم نمایند کہ تہمت ترک مذہب اہل سنت واختیار شیعت نسبت بحضور بستہ صدور بعض امور منافی آئین دین اسلام راکہ جز گمرہی دارند وثمرہ از آں مترتب نگردد بہ بندگان خلافت منسوب کردہ اند کہ میاں نظر بملاحظہ دراند از آں جاکہ مساحت عقیدہ راسخہ حضور بفروغ ادعان وایقان از ظلمتصور این اندیشہ باطل کہ غیر از ضلالت و گمراہی نتیجہ نتواند دادی فرسنگ درازست معاذ اللہ کہ خیال فاسد ہیچ گاہ بہ ضمیر منیر چہ طور کردہ باشد تابہ اختیار این طریقہ ضلالت چہ رسد سوگند بخدای کریم وانہ لقسم لوتعلمون عظیم کہ درعقائد حضور پرنور کہ بروقف طریق اکابر دین واسلاف والاتمکین است۔ اصلاً ومطلقاً فتور راہ یافتہ باشد این ہمہ افتراہای دروغ مرزا حیدر شکوہ ومرزا نورالدین است کہ محض از راہ حسد

برای بدنام ساختن حضور کرده اند واگر خدانخواسته درواقع اثری ازین معنی می بوددرادای این امور درآنجا کدام مانع بود که درلکھنو بظہوری آمد ہمیں معنی بنا بر بطلان این اخبار باطله کافی تواند بود باجمله آن حقائق دستگاهان برافترای این باطل که نسبت بحضور بسته اند هر که اعتماد نکنند که این محض دروغ وبی اصل وبانان که استفسار این امراز ایشان نموده باشند ازین معنی اطمینان خاطرنموده دهند بدین وسیلت تکذیب مدعیان این دعویٰ باطل نمایند۔ فقط

....

(76)

NAI - Document No. B-100 F.167 undated.

نورچشم مرزا ظہیرالدین معلوم نمایند پسر زمان شاه مرحوم از دوسه روز حاضرنشده بود۔ امروز انتقال کرد۔ یک صدروپیه براے پرداخت ایشان فی الفورمرحمت شود از حساب نرینه یومیه تحریر بنویسد۔

....

(77)

NAI - Documet No. 104/45 undated . مہر (پڑھی نہیں جاسکی)

جناب کوتوال صاحب غریب فرمای بنده سلامت

حسب الدعاء شریف برقنداز امروز بطلب سوجی رام ورگناتھ سنگھ فرستاده بودم صاحب ہمون وقت رگھناتھ سنگھ آمده مظہرند که سوجی رام برادرم بیماراست ومن حاضرنیستم

لہذا رگھناتھ سنگھ راہمراہ چپراسی روانہ کوتوالی نمودہ شود

....

(78)

NAI - Document No. 195 F.05 Dated 23rd March, 1857.

نقل چھاپہ صادق الاخبار نمبر ۱۲ مطبوعہ ۲۳ مارچ ۱۸۵۷ء جلد ۳ مطبع جمیل الدین کے بطور انتخاب اشتہار نام نہاد شاہ ایران۔

درینولا کسی شریر مفسدہ ذرہ رذیلی نے اپنی عیاری سے سرخروئی سمجھ کر تازہ شہرت دی یعنی ایک اشتہار ترغیب عام بنام نہاد شاہ ایران پشت جامع مسجد دہلی پر اس مضمون کا چسپاں کیا ہے کہ اہل اسلام وہنود معاونت نصاریٰ سے باز رہیں قریب ہے کہ میں ہندوستان کو تسخیر کروں اور رعایا برایا کو انعام واکرام سے شاد اور باد رکھوں اور نام مشتہر اشتہار کا محمد صدیق خاں مرقوم ہی سنا گیا کہ حکام اس دردغم بے فروغ سے آشفتہ ہورہے ہیں۔ ہم یقین کرتے ہیں کہ جو کوئی اوس بدبخت کو لغو کو گرفتار کر لائے گا کچھ روپیہ انعام پائے گا واللہ اعلم۔ اگر اب میاں صدیق خاں جعلی جنہوں نے چالاکی سے یہ اشتہار دیا ہے سرکار کے ہاتھ آگئی تو یقین ہے کہ اونکی گنجی ٹٹری پر دہای تلی کا منڈا سر کہ بھگو کر پورا پڑے گا اور ایک ایک بال بکھرا بکھرا پڑے گا پھر میاں فرضی کو معلوم ہوگا کہ اینٹ کا گھر مٹی یوں بن جاتا ہے اور یہ چالاکی اور ڈھکوسلے بازی سب زکام کی راہ نکل جاتی ہے اور یالوگ یوں ناکھن دم لاتی ہیں۔

(79)

U.P States Archives,

Etawah File No. 1 Page 25

عزت آثار۔۔۔سنگھ داروغہ جیل خانہ ضلع اٹاوہ بہ عافیت باشند بموجب حکم پروانہ ہذا عمل میں لاؤ

تاریخ وماہ وسنہ۔۱۹/اپریل ۱۸۵۸ء۔نمبر پروانہ ۲۳۲ نام تھانہ ------- دستخط حاکم۔ (انگریزی میں دستخط ہیں) نام مدعی۔سرکار۔نام مدعا علیہ، بلدیو۔علی احمد جرم بغاوت و لوٹ۔عمر۔۳۷ سال۔۴۸ سال۔نام باپ کا بقید ذات و پیشہ۔بکرسی برھمن 'نوکری' محبّ الہ خاں۔سکونت۔شاہجہاں پور۔بجنور۔خلاصہ حکم بقید تاریخ گذرنے میعاد۔حسب صدور اسپیشل کمشنر ضلع اٹاوہ مورخہ ۱۹/اپریل ۱۸۵۹ء۔حکم کہ مجرمان بلدیو اور علی احمد مدعی بحکم سات سات برس قید بامشقت بہ عبوری دریای شور۔

....

(80)

سرچارلس ڈلک۔گزیٹر برٹن، مطبوعہ ۱۸۵۸۔لندن صفحہ ۲۲۳۔

یہ بالکل یقینی بات ہے کہ غدر ۱۸۵۷ء کے فرو کرنے میں صدہا ہندیوں کو ان انگریز افسروں نے پھانسی پر لٹکوادیا جو کسی دیسی زبان کا ایک حرف تک نہ جانتے تھے اور نہ شہادت کو سمجھ سکتے تھے نہ صفائی کے بیانات کو۔۔۔میں نے ایک افسر سے جوان دنوں

بنارس کے قریب سکردل کی چھاونی میں متعین تھا کہا کہ میرا گمان ہے تم اس بات سے خائف رہتے ہوگے کہ بنارس کے لوگ تم پر حملہ نہ کردیں تو اس کے جواب میں وہ افسر کہنے لگا کہ سچ پوچھیے تو میں دل سے چاہتا تھا کہ بنارس والے حملہ کریں تاکہ ہمیں انہیں سزا دینے اور شہر کولوٹنے کا موقع ملے جو دو صدی سے نہیں لٹا تھا۔

....

(81)

Letter No. 32

من جانب جارج کوپر صاحب،

سکریٹری چیف کمشنر اودھ

بخدمت بی ایف ایڈمنٹن صاحب، سکریٹری 'حکومت ھند'

لکھنؤ یکم دسمبر ۱۸۵۷

جناب عالی!

بہ سلسلہ مکتوب چیف کمشنر بنام گورنر جنرل بہادر مورخہ ۱۴ر ستمبر جس میں انہوں نے پچاس ہزار روپے کی رقم بریلی کی ھندو آبادی کو مسلمان باغیوں کے خلاف آمادہ پیکار کرنے پر صرف کرنے کی اجازت دی ہے۔ مجھے کپتان گوں کے خط مورخہ ۱۴ر کا اقتباس پیش کرنے کی ہدایت کی گئی ہے جس سے حضور والا کو یہ علم ہوگا کہ یہ کوشش ناکام رہی اور اس کو ترک کر دیا گیا اور اس پر کوئی رقم صرف نہیں ہوئی۔

آپ کا خادم

جارج کوپر

سکریٹری چیف کمشنر،

عالم باغ، لکھنؤ

یکم دسمبر ۱۸۵۷ء

....

(82)

U.P States Archives Box No.1 Documnet No. 13, Etawah File.

UPSA

غریب پرور سلامت۔

پروانہ کرامت بسامہ مجھکو یہ ۶/ مصدورہ ۸/ جنوری ۱۸۵۹ء بمہری ایک بہ مطلب جواب بلدیو سنگھ باغی کہ جو بہ مقام سہسون بتاریخ ۱۱/ دسمبر ۱۸۵۸ء کو گرفتار ہوا تھا صادر ہوا۔ سابق بے حال یہ ہے کہ وقت شب بہ مقام چوکسی جناب لفٹنٹ کرنیل فارنس صاحب بہادر خود بلدیو سنگھ مذکور دیتا گیا وہ صاحب ممدوح اپنے ہاتھ سے تحریر فرماتے گئے۔ کمترین درمیان صاحب موصوف اور بلدیو سنگھ مذکور کے بیٹا تھا۔ جوبات بلدیو سنگھ مذکور نہیں سمجھتا تھا اسکو سمجھا دیتا تھا اور وہ کاغذ جوابات بلدیو سنگھ مذکور کا پاس جناب کرنیل صاحب بہادر کے

تھا۔سوای اس کےاورکوئی کاغذ فارسی میں بہ مقدمہ بلدیوسنگھ باغی علحدہ تحریر نہیں ہوا کہ ترسیل کرتا۔علیٰ الصباح بلدیوسنگھ مذکورکو بموجب ارشاد حضور روانہ اٹاوہ کردیا تھا۔حال یہ تھا کہ گذارش کیا عرض تحریری اطلاعاً ترسیل حضور پرور۔فقط زیادہ حداداب۔مفروضہ جنوری ۱۸۵۹ء۔

....

(83)

UPSA

نقشہ مجرمان مفرورکہ جنھوں نے باایام غدرنوکری بادشاہی کری اور نیز مفسدی کری از ابتداءاگست ۱۸۵۷ء

دہلی خاص۔روشن ولدیت اکبر خاں۔قومیت پٹھان۔سکونت ،ضلع متھرا ،عہدہ ،برقنداز چوکی غازی آباد، جرم ، کرنا نوکری بادشاہی ۔(کل تعداد ۱۱۶۰۔لوگوں کی ہے۔فہرست میں آخری نام نجف علی کا ہے۔بہت کم نام ہندووں کے ہیں زیادہ تر نام مسلمانوں کے ہیں۔)

درگورنمنٹ پریس دہلی باہتمام بندہ تراب علی طبع شدہ۔

....

(84)

Haryana States Archives.

حکم نامہ مورخہ ۸ر نومبر ۱۸۵۸ء

سوای ان لوگوں کے کہ جن کی نسبت ثابت ہوا ہو یا آئندہ ثابت ہو کہ وی رعیت سرکار انگریزی کے قتل میں بذات شریک ہوئے دوسروں کی نسبت ترحم ظاہر کیا جاوے گا مگر یہ نسبت شرکاء قتل کی انصاف مقتضی اس بات کا ہے کہ اول ترحم نہ ہو۔

جن لوگوں نے جان بوجھ کے قاتلوں کو پناہ دی ہو یا جو لوگ باغیوں کے سردار ہوئے ہوں یا ترغیب دینے والے ہوے ہوں ان کی نسبت صرف یہی عہد ہو سکتا ہے کہ ان کی جان بخش ہو رہی لیکن ایسے لوگوں کی سزا کی تجویز میں اول سب احوال پر جن کی اعتبار سے دی اپنے اطاعت سے پھر گئی غور کیا جاوے گا اور ان لوگوں کی نسبت جو بے سوچے مفسدوں کی جھوٹی باتوں پر اعتماد کر کے مجرم ہوئے بڑی رعایت ظاہر کی جائے گی۔

دوسری اور سبھوں کو جو سرکار کی مخالفت میں ہتھیار بند ہیں وعدہ ہوتا ہے کہ ان کی تقصیر سرکار کی نسبت اور ہماری سلطنت اور مزلت کی نسبت بلا شرف معاف اور عفو اور فراموش کی جائیں گی مگر وہی اپنے اپنے گھروں میں جائیں اور اپنی اپنی پیش صلح و سواد میں ہاتھ لگاویں۔

ہماری یہ مرضی شاہانہ ہے کہ رحم اور عفو کی یہ شرائط اول سبھوں سے متعلق ہوگی جو قبل تاریخ پہلی جنوری ۱۸۵۹ء کی شرائط مذکور کے مطابق عمل کریں۔

جب ملک میں خدا کے فضل سے پھر امن چین ہووے تو یہ دل و جان ہماری آرزو ہے کہ ملک ہند میں صنعت کاری کی تقویت ہووے اور افادہ خلائق کے لیے کارہا مسل تیاری سڑک و نہر وغیرہ مرتب ہوں اور ملک کا انتظام منظر افادہ ہماری رعایای باشندہ ملک مذکور کی

ہوتا رہے۔ رعیت کی فراغ بالی سے ہمارا اقتدار اور اس کی قناعت سے ہماری بے فطری حاصل اور ان کی شکر گذاری ہمارے لیے پورا صلہ ہے اور خدای قادر ہم کو اور ہمارے حکام ماتحت کو ایسی قدرت دیوے کہ واسطہ افادہ خلایق کی اذیتیں ہماری مرادوں کو اتمام میں پہونچا دیں۔

کمشنر بہادر پانی پت نے حسب شرائط مندرجہ دفعات دس اور گیارہ چٹھی گورنمنٹ مورخہ ۸/نومبر ۱۸۵۸ء موسومہ صاحب سکریٹری گورنمنٹ بنگال کے بابت تعمیل حکم معافی ملکہ معظّمہ کے جرم سے معافی عطا کی اور شرائط مذکور بموجب حکم نامزد کو سنائی گئی۔

حسن خاں چپراسی، اصالت خاں، مہر نرائن، عبدالرزاق، سعداللہ، محمد حسین خاں، احمد علی خاں، علیم الدین، کلو، زبردست خاں، منگلی، سرجن، ہرچند، پت رام جاٹ، روپ رام، مغل دار رانگڑ۔

....

ملکہ وکٹوریہ کے منشورات کا جواب ۱۰/اکتوبر ۱۸۵۸ء کو بیگم حضرت محل نے اپنے فرزند برجیس قدر کی جانب سے شائع کرایا۔

"انگریزوں کے وعدہ عفو پر ہرگز اعتبار نہ کروان کا شیوہ ہی یہ ہے کہ کسی کا جرم معاف نہیں کرتے"

قیصر التواریخ

....

(85)

Haryana States Archives.

نمبر۹۱مورخہ ۲۵/مارچ نقل ۱۸۶۱ء

از جانب انڈر سکریٹری صاحب بہادر گورنمنٹ آف انڈیا بنام سکریٹری صاحب بہادر بنگال آپ کی چٹھی نمبری ۱۳۸مورخہ ۱۳ماہ رواں مشعر اس امر کے کہ فارسی جنتریوں میں کہ جو واسطہ استعمال عدالتوں اور سرکاری اہلکاروں کے ہر سال چھپتی ہیں سنہ جلوس یعنی سلطنت شاہنشاہ مغل یا بادشاہ دہلی کے چھاپنے سے دقت عائد ہو سکتی ہے اور مغالطہ پڑ سکتا ہے۔ موصول ملاحظہ گورنمنٹ انڈیا ہووے۔

۲۔اوس کے جواب میں حسب ہدایت آپ کی خدمت میں گذارش ہے کہ آئندہ کو سنہ جلوس کا چھاپنا فارسی جنتریوں میں بند اور ممنوع کیا جاوے اور سنہ ملکہ معظّمہ کی سلطنت کا جملہ جنتریوں میں کہ جو قلم رو سرکار میں چھپتی ہیں سند جلوس کے عوض چھاپا جاوے۔

دستخط ایم یو سرون انڈر سکریٹری گورنمنٹ آف انڈیا وگسٹ نمبر ۶۷۲ مورخہ ۳/اپریل ۱۸۶۱ء

اطلاعاً اور ہدایتاً اور بہ مراد اطلاع صاحبان کمشنر جن کی قسمت میں فارسی چھاپہ خانی واقع ہیں مطبوعہ نقول حکم سپریم گورنمنٹ درباب نہ چھاپہ جانی سنہ جلوس کے جنتریوں میں کہ جو ہر سال چھپتی ہیں اور درباب چھاپہ جانے آئندہ کو سنہ سلطنت ملکہ معظّمہ سنہ جلوس کے عوض

میں بھیجی جاتے ہیں۔

بحکم آر۔ایچ دبوس، سکریٹری گونمنٹ پنجاب

....

(86)

UPSA Document - No.91 dated 25th March, 1861.

فتویٰ جہاد ۱۸۵۷

درصورت مرقومہ یہ فرض عین ہے اوپر تمام اس شہر کے لوگوں کے اور استطاعت ضرور ہے۔اس کی فرضیت کے واسطے چنانچہ اب شہر والوں کو طاقت مقابلہ اور لڑائی کے ہے بسبب کثرت اجتماع افواج کے اور مہیا اور موجود ہونے آلات وحرب کے تو فرض عین ہونے میں کیا شک رہا۔اور اطراف وحوالی کے لوگوں پر جو دور ہیں باوجود خبر کے فرض کفایہ ہے اگر اس شہر کے لوگ باہر ہو جائیں مقابلہ سے یا سستی کریں اور مقابلہ نہ کریں تو اس صورت میں ان سبھی پر فرض عین ہو جائے گا۔اور اسی طرح اسی ترتیب سے سارے اہل زمین شرعاً اور حرباً فرض عین ہوگا اور جو عدد بستیوں پر ہجوم اور قتل وغارت کا ارادہ کریں تو اس بستی والوں پر فرض ہو جائے گا بشرط ان کی طاقت ہے۔دستخط مواہیر رحمۃ اللہ سید محمد نذیر حسین، نور جمال، عبدالکریم، سکندر علی، مفتی صدرالدین، مفتی اکرام الدین، محمد ضیاء الدین، احمد سعید، محمد عنبر خاں، محمد کریم اللہ، سعید شاہ نقشبندی، عبدالقادر، مولوی عبدالغنی، محمد علی، سرفراز علی، سید محبوب علی جعفری، محمد حامی الدین، مولوی سعید الدین، فرید الدین، سید احمد، الٰہی بخش، محمد انصار

علی، حفیظ اللہ خاں، نور الحق، محمد رحمت اللہ خاں، عدالت العالیہ، محمد علی حسین قاضی القضات، سیف الرحمٰن، محمد ہاشم، سید عبدالحمید، سید محمد۔

....

(87)

کھیر

راؤ بھوپال سنگھ کو برطرف کر کے پھانسی دی گئی۔

علی گڑھ

....

(88)

۴ر جولائی ۱۸۵۷ء میں ایک میٹنگ کوتوالی میں ہوئی۔ منشی دیا شنکر، ڈپٹی کلکٹر تھانیسر لالہ چھوٹے لال، نند کشور، جانی آسا شنکر، لالہ تلسی پرشاد، منشی محمد داؤد، حکیم تفضّل حسین، شیخ ضیاء اللہ اور خواجہ نجف علی پنچ مقرر ہوئے اور سر پنچ منشی محمد داؤد اور منشی دیا شنکر بنائے گئے۔ ۶ر جولائی کو ڈاکٹر کریم بخش جنہوں نے نویں پلٹن میں بغاوت پیدا کی تھی وہ کوتوال شہر بنائے گئے۔ ۱۰ر جولائی کو صبح سوار و پیادہ پلٹن چھاؤنی جھانسی معہ تین توپوں کے علی گڑھ میں داخل ہوئیں۔ منا لال پسر چنی لال خزانچی مقرر ہوئے۔ پلا، صاحب آباد، سندھولی، عیسن پور اور داؤد وغیرہ مواضعوں کے ملکانی میواتی اور برہمن نوکر ہوئے اور شہر کے کوتوال حسین خاں میواتی بنائے گئے۔ ۲۱ر اگست کو خبر ملی کہ انگریزی فوج آگرہ سے غوث خاں کے اقتدار

کو ختم کرنے کے لیے آرہی ہے۔ اسی دن نماز جمعہ، جامع مسجد میں مولوی عبدالجلیل نے مسلمانوں کو جہاد کی تلقین کی، مولوی عبدالجلیل لڑتے ہوئے مارے گئے۔

۲۹/اگست کو مولوی نسیم اللہ، مولوی عبدالجلیل، نیاز احمد خاں اور محمد یوسف کا مال و اسباب قرق کر کے سرکاری مال خانہ میں داخل کیا گیا۔ مولوی شمیم اللہ نے پھر اکبرآباد، بھیکن پور، دتاولی، ایٹہ، اترولی اور چاند پور سے فوج بھرتی کی دوسرے روز نسیم اللہ نے بنادیبی اور سرائے حکیم پر مورچہ لگانے کا ارادہ کیا۔ ۱۹/اکتوبر ۱۸۵۷ء کو انگریزی فوج کا علی گڑھ پر قبضہ ہوگیا۔ مولوی نسیم اللہ کو گولی کا نشانہ بنایا گیا۔

....

(89)

UPSA.Box No. 05 F.No. 16

(مہر۔ پڑھی نہیں جاسکی) بحکم مسٹر ہنری ڈیوس ڈلک صاحب بہادر

عزت ایار پرشن سنگھ تھانہ دار تھانہ بہ عافیت باشند۔ آج ہٹے صاحب کمشنر بہادر نمبر ۱۰۲۲ مرقومہ ۲۲/ماہی معہ نقل چٹھی سکریٹری گورنمنٹ مشعر منظوری انعام مبلغ پانچ ہزار روپیہ واسطے گرفتاری مولوی لیاقت علی باغی سرکار بحکم صاحب گورنر جنرل بہادر موصول ہو کر حسب الحکم روبکار امروزہ قطعہ اشتہار نامہ ذریعہ پروانہ ہذا پاس تمہارے بھیجا جا کر لکھا جاتا ہے کہ تم بجوالے تمام مضمون اشتہار مذکور نہادی وبجت کروگے مشتہر گاہ عالم آویزاں کرادیو تاکید جانو و کیفیت اور ہذائے اشتہار بقید تاریخ جلد بھیجو۔ فقط مرقوم ۲۵/جون ۱۸۵۸ء

(اس کی پشت پر لکھا ہے۔)

۲۶رجون کو حسب الحکم حضور صدور پروانہ ہذا کے بعد شہر قیاس عملہ گرفتاری مولوی لیاقت علی باغی سرکارو مرحمت ہونے فی پانچ ہزار روپیہ گرفتار کنندہ کو بخوبی تمام متعلقہ علاقہ تھانہ دہی کرا کے اشتہار شد کہ پروانہ ہذا کو بہ نظر گاہ خاص و عام راقم سرک بازار تہانہا میں پرویزاں کردیا اطلاعاً حضور والا گذارش ہے تمتہ ۲۶رماہ جون ۱۸۵۸ء بقلم ہذا تحریر

العبد

پرشن سنگھ تھانہ دار تھانہا

....

(90)

Aligarh Documents

UPSA - File No. 13 List of rebels of 1857

۱۔اعجاز علی ۲۔حسین خاں ۳۔حسن خاں کوتوال ۴۔محبوب خاں،کول ۵۔ داود خاں، جمعدار ۶۔امام بخش ۷۔حسینا ۸۔حسنا ۹۔پیرا ۱۰۔خدا بخش سوار بہ علت بغاوت بحکم میجر صاحب ۸رمارچ ۱۸۵۸ء۔

۱۔رسول خاں، ۲۔خدا بخش کلو، ۳۔عبدالجلیل، بالای قلعہ کول، جہاد و مقابلہ فوج، ۴۔نسیم اللہ، بالای قلعہ کول۔ ۵۔مرتضی خاں۔ بالای قلعہ کول، ۶۔بولی خاں۔ چاہ گرمایۂ کول بموجب روبکار ۲۹راگست ۱۸۵۷ء اجلاس۔

مکان مسمار ہوا۔ ا۔غوث خاں کوتوال شہر، محلّہ افغانان ۲۔ مہدو خیاط ۳۔خوب خان ۴۔امام بخش جمعدار ۵۔ ارادت خاں ۶۔ میر خاں کوچوان ۷۔ نائب خاں ۸۔ امین الدین ۹۔ بولاقی۔ بازار میان گنج ۱۰۔ سلیم الدین، مدار دروازہ۔ ۱۱۔ میاں جاں سوار، دماہی دروازہ ۱۲۔ مفتی عنایت احمد، بالای قلعہ کول ۱۳۔ گلاب خاں ۱۴۔ احمد خاں کول، محلّہ سرای سلطانی ۱۵۔ شیخ لال محمد، بالای قلعہ کول، ۱۶۔ امیر الدین، تاج گنج آگرہ۔ ۱۷۔ احمد دوی، ماموں بھانجہ ۱۸۔ مکن قصاب ۱۹۔ احمد خاں ۲۰۔ ننّو جولاہہ۔

....

(91)

UPSA - File No. 28

سرکار مدعی ظہوری ولد امامی۔ ذات جولاہہ مدعا علیہ۔ جرم بغاوت ولوٹ، سکونت بالای قلعہ کول۔ حسب صدور وارنٹ رقم زدہ ۴ رنومبر ۱۸۵۸ء

بتاریخ ۴ رنومبر ۱۸۶۳ء کو معیاد قید منقضی ہوگئی۔

....

(92)

UPSA - File No. 37

فہرست مسلم غدر سرکار مدعی بنام کریم بخش مدعا علیہ جرم شامل ہونے جہاد میں ۸ رنومبر ۱۸۵۷ء۔

(93)

NAI - Document No- B-101 F. 13 12th July, 1857.

حضرت جہاں پناہ سلامت

بعز عرض میرساند۔ چونکہ کنیز بر گودام چونہ انگریزی بیرون شہر متصل اجمیری دروازہ یک پہرہ مقرر ساختہ محافظت کنانیدہ است صرف بہ خیال این معنی کہ اکثر چونہ برای مرمت مکانات قلعہ معلیٰ خواہ دیگر مکانات سلطانی مطلوب می شود بکار خواہد آمد۔ اکنوں کہ چیزی چونہ بہ جہت مرمت درکار است زبانی مردمان معلوم شدہ کہ مرزا مغل بہادر مخالفت برداشتن چونہ دادہ اند لہذا امیدوار فضل و کرم خسروانہ آنست کہ حکم قضا شیم بنام بہادر مسطور مزین بدستخط خاص فرمودہ شود کہ مردمان نوعی مزاحمت نرسانند و چند چھکڑہ ہانزد مرزا مغل بہادر ہستند منجملہ آں پنج چھکڑہ بہ کنیز دہانیدہ شود کہ بہ کاروبار مرجوعہ بکار خواہند آمد واجب دانستہ بہ پایہ عرض بندگان عالی متعالی رسانید زیادہ حد ادب

الٰہی آفتاب دولت و سلطنت تاباں و درخشاں باد

عرضی

کنیز زینت محل

معروضہ ۱۹/ ذیقعدہ ۲۱ سنہ معلیٰ

حکم ہوا کہ حسب الحکم حضور والا برای عندمزاحمت خود پروانہ بنام افسران پلٹن رشتہ متعینہ اجمیری دروازہ برای دادن پنج مرا چھکڑہ پروانہ بنام غلام علی داروغہ فراش خانہ جاری ہو۔ ۲۰/ذی قعدہ ۲۱

اخبار الظفر دہلی۔ ۱۲۷۴

....

(94)

اخبار الظفر

ظلم کفار بدکردار

مردمان بیرونجات کی زبانی سنا جاتا ہے کہ اب نصارائے کفار نے بہت تنگ کر رکھا ہے۔ رعایا کو خصوصاً اہل اسلام کو زیادہ تنگ کرتے ہیں جہاں قابو پاتے ہیں پھانسیاں دیتے ہیں قتل کرتے ہیں۔ گانو کے گانو اڑادیتے ہیں۔ اودھر سونی پت میں ایک مولوی صاحب کو پھانسی دے دی جن کا حال خبر سونی پت میں لکھا جاتا ہے اور گلاوٹی سادات کو بہت تکلیف دی۔ بعضے تو کہتے ہیں کہ گانو اوڑا دیا اور زر تحصیل مال آیندہ کا مانگتے ہیں اور اس سال کا وصول کر لیا تھا۔

....

(95)

اخبار الظفر

تدبیر مناسب

دہلی

عقلای کامل کے یہی رائے ہے کہ جو فوج منبئی اوراندور وغیرہ کی ابھی رستہ میں ہے ان کے یہاں بلانا عبث ہے بلکہ باعث تردد وتکلیف بندگان والا دعایا ہے۔۔۔لیکن ہر جگہ بقدر مناسب پلٹن یا پلٹن قیام پذیر رہیں اس میں شک نہیں کہ بغیران تدابیر کے اوراس قسم کے انتظام کے روسای گرد ونواح ودیار وامصار کے دل حکومت کفار کا اثر نہیں جانے کا اور ان کی حکومت ان کے دل سے منقطع نہیں ہوگی اور خود نصارائے کفار کے دانت بھی بغیراس کے کھٹے نہ ہونگے۔ علاوہ اس کے پانی دانہ ہماری خاص حضرت دہلی کا وہ ہے کہ جو فوج بیرون جات میں جرات کے کام کرسکتی ہے اور پہلے حملہ میں کفار نابکار کو دارالبوار جہنم کو پہونچاتی ہے جہاں پانی یہاں کا پیا اور چاندنی چوک کا ایک گشت کیا اور دریبہ خورد وکلاں کے دو پھیرے اور جامع مسجد کے چارطرف دورہ عمل میں آیا گھنٹے والے کا قلاقند اور لڈ ونوش جان فرمائے پھرتمام عزم وقصد دشمن کشی اور جرات وشجاعت کا خاتمہ ہے از روے تجربہ کے اور سیر وتواریخ سے اسی طرح واضح ہے کہ قیام پذیری اور آرام گیری اس مقام تعیش القیام کے مخل انتظام ومہام ملک گیری پائی گئی یہی جہت ہے کہ قیام فوج عدوکش کو اس فن کے کار آزمودوں نے اس شہر کے اندر نہیں مرعی رکھا اور سلاطین ملک گیر نے بھی اس آرام گاہ کو واسطے قیام دوام کے ناپسند جانا اور تجربہ روزمرہ شاہد حال ہے اس رائے اور مقال کا واللہ المعین المقال

....

(96)

اخبار الظفر ۔ دہلی بتاریخ اتوار ۔ ۲ شہر محرم الحرام ۱۲۷۴ھ ۔ جلد ۱۹ نمبر ۲۴۔

اشتہار

رسالہ جہاد جورد میں اشتہار نصاریٰ کے کفار کے لکھا گیا ہے بالکل چھپ کے طیار ہو گیا۔ قیمت چار آنہ ہیں جن صاحب کو خریداری منظور ہو لے سکتے ہیں اور امیران ذی استطاعت سو، سو (۱۰۰) دو دو سو لے کر فوج اور مجاہدین شہر و بیرونجات میں تقسیم کریں تو مقتضی حسنات بے غایات ہے۔ لیکن نہایت افسوس ہے کہ ہمارے ملک والوں کو اصلاً و مطلقاً توجہ طرف امور خیر کے نہیں رہی اور زیادہ تر تعجب و افسوس کا یہ مقام ہے کہ اس حال و ہنگام میں کہ صبح و شام مدت اور غارت نمایاں ہے اور مارتے میان دکھلائی دیتی ہیں تو بھاگتے دوڑتے دینے کو موجود اور مضمون ان الحسنات یذھبن السیئات اور الصدقات رد البلیات کہ ارشاد خالق ارض و سماوات و رسول سرور کائنات سے ہے بالائے طاق نسیان الحق یہ جو حالات ظاہر و نمایاں ہیں یہ صرف ہمارے اعمال کا نتیجہ جانا چاہیے کہ معبود اپنا ہوائے نفس کو گردانا ہے۔ بیشتر ایک آدمی کے کہنے کے برابر یہی حکم خدا اور رسول نہیں شمار کیا جانا۔

بعض حاجی صاحبوں سے سنا گیا کہ نصاریٰ کفار اوس نواح کے صغار و کبار دار البوار جہنم کو بھیج دئے گئے۔ کچھ جہازوں پر بیٹھ کر راہ فرار دیکھا چاہتے تھے سو وہ بھی انہیں نصیب نہ ہوئی اور فوج ایران مبنیٔ اور کھمبات وغیرہ کی طرف اوتر آئی والعہدہ علی الراوی

....

(97)

گوالیار

سنا گیا کہ بیجا بائی نے ظاہر آخیر خواہی نصاریٰ سے دست برداری نہیں کہ فوج منصورہ جبل پور واندور وغیرہ کے جو آتے تھے اس میں اور بگڑ گئے اور مشہور تو یہ ہے کہ بیجا بائی کو قید کرلیا اور اس کی اپنی فوج بھی بپاس دین ہمراہ فوج منصورہ اسلامی کی یک جان ہوگئی اور بعضے یہ کہتے ہیں کہ اس نے خریطہ بھیجا ہے آگرہ کو کہ فوج میرے قابو میں نہیں رہی۔ بہر کیف فوج اسلامی ہر طور بہ عنایت الٰہی ظاہر و باہر ہے بلکہ روایت قید بیجا بائی میں یہ بھی مشہور ہے کہ گوالیار خوب لوٹا گیا بشرطیکہ مثل جے پور کے خبر کے نہووے اور انجام کو یہ بھی سنا گیا کہ بیجا بائی سے فوج منصورہ نے وہ نصارا سے مانگی تھی جو اس کے ہاں چھپے تھے سو بیجا بائی نے مکان بتلا دیا اس گفتگو کے درمیان کچھ گوالیار بھی لوٹا گیا مگر درحقیقت بیجا بائی دل سے نصاریٰ سے موافق نہیں تھی۔ فوج کو نصاریٰ بتلا دی انہوں نے مار ڈالا پھر چین چان ہوگیا یہ امر قرین قیاس ہے اور توفیق بھی دونوں خبروں میں دیتا ہے۔

....

(98)

جبل پور

سنا گیا کہ اوس طرف ایک کا فرزند نہیں چھوڑا اور سب اس نواح کے فوج معہ فوج اندور وغیرہ گوالیار کو آئے ہیں جس کا حال ابھی گوالیار میں لکھا گیا

(99)

جھجر

ایک دوست وہاں سے آئے ہوئے تھے بیان کرتے ہیں کہ اول اول فوج جھجر کا ایسا حال ظاہر اور مشہور تھا کہ اگر ذرا اشارہ وایما تخت اسلامی کا پہونچے تو بہ سر و چشم حاضر ہوویں لیکن جب یہاں سے کچھ سوار اور رسالہ دار افواج منصورہ مرسلہ بندگان اقدس گئے تو فوج جھجر کا وہ مقولہ پاستانی محض زبانی ظاہر ہوا اور مصداق مضمون **یقولون بافواھھم مالیس فی قلوبھم** اور **لم تقولون ما لا تفعلون** معلوم ہوا۔ ہر چند ناقل تو بہت طول کلام سے بیان کرتے ہیں مگر مختصر لکھا جاتا ہے کہ انجام کو رئیس اور ان کی سپاہ نے عدم حضوری کے عذر میں تو انتظام کا اپنی ملک کے بہانہ پیش کیا اور زر مطلوبہ کے ادا میں وعدہ احضار بغور وصول زر دیہات اور اغلب ہے کہ پانچ لاکھ کے طلب میں ایک لاکھ انجام کو ادا ہو۔

....

(100)

خلاصۃ الاخبار دربار مطبع حضرت ظل سبحانی خلیفہ الرحمانی فروغ خاندانی عالی شان گورگانی چراغ دودمان بخدمت نشان صاحب قرانی خلد اللہ ملک وسلطنتہ۔

روز شنبہ ۱۷ ربعد ادای فرائض وسنن معمولات مستمرہ بندگان اقدس مشغول اوراد اور مناجات بارگاہ حضرت رب العباد تھی کہ خصال دربار مثل صمصام الدولہ نواب احمد قلی خاں بہادر و معین الدولہ وسرفراز الدولہ ونواب حسن علی خاں ونواب امین الدین احمد خاں ومیر

عدل بہادران وغیرہ خوانین واہلکاران ناصیہ سای بارگاہ جہاں بانی ہوئے۔ آداب وکورنش عرض کر بھیجا۔ چونکہ مزاج اقدس مکدر ومنقبض تھا برآمد نہیں ہوئے سب اہل دربار مرخص بعد اس کے مرزا خضر سلطان بہادراور مرزا ابوالحسن عرف مرزا عبداللہ بہادر وغیرہ فرزندان نامدار باریاب حضور ہوئے اور عرض معروض عمل میں آئے مگر بسبب برہم مزاجی کے بسبب سانحہ احترام الدولہ بہادر کے طبیعت فیض طویت بہت برہم رہی بسبب بے رغبتی کے طعام بھی ہضم نہیں ہوا۔ شاہزادگان والاتبار کوارشاد ہوا کہ احترام الدولہ بہادر کوتنہا نہ چھوڑیں اور مرزا محمد ظہیر الدین بخت بہادر کوفرمان ہوا کہ مال واسباب مفروقہ احترام الدولہ بہادر معرفت اہل پولس کے ہر جگہ سے بہم پہونچا کے حضور میں حاضر کیا جاوے۔ بعد عصر بھی نظر برانحراف طبیعت کے سیر وتفرج ظہور میں نہیں آئی اور رات کو بھی نیند کم آئی حکمت پناہ نے دواہای مناسب عرض کر بھیجیں وہ استعمال میں آ گئیں۔

....

(101)

سونی پت

سنا گیا کہ کفار نے ایک مولوی کو جس نے ایک انگریزن اور بچوں کو اس کے مارا تھا پھانسی دے دی اور اہالی سونی پت سے پیغام ہے کہ کوٹ کو خالی کردیویں وہ مقام بہت بلندی پر نمونہ پہاڑ کا ہے۔ کفار اس لئے مورچہ بنانے کو کہتے ہیں۔ تین دن کی مہلت دی گئی ہے اور حکم دیا ہے کہ اس عرصہ میں آپ اسے خالی کردیں تو بہتر ہے نہیں تو سب مکانات اڑا

دیئے جائیں گے سو باشندے وہاں کے سخت حیرت و پریشان ہیں۔ ہم بہت افسوس کرتے ہیں کہ ہمارے اس رائے کے بموجب ہمارے اہل اسلام کی طرف سے یہ بات نہ ظہور میں آئی کہ ہمارے ہاں کا مورچہ وہاں بنایا جاتا تو سب طرح کا انتظام بھی عمل میں آتا رسد کفار کی بند کی جاتی اور تحصیل کو مدد ہوتی اور روپیہ بھی بہت نہیں تو کچھ نہ کچھ وصول ہوتا۔ اب جس وقت کہ کفار نے وہاں مورچہ اور ملجا وا وہاں بنالیا تو ہمارے اہل اسلام کو بہت مشکل ہوگی۔ لیکن ابھی بھی کچھ نہیں گیا۔ اب بھی جتنی تعجیل مدافعہ وغیرہ مراتب میں عمل میں آویں بہتر اور مناسب ہے۔ امید ہے اللہ تعالیٰ سے کہ اب کفار کو یہاں سے ناامیدی حصول مرام حاصل ہوئی ہے کہ اب یہ تدبیر سوجھی ہے یا حفظ ماتقدم سمجھی ہے بہر کیف یہاں کے حرب و پیکار روز مرہ سے وہاں کا مورچہ اور ادھر سے رسد اور مسدود دے راہ کفارِ گمراہ عندالعقل بہتر ہوتا ہے واللہ اعلم بالصواب والیہ المرجع والماب۔

....

(102)

پنجاب

لاہور کی طرف آنے والوں سے قتل و قمع کفار ناہنجار کا اگرچہ سنا جاتا ہے لیکن بعض بعض بچشم دیدہ قلعہ بندی اور دن کو پھرنا چلنا بھی بیان کرتے ہیں اور اس نواح سے بالکل ابھی صفائی نہیں بیان کرتے جیسے کہ عنایت الٰہی سے پورب کی طرف سے صفائی ظاہر ہے لیکن اس مین شک نہیں کہ عمل داری بھی کفار کے پنجاب میں ہرگز نہیں رہی۔ پٹیالہ والہ وغیرہ

نمک حراماں تخت کی حمایت واعانت سے اب ان کا وجود ہے۔ علی الخصوص پٹیالہ والہ جتنا ان کا ساتھ دے رہا ہے اتنا کوئی نہیں۔

....

(103)

روز چہار شنبہ ۲۱۔ بعد فرض و سنن و اوراد معمولی جلوہ آرای دربار ہوئے سب حضار دربار آداب و مجرا بجالائے۔ مرزا ظہیر الدین بہادر کو فرمان قضا جریان صادر ہوا کہ نواب سید حامد علی خاں اور احمد مرزا خاں اور راجہ دیبی سنگھ اور سالگ رام قلعہ مبارک میں نہ آویں۔ مسدود کیے جاویں۔ چنانچہ حسب الحکم عمل میں آیا۔ بعد نماز پیشین بندگان اقدس رونق بخش تسبیح خانہ ہوئے حکمت پناہ کو نبض شناسی کے لیے بلاکر بعد شرف بخشنے نبض شناسی سے رخصت فرمایا۔

....

(104)

لشکر ایران

بعض لوگ آیندگان طرف پشاور و پنجاب کے زبانی بیان کرتے ہیں کہ لشکر ایران اٹک تک پہنچ گیا ہے اگر چہ اس کا وثوقِ تصدیق ہم کو نہیں ہے لیکن بہ طریق گپ جو سنا گیا لکھا گیا۔ کیونکہ ممکنات سے ہے کچھ محال نہیں کہ بالکل کذب کا حکم قائم کیا جائے اور صرف جھوٹ تصور کیا جاوے لیکن اب حال لوگوں کا یہ ہوگیا ہے کہ کسی خبر پر یقین واعتماد نہیں ہوسکتا

اورتعریف خبر میں سے شق احتمال صدق حذف کی جاوے تو بجا وزیا ہے۔

....

(105)

سنا جاتا ہے کہ اس طرف کی فوج ہندوستانی وغیرہ اور فوج کنٹن جنیٹ نے سب کفار ناہنجار کو تہہ تیغ آبدار کرڈالا۔ اور غالبًا اور کچھ پنڈاری بھی اس طرف کو روانہ ہوئے ہیں اور خزانہ بھی تیس لاکھ روپیہ طرف مہد پور کا لکھا ہے۔

باہتمام بندہ سید عبداللہ مہتمم دہلی اردو اخبار میں چھپا

....

(106)

UP State Archives, Allahabad. F. No. 1568

بحضور سرکار صاحب بہادر

۲۶ رجولائی ۱۸۵۸ء (انگریزی میں دستخط)

۸ ے غریب پرور سلامت، جناب عالی حالِ مسمار قلعہ پختہ جہانگیر آباد کا یہ ہے کہ آج کی تاریخ بسبب شدت بارش مزدوران بہم نہ پہونچے اور مسماری میں ہرج ہوا۔ کچھ مزدور جن کا ٹھیکہ تھا مگر اون سے بھی بسبب بارش محاری دیوار ہای نہ ہوئی۔ اب قلعہ میں سالم ایک برج اور ایک دیوار و دو کاری۔ کمترین مدوم تحصیل جہانگیر آباد خانپور۔

مروضہ ۲۵ رجولائی ۱۸۵۸ء

(107)

NAI - Document No. B111C F. 31 Dated 28th July, 1857.

شجاعت نشان مبارک شاہ خاں کوتوال شہر معلوم نمایند چوں آن فدوی حسب صدور شقہ خاص دیروزہ منادی در تمام شہر کنانیدہ ممانعت قطعی برای مذبوحی وقربانی گاو شدہ است حالا عز ارقام می رود کہ بر دروازہ ہای شہر اتحبان بندوبست نماند کہ کدام بیوپاری فروشندہ گاو از امر درباب بابتہ روز بقرعید در شہر گاو گلومیسن را برای فروخت آوردن نتواند وبہ مکان کسانی کہ گاوہای پروردہ از اہل اسلام باشند آنرا گرفتہ در کوتوالی بہ بند وبہ مکان محروس آں فدوی آن را محفوظ دارد اگر کسی خفیہ یا علانیہ قربانی گاو پروردہ خانہ خود ہم خواہد ساخت بموجب ہلاکت آن شخص خواہد شد۔ درباب انتظام این امر گاوکشی کہ بہ فروختن باہم در شہر نیایند و گاوہای پروردہ ہم نکشند بانتظار کوتوال از خانہ اہل اسلام درین روزہای عیدالضحی بہ آن قدور ہر قدر کہ اجتہاد خواہد نمود بموجب خوشنودی خاطر والاست۔ زیادہ تفصلات صادر شد۔ مرقوم ہفتم ماہ ذلحجہ ۲۱ معلیٰ نقل پروانہ تو برای ارسال پیش والاست شہر فقط ۷ ذلحجہ ۲۱ معلیٰ و بجواب ہذا عرضی ہم ارسال شدہ۔ فقط

ایضاً

....

(108)

Haryana State Archives, Chandigarh, D No. 123, 124

رجسٹر جس کو صاحب ڈپٹی کمشنر بہادر پانی پت نے حسب شرائط مندرجہ دفعات دس اور گیارہ جسے گورنمنٹ طرح۔ مورخہ آٹھویں نوامبر ۱۸۵۸ء موسومہ صاحب سکریٹری گورنمنٹ بنگال کے بابت تعمیل حکم معافی مشیرہ ملکہ معظّمہ کے جرم سے معافی عطا کی اور شرائط مذکور بموجب حکم کے نامزد کو سنائی گئی۔

نام اور عہدہ اور فارم رجمنٹ کا جس میں باغی یا مفرور رہوا	عمر	قوم	سکونت	تاریخ حاضری	سبب غیر حاضری

حسن علی خاں چپراسی پرمٹ مہم ضلع رہتک	۳۰ برس	بلوچ	سونی پت	خود بخود حاضر آیا	بیان حسن علی خان کا یہ ہے کہ ایک شخص حسن خاں نامی پرمٹ حصار سے آیا تھا اوسکی گرفتاری کے واسطے حکم حصار سے آتا تھا۔ مجھ کو یہ دہشت ہوئی کہ کوئی مجھ کو نہ پکڑے اور پرمٹ مہم کے جب سب لوگ چلے آئے تب میں چلا آیا تھا اور جا بجا پھرتا رہا۔

۲۔ اصابت علی خاں شتربان غائب ہے	۵۵ برس	دوگڑ	سونی پت	۲۹ نوامبر ۵۸ء کو ازخود سونی پت میں حاضر ہوا کہ تھانہ دار نے اوسی تاریخ بذیعہ عرضی کے عدالت میں بھیج دیا۔	اس کا اظہار یہ ہے کہ میں تین پشت سے بادشاہی اونٹوں پر نوکر تھا جب سرکار نے دہلی فتح کر لی تب میں خوف سے بھاگ گیا کہ اسوقت آدمی جان سے مارے جاتے تھے اور سرشتہ سے جو حال دریافت کیا تو بجز اوسکے کہ نام اوسکا غیر حاضران سونی پت میں درج تھا اور کوئی جرم درج نہیں ہے۔
۳۔ ہرنرائن ولد روپ رام	۵۵ برس	بیراگی	بہنڈاری پرگنہ پانی پت	۹ نوامبر	

۴۔عبدالرازق	۳۰سال	چھینی	پانی پت	۹/نوامبر	کتاب بیچنے لدھیانہ وغیرہ سہارنپور کی طرف گیا تھا اون ایام میں عذر ہو گیا اور خدمت غیر حاضران میں میرا نام لکھا گیا اس خوف سے میں حاضر نہیں ہوا تھا۔
۵۔سعداللہ خاں	سوبرس	پٹھان	پانی پت	۸/نوامبر خود بخود حاضر عدالت ہوا	بیان یہ ہے کہ کسی دشمن نے عرضی گم نام دیدی تھی کہ یہ شخص دہلی گیا ہے اور میں سوداگری بیل و گاڑی ریز کے کرتے تھے اس وقت دہشت سے بھاگ گیا ۔غیر حاضر ہوگیا۔

٦۔ محمد حسین خان	٢٦ برس	پٹھان	پانی پت	٢٩ر کو خود بخود حاضر عدالت ہوا۔	بیان اسکا یہ ہے جس روز صاحب کمشنر بہادر نے پانی پت میں اپنی بخشی و کوتوال پانی پت سود پال سنگھ ڈپٹی کلکٹر مردمان شہر کو پکڑا تھا میں بہ خوف ہتک عزت کے غیر حاضر ہوگیا اور آوارہ پھرتا رہا۔

۷۔احمد علی خاں	۲۰برس	پٹھان	پانی پت	۲۹ر کو خود بخود حاضر عدالت ہوا	بیان یہ ہے کہ میں دہلی گھوڑا بیچنے گیا تھا جب وہاں گھوڑا نہ بکا تو میں واپس گھوڑا لے طرف کانپور و باندہ چلا گیا اس عرصہ میں عذر ہو گیا پھر باندہ سے چل کر راستہ میں لوٹ گیا اور پانی پت میں آیا تو گھر کے آدمیوں نے کہا کہ تو غیر حاضر لکھا گیا تھا نہ دار پکڑ کر بھیج دیگا تو میں اس سبب سے چلا گیا اور آوارہ پھرتا رہا ۔

۸۔علیم الدین	۴۰برس	شیخ	کہوڑہ	۳۰/ دسمبر ۵۸ کوخودبخود حاضرعدالت آیا۔	اظہار یہ ہے کہ میں چوکی دار سنولے میں تھا اور ایام مفسدہ میں بیمار ہوکر اپنے گھر چلا گیا سنولی والوں نے غیر حاضر لکھا دیا اس خوف سے بھاگ گیا اور آوارہ پھرتا رہا۔
۹۔کلو	۲۵/برس	بلوچ	کھپوڑہ	۳۰دسمبر۵۸ کو خودبخود حاضرعدالت آیا۔	اس کا بیان یہ ہے کہ کسی مخبر نے لکھوادیا تھا دہلی گیا ہے اس خوف سے بھاگ گیا اور ضلع سہارنپور میں پھرتا رہا۔

۱۰۔ زبردست خاں	۲۵ برس	بلوچ	کھپوڑہ	۳۰ دسمبر کو خود بخود حاضر عدالت آیا۔	بیان اس کا یہ ہے میں مرحلہ قماشپور میں نوکر تھا بیمار ہو کر اپنے گھر چلا گیا کسی نے کہہ دیا کہ دہلی گیا ہے اس خوف سے غیر حاضر ہو گیا تھا۔

ضلع	نمبر	نام اور عہدہ اور نام رجمنٹ کا جس میں غیر حاضر یا مفرور رہوا	عمر	قوم	سکونت	تاریخ حاضری	سبب غیر حاضری

حلب	۱۱	منگلی	۲۶ برس	بلوچ	شاملی	۱۰ دسمبر کو خود حاضر آیا۔	بیان اسکا یہ ہے کہ میری سولہ کشتی پل میں لگ رہی ہیں اور میں طرف سہارنپور گیا اس عرصہ میں فساد ہوگیا میں دہشت گوجران سے ٹھہرا رہا اور اک روپیہ کرایہ کے جھوٹی نالش کرائی میں نے کچھ فساد نہیں کیا۔

پانی پت	۱۲	مغلا رانگڑ	۴۰ برس کی	رانگڑ	گھرونڈہ	۳۰ دسمبر ۵۸ کو تحصیل گھرونڈہ میں خود بخود آیا۔	بیان اس کا یہ ہے کہ میں رہتک کی طرف بیل لینے گیا تھا ۔گھرونڈہ والوں نے میرا گاؤں پھونکوا دیا میں اس طرف سے بھاگ گیا تھا اور گاؤں بہ گاؤں پھرتا رہا میں کوئی فساد نہیں کیا۔

پانی پت	۱۳	سرجن مندی	۵۰ برس	جاٹ	اولدی پور	۲۹ اپریل ۵۸ کو گرفتار آیا۔	یہ مدعا علیہ بہ علت بغاوت یعنی جانے دہلی میں سپرد عدالت شش ہوئی تھی اور اب حسب منشاء اشتہار کہ اوسکا یہ منشا تھا جو لوگ اس قسم کے ہیں وہ رہائی پاویں چنانچہ بموجب حکم ۳۱ دسمبر ۵۸ صاحب کمشنر بہادر دہلی بتاریخ ۴ جنوری ۵۹ کو رہائی پائے کہ نوامبر سے جیل میں تھے۔

پانی پت	۱۴	ہرچند منسی	۴۵ برس	جاٹ	اولدی پور	۲۹ اپریل ۵۸ کو گرفتار آیا۔	یہ مدعا علیہ بہ علت بغاوت یعنی جانے دہلی میں سپرد عدالت شش ہوئی تھی اور اب حسب منشاء اشتہار کہ اوسکا یہ منشا تھا کہ جولوگ اس قسم ہیں وہ رہائی پاویں چنانچہ بموجب حکم ۳۱ دسمبر ۵۸ صاحب کمشنر بہادر دہلی بتاریخ ۴ جنوری ۵۹ کو رہائی پائے کہ نوامبر ۵۸ میں زیر تجویز تھے۔
پانی پت	۱۵	پت رام جاٹ مدے	۴۰ سال	جاٹ	براٹھد ینہ	۲۹ اپریل ۵۸ کو گرفتار آیا	ایضاً

پانی پت	۱۶	روپ رام مدے	-	جاٹ	رسوئی رسولے	۲۹/اپریل ۵۸ کو گرفتار آیا	ایضاً

(109)

بحضور جہاں پناہ! (تاریخ نہیں ہے)

التماس ہے کہ فدیوں نے دوروز پہلے علی گڑہ اور بابوگڑہ کے انتظامات کے متعلق ایک عرضی دی تھی لیکن اب تک حکومت نے فوج نہیں بھیجی جس سے بندوبست ہو جاتا۔ شہر مذکور کے انتظام میں عجلت نہ کرنے سے حکومت کا نقصان ہوگا اور اسکے سوا خزانہ بھی ضائع ہو جائے گا۔ جو بابوگڑہ، علی گڑھ اور چتوڑ اور دیگر مقامات میں محفوظ ہے۔ غریب پرور! بابوگڑہ چوبیس فوجی سپاہیوں کے زیر حفاظت بیس ہزار روپیہ موجود ہے اور چنار میں مروان خاں کے بیس لاکھ روپیہ امانت ہے جس کی چھ سو جاٹ حفاظت کررہے ہیں علی گڑہ کا خزانہ تین قواعدداں پیادہ رجمنٹوں کے حفاظت میں عنقریب ارسال کیا جائے گا مزید برآن بابوگڑہ سب مع سامان رسد کے پندرہ سو گھوڑے موجود ہیں اگر مقامات مذکورہ میں سپاہیوں کو بھیجنے اور امن قائم کرنے میں تعجیل سے کام لیا جائے تو یقین ہے کہ کل سامان بہ حفاظت تمام حضور عالی کے قبضہ میں آجائے گا۔ لیکن اگر ایک یا دوروز کی بھی دیر کی گئی تو بلاشبہ سارا سامان ہاتھ سے جاتا رہے گا۔

....

(110)

مہر۔روشن سنگھ ۱۲۵۳ھ

حکم شاہی پنسل سے

مرزا مغل۔فوراً افسران پیدل کے نام احکام جاری کیے جائیں تا کہ وہ روانہ ہو کر جواہر سنگھ کی درخواست کے بموجب عمل کریں۔

....

(111)

بادشاہ جہاں پناہ

مودبانہ عرض ہے کہ انگریزوں کو مظفر نگر میں کر کے ۲۳ جون ۱۸۵۷ء کو غلام دولت خانہ پر حاضر ہو گیا ہے اور اب حضور کے لیے نہایت وفادارانہ خدمات انجام دے رہا ہے۔غلام کے آباءواجداد سے ہی مبتد عالم ہی کے نمک خوردہ تھے۔

مہر غلام عباس

(انہیں انگریزوں نے قتل کر دیا۔)

....

(112)

حکم شاہی

مورخہ ۱۱راگست ۱۸۵۷ء

بنام جملہ ھنود و مسلمانان جو مذہب وملت کی بہبودی کے خواہاں ہوں۔انہیں معلوم ہو کہ ملک الدین شاہ ان میں سے ہیں جنہوں نے مذہب اسلام کی خاطر کفار سے جنگ و جدل کرنے کے لیے اپنی جانیں وقف کر دی ہیں۔ جو لوگ راہ مذہب میں ان سے متفق ہوں گے اجر عظیم کے مستحق ہوں گے اور جو عیسائیوں کے شریک ہوں گے جان ومال سمیت برباد ہو جائیں گے۔

....

(113)

فہرست سامان مطلوبہ

رئیس جیوڑی۔ پانچ ہزار روپیہ۔رئیس قصبہ پراورے دس ہزار روپیہ، رئیس قصبہ دھرم پور پانچ ہزار روپیہ۔ رئیس دان پور کو پانچ ہزار روپیہ۔رئیس پہاسو۔ پانچ ہزار روپیہ۔رئیس دتاولی دو ہزار روپیہ۔رئیس بھیکم پور۔دس ہزار روپیہ۔رئیس بدایوں۔دس ہزار روپیہ۔رئیس قصبہ پانچ ہزار روپیہ۔تاجران شہر متھرا۔ پانچ ہزار روپیہ۔راجہ بلب گڑھ، دس ہزار روپیہ غلام حسین والی اترولی۔بیس ہزار روپیہ۔راجہ بھرت پور۔ پانچ ہزار روپیہ۔

میزان ۱۲۴۵۰۰۰

....

(114)

بحضور بادشاہ جہاں پناہ

۲/اگست ۱۸۵۷ء

مودبانہ عرض ہے کہ خاکسار ٹونک سے اس شہر میں وارد ہوا ہے اور پانسو سپاہیوں کو ایک کمپنی بن گئی ہے اور ۱۵۰۰ مجاہدین کو ہمراہ لایا ہے جنہوں نے اپنی جانیں مذہب پر فدا کرنے اور کفار سے لڑنے کے لیے وقف کر دی ہیں۔

عرضی غلام محی الدین خاں رسالدار خاص

حکم جنرل محمد خاں مع ان کی سرکاری مہر کے

بنام افسران سکھ رجمنٹ

مورخہ ۲۳ اگست ۱۸۵۷ء

اعلیٰ حضرت ظل سبحانی نے ابھی ہمارے جناب عالی کے ارشاد کیا کہ سکھوں کی رجمنٹ پر انہیں بہت اعتماد ہے اور وہ بہت مردانگی سے جوہر دکھائے گی۔

سرکاری مہر (جنرل صاحب)

....

(115)

بحضور بادشاہ غریب پرور

مورخہ ۹ ستمبر ۱۸۵۷

نیازمندانہ التجا ہے کہ حضور کی خدمت ہی سے جدا ہو کر خادم غازی آباد پہونچا جہاں

معلوم ہوا کہ کل بتاریخ ۸ ستمبر کچھ انگریزوں نے جاٹوں کی مدد سے پلکھوا کو تاخت و تاراج کر کے جلا ڈالا اس تباہی میں حصہ لینے والی فوج میں تیس انگریز اور قوم دھیا کے تین سو جاٹ تھے۔ پچاس انگریز مع جاٹوں کے ہنڈن کا پل توڑ دینے کے لیے بیگم آباد میں جمع ہوئے ہیں پلکھوا سے جو رسد دہلی جاتی تھی اسے منقطع کر دیا ہے۔

عریضہ غلام۔ احمد خاں مقیم غازی آباد

....

(116)

بحضور بادشاہ جہاں پناہ (تاریخ نہیں)

خداوند۔ غلام دیسی پیادہ رجمنٹ نمبر ۹۵ کی ساتویں کمپنی میں سپاہی تھا جو امرتسر میں مقیم ہے۔ انگریزوں نے تمام آدمیوں سے ہتھیار چھین لیے اور مقید کر دیا مگر جنہیں موقع ملتا گیا فرار ہوتے رہے چنانچہ غلام سے بھی امرتسر میں ہتھیار لیے گئے اور جو ذاتی سرمایہ تھا گوجروں نے لوٹ لیا۔ اب اس کے پاس روزمرہ خرچ تک کے لیے ایک پیسہ نہیں ہے۔

عرضی قاسم الدین سپاہی

....

(117)

حکم زیر مہر شہنشاہ

ظل السادات سید عبدالحسین　　　　　　مورخہ ۲۵ مئی ۱۸۵۷ء

جانو کہ جب سے تم رہتک گئے وہاں کے معاملات کے حالات کا کوئی مراسلہ نہیں بھیجا لہٰذا تمہیں لکھا جاتا ہے کہ اس فرمان خاص کے پہونچتے ہی فوراً اس ضلع کی مفصل حالت لکھ کر اور یہ کہ زیر نگین لانے میں دونوں کامیاب ہوئے یا نہیں۔ اس معاملہ کی کیفیت بغیر دیر کے فوراً ارسال کرو اور نہایت ضروری فرمان جانو۔

....

(118)

بحضور بادشاہ جہاں پناہ

مورخہ ۱۹ جون ۱۸۵۷

مودبانہ التماس ہے کہ ان مبارک دنوں ہم غرباء باشندگان جے سنگھ پورہ شاہ گنج المعروف بہ پہاڑ گنج و دیگر مقامات حضور کے ظل عاطفت میں پناہ ڈھونڈتے ہیں تا کہ تمام ظلموں سے چھٹکارا ملے۔ قصبہ شاہ گنج ہمیشہ بادشاہ کے نام سے پکارا جاتا ہے تا ہم افواج شاہی اجمیری دروازہ سے نکل کر یہاں گھس جاتی ہیں اور دوکانداروں کو بے قیمت دیے جبراً سامان لے جاتی ہیں اور نادار و تہی دستوں کے مکانوں میں گھس کر بستر ے، لکڑیاں اور برتن چھین لے جاتی ہیں۔ اور جو لوگ انہیں بہ منت باز رکھنے کی کوشش کرتے ہیں انہیں ہتھیاروں سے زخمی کرتے ہیں ان کے ظلم و تعدی سے تنگ آ کر ہم لوگ مجبور ہیں کہ حضور والا سے عرض کریں کہ ہماری زبوں حالت اور عدل پروری کو مدنظر رکھ کر سپاہ سے جواب

طلب کیا جائے اور انہیں حکم امتناعی ہو کہ وہ ہم پر اور ساکنان پہاڑ گنج پر ظلم کرنے سے دست بردار ہوں

عریضہ۔ نیاز

چاند خاں وگلاب خاں

....

(119)

(بادشاہ کا دستی حکم)

مرزا مغل۔ ایسی تدبیر اختیار کی جائے کہ یہ مفسد لوٹ مار سے باز رہیں اور ہماری رعایا ظلم کا شکار نہ بنے۔

....

(120)

بحضور بادشاہ جہاں پناہ

مورخہ ۴ جولائی ۱۸۵۷ء

مودبانہ التماس ہے کہ کچھ عرصہ سے مرزا ابوبکر صاحب شہزادی فرخندہ زمانی کے مکان میں جو بہرام خاں کے تراہے پر ہے فاسد ارادوں سے جایا کرتے ہیں اور ان تمام سیاہ کاریوں کے مرتکب ہوتے ہیں جو مے نوشی کے لازمی نتائج ہیں کل دو پہر کے مثل وہ موافق معمول آئے اور تمام دن شہزادی مذکورہ کے مکان میں اسپرٹ دار شرابیں پیتے اور ناچ

مجرا یکھتے رہے۔ غروب آفتاب کے ڈیڑھ گھنٹہ کے بعد وہ جانے کے لیے آمادہ ہوئے۔

عرضی احسان الحق

....

(121)

بحضور بادشاہ جہاں پناہ (تاریخ نہیں ہے۔)

نہایت ادب سے گزارش ہے کہ سوار چاندنی چوک میں آکر بسے ہیں اور دوکانوں کے سامنے اپنے گھوڑے باندھتے ہیں۔ بہتیرے کرایہ داروں نے دکانیں خالی کردی ہیں اور جو رہ گئے ہیں وہ بھی ان کی تقلید کرتے جاتے ہیں یہ سب لوگ سواروں سے خائف ہیں اور دوکانوں کے کرایہ کا بہت نقصان ہو رہا ہے غلام عرض کر کے امیدوار ہے کہ بمرضی شاہی ان کے نام حکم جاری کیا جائے۔

عرضی منجانب رتن چند داروغہ باغات شاہی و جائداد خانگی شاہی متعلقہ صاحب آباد

....

(122)

حکم شاہی

بنام مرزا مغل۔ تمہیں یہ ہدایت کی جاتی ہے کہ ان رسالہ داروں کو وہاں سے نکال کر دوسری جگہ ٹھہرادو تا کہ رعایا کی آمدنی میں کوئی کمی واقع نہ ہو۔

....

(123)

بنام مرزا مغل

مورخہ ۱۷ جولائی ۱۸۵۷ء

فرزند۔ شہرہ آفاق دلاور ظہور الدین عرف مرزا مغل بیگ بہادر جانو کہ سید حسین علی خاں پولس آفیسر کی درخواست جس میں ایک جمعدار اور چند سپاہیوں نے علی گنج، پلنجی، حسن گڑھ اور علا پور کے گوجروں کے ہاتھوں خوفناک زخم کھائے ہیں پڑھ کر ایک خاص حکم و درخواست مذکورہ تمہیں روانہ کی گئی تھی آج پولس افسر مہرولی کی عرضی سے معلوم ہوا کہ وہی گوجر وہاں بھی شورش کر رہے ہیں اور تمام دیہاتوں میں غارت گری کرتے پھر رہے ہیں ایسی قانون شکنی از حد خطرناک ہے لہذا تمہیں ہدایت کی جاتی ہے کہ ایک پیدل کمپنی اور ۵۰ سوار فوراً روانہ کر دو تاکہ یہ لوگ گوجروں اور گاؤں کے صدر نمبردار کو گرفتار کر کے لائیں۔

....

(124)

مہر

ابوالظفر سراج الدین بہادر شاہ بادشاہ غازی ۱۲۵۳ ہجری و یکم جلوس

امیر الدولہ، ضیاء الملک محمد محمود خاں بہادر مظفر جنگ ہمارے ملازم خاص، حدود الطاف و نگہداشت ہماری مہربانیوں کے مقصود۔ جانو کہ تم خاص ملازم عرض مشتمل بہ حالات مفصلہ، مع تفصیل معلوم کے تمام پرگنوں کی خراب حالت کے جو لٹیروں اور بدمعاشوں نے

کر رکھی ہے اور انسداد کے لیے جو طریقہ اختیار کیا گیا ہے کہ جتنے پیدل اور سوار مل سکیں بھرتی کر کے حالت درست کی جائے۔

۲۸ ذیقعدہ بست و یکم سال جلوس خود بدولت مطابق ۲۱ جولائی ۱۸۵۷ء

....

(125)

بحضور بادشاہ خداوند و کرم گستر۔ ۲۲ جولائی ۱۸۵۷ء

مودبانہ التجا ہے کہ آٹھ یا دس روز ہوئے کہ گیارھویں پیدل کے خفیہ ملازم جواہر بخش نے سڑک مسمی قاضی کے حوض سے فدوی کی جو خچر مادیاں چرالی ہے۔ غلام نے پانچ روز تک بڑی دقت اور تلاش کے بعد اس مادہ خچر کا پتہ لگایا اور جواہر بخش مذکورہ نے گیارہ روپیہ لینے کے بعد اسے واپس کیا۔ تین روز کے بعد پھر مذکورہ خفیہ پولس اپنے ایک ہمراہی کو لیے ہوئے غلام کے دکان پر آیا جو ترکمان پولس حلقہ میں ہے۔ اور بطور مجرم گرفتار کر کے مرزا خیر سلطان بیگ ڈاکٹر پیادہ نمبر ۱۱ کے روبرو پیش کیا جائے۔ ڈاکٹر غلام کو حوالات کر دیا اور کہا کہ یہ اسی کا خچر ہے پس یا تو اسے لا کر چھوڑ دیا جائے ورنہ حوالات رہے۔ چنانچہ فدوی نے اپنی قریب المرگ اہلیہ کو چھوڑ کر فی الفور خچر لے جا کر اس کے حوالہ کیا اور گیارہ روپے اسنے مجھے واپس کر دیے۔ حقیقت یہ ہے کہ پانچ مہینے گزرے جبکہ غلام نے مویشی مذکورہ کو رمضان خاں رسالدار پانچوں ترپ رجمنٹ بے قاعدہ سواران نمبر ۸ سے جو دہلی کے باشندے ہیں خرید کیا۔ غلام ملتجی ہے کہ اعلی حضرت بلی غریب پروری و حفاظت جو حضور کے خاص اوصاف

ہیں رسالدار مذکورہ اوران کی رجمنٹ کے چار پانچ افسروں سے تحقیق فرمائیں تاکہ غلام انصاف کو پہونچے اور ہمیشہ اعلیٰ حضرت کی ترقی سلطنت واقبال کا دست بدعا رہے۔ واجب تھا عرض کیا۔

عرض کمترین کریم بخش عرف نھوامالک خچر اور انصاف کا خواستگار

....

(126)

بحضور بادشاہ جہاں پناہ مورخہ ۱۷جولائی ۱۸۵۷ء

بادشاہ جہاں پناہ

نہایت ادب سے التماس ہے کہ بدمعاشوں کا بڑا بھاری گروہ فدویوں کی دکان متصل کشمیری دروازہ پر آتا ہے اور بہت بری کاروائیاں کرتا ہے بعض اوقات چیف پولس آفسر کو بعض اوقات سپاہیوں کو بلا لاتا ہے۔ اور فدویوں پر الزام لگاتا ہے کہ دشمنوں سے سازش کی ہے اور انہیں رسد پہونچاتے ہیں حضور کو معلوم ہو کہ فدویاں خانہ زاد غلام ہین اور ایسی کاروائیوں سے ان کی بربادی یقینی ہے بس ملتجی ہیں کہ ہماری دوکانوں پر سرکاری قفل لگا دیے جائیں تاکہ ہمیں بھی امن وچین نصیب ہو اور دکانیں بھی محفوظ ومامون رہیں۔

عرضی شیودیال وشادی رام سوداگران

(پنسل کا لکھا ہوا بادشاہ کا دستی حکم)

مرزا مغل۔ درخواست کنندگان کی حفاظت کا انتظام کیا جائے۔

پشت پر نوٹ۔ نمبر ۵۵۷

پشت پر حکم مرزا مغل

عرضی ہذا آج پہونچی جس پر بادشاہ کا تحریری حکم ہے کہ انتظام کیا جائے۔ سائلوں کی استدعا ہے کہ ان کی دکان پر سرکاری قفل جڑ دیا جائے۔ پس حکم دیا جاتا ہے چیف پولس آفسر کے نام ایک حکم جاری کیا جائے کہ درخواست کنندوں کی دکان پر سرکاری قفل جڑ دیا جائے اوران کی خبر گیری کی جائے۔

....

(127)

حکم پر شاہی عدالت کی مہر ثبت ہے۔

بنام

نشان الوالعزمی چیف پولس آفیسر دہلی

مورخہ ۲۲ جولائی ۱۸۵۷ء

پانچ ملزموں میں سے جنہیں تم نے روانہ کیا ہے دفتر ہذا میں دو کے فائل موجود ہیں۔ تفصیل ذیل میں درج ہے لیکن یہ تین فائل یہاں موجود نہیں۔ پس اگر تمہارے پاس عدالت شاہی کی کوئی تحریر رسید بابت گم جانے اوران تینوں فائلوں کے موجود ہو تو عدالت ہذا میں پیش کرو۔ آیندہ کے لیے خیال رہے کہ کوئی بھی ملزم جو عدالت میں پیش کیا جائے فرد ارتکاب جرائم بھی اسکے ہمراہ ہونی چاہیے۔

فہرست مقدمات۔ فائل موجود ہیں۔ مقدمہ گمانی مدعا علیہ مقدمہ رحم اللہ مدعا علیہ فائل جو موجود نہیں۔ ہر سکھ، غلام علی اور خدا بخش۔

....

(128)

بحضور بادشاہ جہاں پناہ مورخہ ۲۲ جولائی ۱۸۵۷ء

ظل السبحانی جہاں پناہ

نیاز مندانہ عرض ہے کہ فدوی کا گھوڑا بسبب سم پھٹ جانے کے بالکل ناکارہ ہوگیا ہے چونکہ خانہ زاد پر حضور کی عنایات قدیمی ہیں لہذا نمک خوار ملتجی ہے کہ ایک ماہ کی رخصت دی جائے تاکہ وہ کوئی اور گھوڑا اتلاش کرلائے۔

عریضہ کمترین خانہ زاد امام اللہ خان بارگیر

بادشاہ کے ہاتھ کا پنسل سے لکھا حکم۔ افسران محکمہ تنخواہ۔ ایک ماہ کی رخصت دیدی جائے۔

....

(129)

بحضور بادشاہ جہاں پناہ

۱۸/اگست ۱۸۵۷

مودبانہ التماس ہے کہ حضور عالی نے حکم دیا تھا کہ پل کی مرمت کے لیے دوسو روپیہ

صرف کیا جائے چنانچہ روزانہ مزدوروں کو شام کے وقت اجرت دیدی جاتی ہے اور چونکہ کسی کو ٹھیکہ نہیں دیا گیا ہے لہذا دو سو روپیہ کے خرچ کی ضرورت نہیں۔ واجب تھا عرض کیا۔

عرضی غلام ظہور الدین

....

(130)

مہر شاہی ثبت ہے

مورخہ ۱۲/اگست ۱۸۵۷ء

بنام مرزا صفی سلطان حیدر مرزا صفی تہماسپ مرزا ضیاء الدین بخت و مرزا عثمان معلوم ہو کہ تمام صعوبتوں وشاہیوں اور سختیوں کا جو تمہیں صوبہ اودھ میں جھیلنی پڑی ہمیں معلوم ہوا۔ حیرت انگیز انقلاب واقع ہو رہے ہیں خدا کی مرضی یونہی ہے ان تمام واقعات کو سن کر ہمیں بے حد صدمہ پہونچا۔ قادر ذوالجلال نے اپنی مرضی پوری کی ہے اس نے جو کیا اچھا کیا اور جو بعد میں ہوگا اچھا ہوگا ہر حالت میں شاکر وصابر رہو اور ایک دوسرے سے بغض وعناد نہ رکھو اور لکھنو کے موسومہ امین آباد میں توقف کرو اور موجود خطرات سے بچ کر اپنے دن کاٹو۔ الھم ارحم۔ موجودہ نازک حالت اور بے چینی بتائید یزدانی فی الفور ختم ہو جائے گی۔ ہماری مہربانیوں کا یقین رکھو۔

....

(131)

بحضور ظل سبحانی غرباء پرور سلامت۔

مودبانہ التماس ہے کہ حضور پر واضح ہے کہ انصاف خلاق عالم کا پسندیدہ ہے اور ظالمانہ کاروائیاں ممنوع، لہذا التجا ہے کہ اگر اعلی حضرت افسران فوج کو اجازت دیدیں گے جو حضور سے قیدی عورتوں مردوں اور بچوں کے قتل کا مطالبہ کرتے ہیں اور جن کے سروں پر عرض معروض سن کر اعلیٰ حضرت نے اپنا دست شفقت رکھا تو حضور قوانین مذہب سے علیحدہ ہو جائیں گے۔ افسران مذکور کو پہلے مفتیان شرع متین سے فتویٰ حاصل کرنا چاہیے اور اگر یہ قتل کرنے کی اجازت دیں تو وہ لوگ ان قیدیوں کو قتل کر سکتے ہیں مگر اعلیٰ حضرت شرع نبوی کے خلاف کوئی حکم نہ دیں

عرضی نبی بخش خاں

کارندہ اعلی حضرت

....

(132)

حکم شاہی جس پر مہر ثبت ہے

تاریخ نہیں ہے

بنام خادم خاص مورد الطاف وکرم راجہ ناہر سنگھ بہادر۔ ہم نے سنا ہے کہ تم نے ایک تھانہ دار اپنی طرف سے بدر پور میں مامور کیا ہے اور مسمی نظیر الدین خاں سلطنت کی طرف

سے مقرر کیا گیا ہے جو فی الحال عرب سرائے میں موجود ہے پس تم چونکہ مابدولت کے تابعدار ہو اپنے مقرر کردہ شخص کو برطرف کردو۔

....

(133)

بحضور بادشاہ جہاں پناہ بادولت گستر

نہایت ادب سے عرض ہے کہ چونکہ دہلی کی سڑک پر امن نہیں تھا۔ تابعدار نے بموجب اعلیٰ حضرت کے فرمان کے رات اور دن کی کوشش سے کافی بندوبست کرلیا ہے۔

تب بھی موضع پالی کے جرائم پیشہ باشندے جو سرحد بلبھ گڑھ سے متصل ہے جو بہ زمانہ فوجداری اسی ریاست میں شامل تھا۔ قانون شکنی کرتے ہیں اور ایسے قتل و غارت گری پر کمر باندھی ہے کہ مخلوق بالکل عاجز آگئی ہے۔ تابعدار آہستہ آہستہ انہیں راہ پر لاتا ہے لیکن اعلی حضرت کی مدد کے بغیر پوری طور سے کامیاب نہیں ہوسکا۔ اگر حضور سے اجازت مل جائے تو ایسے انتظامات عمل میں لائے جائیں گے کہ موضع مذکور کے باغی اور نافرمان سر نہ اٹھاسکیں گے اور بلبھ گڑھ سے دہلی تک کے راستہ بالکل محفوظ ہو جائے گا۔ دیگر عرض یہ ہے کہ میں نے چند لوگوں سے سنا ہے کہ کسی نے حضور سے چغلی کھائی ہے کہ راجہ بلبھ گڑھ نے دو انگریزوں کو مع انکی عورتوں اور بچوں کو چھپا رکھا ہے۔ خدا شاہد ہے کہ یہ خبر محض غلط اور بے بنیاد ہے حضور کی مرضی اور احکام کے بغیر تابعدار ایسا کرنے کی کیوں کر جرأت کرسکتا ہے۔ ایک ہندوستانی البتہ بارہ سال میرے پاس ملازم تھا جو درمیان میں عیسائی ہو گیا تھا اسے بھی حضور کی خفگی کی

وجہ سے برطرف کردیا گیا۔ مگر اب اس شخص نے عیسویت ترک کر کے مذہب اسلام قبول کر لیا ہے۔ اور اب وہ رحم و معافی کا سزاوار ہے اگر حضور اجازت دیں تو میں پھر اسے اپنے پاس بلالوں

عریضہ تابعدار قدیمی ناہر سنگھ راجہ بلبھ گڑھ

مہر راجہ ناہر سنگھ

....

(134)

بحضور بادشاہ جہاں پناہ خداوند بنی آدم ظل سبحانی

تاریخ نہیں ہے

مودبانہ التماس ہے کہ حضور عالی کا حکم بابت میرے حاضر دربار ہونے اور شہر دہلی کی پولس کا انتظام ہاتھ میں لینے کے موصول ہوا جس کے ساتھ ہی دوسرا حکم حفاظت سڑک پر خادم کو توجہ دلانے اور مسافروں کی سلامتی کے طریقے اختیار کرنے اور رسد وغیرہ کی بابت ملا۔ میں یہ سچ عرض کرتا ہوں کہ ان احکام نے صادر ہو کر مجھے بے حد معزز فرما دیا ہے جس کے لیے خدا کی جناب میں شکریہ ادا کرتا ہوں۔ میری آدھی رات کی دعائیں خدا قبول کرے اور اعلیٰ حضرت کو ہمیشہ باشوکت و شان برقرار رکھے۔

شاہنشاہا۔ اگرچہ حضور کے اقبال و دبدبہ سے غلام کے علاقے میں امن امان ہو گیا ہے جس کے لیے میں شب و روز بندوبست اور امن و امان قائم رکھنے کی کوشش میں سرگرم رہتا تھا

تاہم موضع پالی اور پلول میں جو تابعدار کے علاقے سے ملے ہوئے ہیں چند بدمعاش ایسے پیدا ہو گئے ہیں جنہوں نے قتل و غارت شروع کر دیا ہے اور ایسی ایسی ڈکیتیاں، چوری اور راہزنی کر رہے ہیں جو بیان نہیں کی جا سکتی۔ گو خادم نے خود بھی ازراہ دور اندیشی اور پٹواریوں اور مالگذاری دفتر کے افسروں کی مشورت سے ایک حد تک بندوبست کر لیا ہے اور افسران مذکورہ کو سوار اور پیدل برائے مدد دیے ہیں لیکن بدوں حضور کے فرمان کے تابعدار اور کچھ اور کرنا نہیں چاہتا۔ بلب گڑھ سے دہلی تک کی سڑک کو پر امن بنانے کے لیے میں نے سپاہی بھرتی کیے ہیں اور راشب و روز انتظام سلطنت اور خبر گیری خلایق میں لگا رہتا ہوں میں حضور کا دیرینہ خادم ہوں اور جیسا کہ حکم دیا جائے گا انشاءاللہ تعمیل کروں گا عنقریب حضور کی روبکاری میں حاضر ہونے کا شرف حاصل کرونگا مگر اس وقت جب کہ ریاست میں پختہ طور پر امن و امان قائم ہو جائے گا کیونکہ موجودہ حالت نہایت پر آشوب ہے اور اعلی حضرت کے عتاب شاہی کا بھی خوف ہے واجب تھا عرض کیا۔

عریضہ خانہ زاد غلام ناہر سنگھ راجہ بلب گڑھ

مہر۔ راجہ ناہر سنگھ

....

(135)

عالیجناب

تاریخ نہیں ہے

حضور بادشاہ جہاں پناہ!

مودبانہ التماس ہے کہ جناب راجہ صاحب دہلی میں بموجب حکم حضور حاضر خدمت ہیں اور انھوں نے اپنے کپڑے منگوائے ہیں۔ لہذا عرض ہے کہ پروانہ راہداری عطا فرمایا جائے تا کہ گاڑیاں بلب گڑھ سے روانہ ہو جائیں اور انہیں کوئی روک نہ سکے اور اشیاء مذکورہ روانہ کر دینے کے بعد کوئی سپاہی دہلی دروازہ پر اندر جانے سے نہ روکے۔ ترقی اقبال کی دعائیں

عریضہ کمترین احمد علی کارندہ راجہ بلب گڑھ۔

مہر کا نشان۔ ''احمد علی'' حکم شاہی

مرزا مغل۔ پروانہ راہداری بنا کر دیدیا جائے۔

....

(136)

عرضی راجہ بلب گڈھ

مورخہ ۲۰ مئی ۱۸۵۷ء

عالیجناب

حضور بادشاہ جہاں پناہ!

نہایت عاجزی اور ادب سے درخواست ہے کہ اس سے پہلے بھی میں نے کئی درخواستیں بھیجیں مگر کسی کے جواب سے بھی مجھے سرفراز نہیں فرمایا گیا۔ میں پھر عرض کرتا ہوں

کہ موضع پالی وغیرہ کے سرکشوں نے بہت اودھم مچا رکھا ہے اور رعیت کو بہت نقصان پہونچا رہے ہیں اگر چہ مذکورہ موضع کو میں آہستہ آہستہ راہ پر لے آیا ہوں لیکن حضور کے احکام بغیر پوری سرکوبی نہیں کرسکتا اور کسی معاملہ میں دخل نہیں دے سکتا۔ میں شب و روز سوار اور پیادوں کے بڑھانے کے فکر میں ہوں۔ میں اس ضلع کے نافرمانوں کے ٹھیک کردوں گا اور پھر حضور کی خدمت میں حاضر ہوں گا۔ میں قلندر خاں رسالدار کو مع کچھ پیدل اور سواروں کے حضور کی خدمت میں، حسب الحکم اعلیٰ حضرت روانہ کیا ہے جیسا انہیں حکم ہوگا تعمیل کرینگے۔

درخواست نمکخوار غلام ناہر سنگھ راجہ بلب گڈھ۔ مہر راجہ رناہر سنگھ بہادر ثبت ہے

....

(137)

درخواست راجہ بلب گڈھ

بعالیخدمت مورخہ ۲۱ رمئی ۱۸۵۷ء

حضور بادشاہ جہاں پناہ!

مودبانہ گزارش ہے کہ بموجب حکم شاہراہ دہلی اور پولس اسٹیشن بدر پور کا انتظام جو خاکسار کے سپرد کیا گیا ہے ہو رہا ہے۔ اگر حضور نے کسی اور تھانے دار کو ممتاز فرمایا ہے تو میں اعلیٰ حضرت کے حکم کی بموجب تمام ماتحت افسران تھانہ مذکور کو برطرف کردوں گا۔ اور حضور کے مامور کردہ شخص کو تنخواہ دیدیا کروں گا۔ قلندر بخش خان رسالدار کو پیادوں اور سواروں کے

ہمراہ حضور کی خدمت میں روانہ کیا تھا مگر جب یہ لوگ حسب الحکم دہلی دروازے پر پہونچے تو محافظوں نے انہیں شہر میں نہ گھسنے دیا اور کہا کہ پہلے ہتیار رکھدو پھر جاؤ۔ حضور کو معلوم ہو کہ صرف ہتیار ہی سپاہی کی زیب وزینت اور اس کا زیور ہیں۔ ان کے بغیر ایک لحہ بھی اس کے لیے بیکار ہے، اسلیے وہ لوگ واپس چلے آئے اور چند روز کے لیے پرانے قلعہ میں ٹھہر گئے ہیں۔ لہذا ایک حکم عطا فرمایا جائے کہ وہ لوگ کھلے بندوں شہر میں داخل ہو سکیں۔ اور خلوص دل سے غلام ہو کر اپنی جانیں حضور پر سے قربان کریں۔ میں، جو حضور کا دیرینہ خادم ہوں سوچا کرتا ہوں کہ حضور کے احکام بجالانا عین سعادتمندی ہے۔ محرر تھانہ بدر پور سے یہ معلوم ہوا تھا اور بغرض اطلاع حضور کو عرض کر دیا گیا۔ (ترقی سلطنت واقبال کی دعائیں)

درخواست خادم دیرینہ ناہر سنگھ بہادر والی بلب گڈھ

مہر کا نشان۔ ''راجہ ناہر سنگھ بہادر''

....

(138)

بحضور بادشاہ جہاں پناہ!

مورخہ ۲۲ رمئی ۱۸۵۷ء

مودبانہ گزارش ہے کہ اعلیٰ حضرت کے احکام نے غلام کو اعزاز بخشا۔ بلب گڈھ سے بدر پور اور وہاں سے دہلی دروازہ تک کی شاہراہ کا بندوبست، موضع پالی، پلول، فتحپور وغیرہ کا انتظام بفضل خدا اور حضور کے اقبال سے بخوبی کر دیا گیا ہے اور پولیس و مالگذاری آمدنی

کے افسران جابجا مامور کر دیے گئے ہیں۔فدوی کی کوشش اور سرگرمی کی بہت دھوم ہے اور عنقریب حضور کے بھی گوش گزار ہوگی۔ جہاں پناہ! چند بے فکرے اس ریاست کے دشمن اور گردن زنی، جنہوں نے حتی المقدور ریاست کو نقصان پہنچانے کی کوشش کی تھی اور اب دہلی میں شہر کے دروازوں کے محافظ پیادوں اور سواروں کو میرے ملازموں کے بر خلاف بھڑکاتے ہیں، وہ لوگ میری تعریف سن کر خوش نہ ہوتے ہونگے۔پس امیدوار ہوں کہ پھاٹک کے سپاہیوں کو ہدایت کر دیجائے گی کہ بلب گڈھ ریاست کے ملازموں سے چھیڑ چھاڑ نہ کریں اور کسی حالت میں انہیں تنگ نہ کیا کریں، کیونکہ اس سے نظم ونسق میں فرق آنے کا اندیشہ ہے جسکے لیے حضور احکام جاری فرما چکے ہیں آگے حضور مالک ہیں اور بندہ تابعدار ہے۔حضور کے احکام کی بجا آوری میں ہمیشہ خدشہ رہتا ہے ہے کہ کچھ کوتاہی نہ ہونے پائے، چنانچہ پیادوں اور سواروں کی بھرتی بدستور جاری ہے اور چند روز بعد پولیس اور دیگر صیغوں کے لیے انہیں روانہ کردوں گا۔تابعدار دل و جان سے خیر خواہ سرکار ہے۔(ترقی سلطنت اقبال کی دعائیں

درخواست خادم دیرینہ ناہر سنگھ بہادر والی بلب گڈھ

مہر کا نشان۔"راجہ ناہر سنگھ بہادر"

....

(139)

بحضور بادشاہ جہاں پناہ!

مورخہ ۲۴ مئی ۱۸۵۷ء

نیاز مند عرض پرداز ہے کہ حضور کا نوازشنامہ پانے کی عزت حاصل ہوئی۔ پھاٹک کے محافظوں کے نام ریاست بلب گڈھ کے ملازموں کو تنگ نہ کرنے کے احکام جاری کرنے اور پیادوں وسواروں کو شاہی قلعہ کے پاس چھاؤنی کرانے اور نہایت الطاف وعنایات سے بندہ کو دربار شاہی میں حاضر ہونے کی ہدایت فرمانے کا احوال اسمیں مندرج تھا۔ مجھے جو اعزاز بخشا گیا ہے اسکے لیے میں بارگاہ ایزدی میں سربسجود ہوں۔ خدا ہمیشہ بادشاہ کو سلامت رکھے۔ جہاں پناہ! حضور کا غلام فرمان شاہی کو بجالانا موجب فخر جانتا ہے لیکن بندوبست کی ضرورت کے لحاظ سے اور موضع پالی وغیرہ کے بدمعاشوں کو نیچا دکھانے میں مصروف رہنے کی وجہ سے غلام حاضر دربار ہونے سے معذور ہے۔ ان کا بندوبست کر کے بہت خوشی سے حاضر ہوں گا۔

عالیجاہ! آج اتوار ہے اور موافق آج میں بھی ہوا کھانے دلکشا باغ میں گیا تھا جب میں وہاں تھا تو مجھے ہلال عید نظر آیا اور یہاں کے تمام باشندوں نے بھی اسے دیکھا چونکہ بندہ حضور کا خانہ زاد غلام ہے۔ لہذا مبارکباد دیتا ہے اور تہ دل سے چاہتا ہے کہ خوشخبری اور وعدوں سے بھرا ہوا دن یعنی عید جو خوشیاں منانے کا دن ہے۔ حضور کی خوش اقبال کا قاصد ہو! (بقائے سلطنت کی دعائیں)

مہر۔ ''مہر راجہ ناہر سنگھ بہادر''

....

(140)

بعالیخدمت

مورخہ ۲۵ر مئی ۱۸۵۷ء

حضور بادشاہ جہاں پناہ!

مودبانہ التماس ہے کہ کل ایک درخواست ارسال کر چکا ہوں جس میں ریاست کے معاملات مرقوم ہیں اور حضور کے علم میں آگئے ہوں گے ۔ خدا کے فضل و کرم سے اور حضور کے اقبال سے دہلی درواز تک اور اس ضلع کے گردونواح کے دیہات میں پورا پورا انتظام ہو گیا ہے ۔ میرے خیال میں نیچے درجہ کا ایک تھانیدار اور دس سپاہی ہنومان تھانہ میں اور ایک تھانے دار و پچیس سپاہی مہرولی میں متعین کرنے نہایت ضروری ہیں ۔ پھر حضور کے دبدبہ شاہانہ سے تمام ضلع میں کامل انتظام ہو جائے گا ۔ اگر حضور کی مرضی ہو اور احکام جاری فرمادیئے جائیں تو دونوں جگہ کا انتظام مکمل ہو جائے گا ترقی دولت وسلطنت کی دعائیں

درخواست خانہ زاد ناہر سنگھ راجہ بلب گڈھ

مہر ۔ ”راجہ ناہر سنگھ بہادر“

....

(141)

بحضور بادشاہ جہاں پناہ!

مورخہ ۲۷ر مئی ۱۸۵۷ء

مودبانہ عرض ہے کہ حضور کے احکام بابت قتل و غارت کے انسداد کرنے اور بیس سواروں کو تھانہ پولس مکندا، اور شہدری میں انتظام اور امن وامان قائم کرنے کے لیے متعین کرنے کے صادر ہوئے اور اعزاز بخشا۔ اس عزت افزائی کو محسوس کر کے سجدۂ شکر بجا لایا۔ میں بہت جلد سواروں کی روانگی کا بندوبست کردوں گا۔ انسداد جرائم کی تدبیروں میں مصروف ہوں۔ لیکن اب گوجروں، میواتیوں اور دیگر اقوام نے بہت بری طرح سر اٹھایا ہے اور روزمرہ فرید آباد اور خاص بلب گڈھ پر اچانک حملوں کی تیاریاں کرتے رہتے ہیں۔

لیکن اگر حضور کا اقبال اور فضل خداوندی شامل حال رہا تو بہت جلد نہایت عمدہ انتظامات کرلوں گا اور پھر حاضر خدمت ہوں گا کیونکہ یہ میری عین تمنا ہے۔ ترقی اقبال کی دعائیں

درخواست خانہ زاد ناہر سنگھ۔ والی بلب گڈھ

مہر۔ ''راجہ ناہر سنگھ بہادر''

....

(142)

عالیجناب

مورخہ ۳۰ رمئی ۱۸۵۷ء

حضور بادشاہ جہاں پناہ!

چندروز سے حضور کی خیریت نہیں معلوم ہوئی جس سے مجھے بیحد فکر رہتا ہے خدا حضور کو

اچھار کھے اور اقبال میں ترقی دے۔ جہاں پناہ کے فرمان سے مجھے بدر پور میں گاڑیاں کے لٹنے کا حال معلوم ہوا۔ میں نے بموجب حکم اعلی حضرت تھانے دار بدر پور کو سخت تاکید لکھی ہے کی تحقیقات کر کے مال اور مدعا علیہ کو بہم پہونچائے۔ خدا چاہے تو معاملہ بالکل تحقیق کرایا جائے گا۔ ابھی بیس سوار حضور کی خدمت میں روانہ کیے ہیں۔ ان سے کام لیجیے۔ اطلاعاً عرض ہے (ترقی سلطنت کی دعائیں)

عریضہ غلام خانہ زاد ناہر سنگھ والی بلب گڈھ مہر "راجہ ناہر سنگھ بہادر"

حکم شاہی پنسل سے لکھا ہوا

مضمون پڑھ لیا گیا یہ شخص مابدولت کا خیر خواہ ہے۔

....

(143)

بعالیخدمت

مورخہ ۲۸؍ مئی ۱۸۵۷ء

باادب ملتجی ہوں کہ کل حضور کے مراسلہ کا جواب ارسال کر چکا ہوں۔ آج خدا کے فضل اور حضور کے دبدبہ شاہی سے تمام ضلع میں امن وامان ہو گیا ہے اور انتظامات پختہ کر دیے گئے ہیں۔ پانچ طلائی مہریں ارسال ہیں۔ خانہ زاد غلام کا خیال کرتے ہوئے بنظر شفقت یہ تحفہ عید الفطر قبول فرمایا جائے۔ (ترقی سلطنت کی دعائیں)

درخواست کمترین ناہر سنگھ

مہر کا نشان۔ ''راجہ ناہر سنگھ بہادر''

حکم شاہی پنسل سے لکھا ہے (پڑھا نہیں جا سکا)

....

(144)

بعالیخدمت

مورخہ ۳۱/ جولائی ۱۸۵۷ء

بادشاہ جہاں پناہ!

مودبانہ التماس ہے کہ حضور پر بخوبی روشن ہے کہ افسران سابق کو میں نے پورا پورا اختیار دیدیا تھا۔ ان لوگوں نے عنایت کی اور ایک لاکھ روپیہ کی مالیت ہضم کر گئے۔ جب انکی بدذاتی کا بھید آشکارا ہوا۔ اور میں نے بھی حساب طلب کیا اور جو کمی واقع ہوئی اسے انکے گھروں سے بھرنے کی دھمکی دی تو یکے بعد دیگرے کچھ نہ کچھ عذر کر کے دہلی چلے گئے اور اب اپنے گھروں میں چین کرتے ہیں۔ حضور کے افسران کے کان میں یہ بات نہ پڑ جائے ۔اس کا ان کو اتنا خوف ہے کہ میری ریاست سے جو حضور کو یقین دلایا ہے کہ میں ظاہرا تو سلطنت کا خادم ہوں مگر باطن میں انگریزوں سے مل گیا ہوں اور فاسد ارادوں سے ذخائر حرب جمع کر رہا ہوں اور یہ کہ میں نے مسافروں اور مال وغیرہ کو شاہراہ پر لے جانے سے روک دیا ہے اب حضور کا رحم ولطف بالکل خفگی اور ناراضگی سے مبدل ہو گیا ہے چنانچہ احمد علی غلام کے ایجنٹ جب حضور کے دربار میں حاضر ہوئے تو حضور سرد مہری سے پیش آئے جسے

دیکھ کر وہ واپس چلے آئے۔ پھر اسی وقت قلندر خان رسالدار کو جو اعلیٰ حضرت کے حکم سے وہاں گیا تھا۔ برطرفی کا حکم مل گیا۔ عالیجاہ! میرے اغیار نے جو چغلی کھائی وہ سراسر بہتان ہے اور ان کا افترا آخر میں عیاں ہو جائے گا۔ وہ حضور کے محبت و خیر خواہی کا ایسا دم بھرتے ہیں کہ گویا بڑے راست باز ہیں حالانکہ اس سے ان کا مقصد یہ ہے کہ انہیں حضور کے افسران کے جواب طلب کرنے سے امن مل جائے اور جو بیش قرار رقم اس ریاست کی اپنی حرامزدگی سے جمع کی ہے، اس سے اپنے گھروں میں بیٹھے مزے اڑایا کریں۔ میرے آباء و اجداد ہمیشہ سے اسی سلطنت کے وفادار غلام رہے ہیں اور اس کے خلاف کبھی سازش نہیں کی نہ حصہ لیا۔ ایمانداری اور وفاشعاری میں میں وہ چاندی ہوں جسے اچھی طرح پرکھ لیا گیا ہو اگر آپ ایکسو بار جانچیں پھر بھی میں کھوٹا نہ اتروں گا۔ میرے دشمن جو چاہیں کہیں میں آپ کا قدیمی غلام ہمیشہ اور ہر حالت میں وہی وفاداری برتونگا۔

میری آنکھیں سوا تمہارے غیر کا چہرہ نہ دیکھیں گی
میرا آئینہ کسی اجنبی کا عکس قبول نہ کریگا

علاوہ ازین تابعدار اگرچہ ہندو مذہب رکھتا ہے لیکن ان لوگوں کے عادات و خصائص دیکھے ہیں جو خدا کو بزرگ و برتر مانتے ہیں۔ میں پیشویانِ اسلام کا معتقد ہوں، میں ایسا معتقد ہوں کہ قصبہ کی بنا کے پہلے قلعہ یا بازار میں مسلمانوں کی کوئی مسجد نہیں تھی۔ میں نے قلعہ میں ایک سنگین جامع مسجد تعمیر کرائی ہے۔ علاوہ ازیں میرے ہاں ایک عیدگاہ بھی ہے جو میرے باغ دلکشاء کے قریب ہے اور عید کے موقع پر وہاں نماز ہوتی ہے۔ یہ اسلیے ہے کہ

مسلمانوں سے اتحاد قائم رہے۔آپکا دیرینہ غلام اشاعت اسلام کی ہمیشہ کوشش کرتا رہتا ہے۔اب حضور کی ناراضگی مہربانی سے مبدل ہوجانی چاہیے۔حضور کی عنایتوں کا متمنی ہوں پہلے کی طرح نظر عنایت سے شاد کام کیجیے اوراغیار کی غلط بیانی اور دروغگوئی پر اعتبار نہ فرمایا جائے

هم جلیسوں ہمیشہ ہوشیار رہنا چاہیے

کیونکہ پانی اگرچہ بظاہر شفاف ہے مگر آئینہ کا دشمن ہے

حضور کی شفقتوں سے امید ہے کہ ان لوگوں کوملازمان سلطنت کے ذریعہ گرفتار کرا کر میرے سپرد فرمادیں گے تا کہ ان کی حرامزدگی کا خاتمہ کردیا جائے اور حضور خفگی کا غبار دل سے دور کردیں۔ایسا کرنے سے میں اپنے نقصانات کا معاوضہ لے سکوں گا جیسا کہ تخمینہ ایک لاکھ روپیہ ہے۔لارڈ صاحب بہادر کورستم علی قرولی نے درخواست دی ہے کہ گینڈہ اور دیگر گیارہ اشخاص دوگاڑی گندم دہلی لئے آرہے تھے۔جنہیں راجہ کے تھانیدار نے چھین کر بلب گڈھ روانہ کردیا ہے۔جہاں پناہ گاڑیاں خالی کرالی گئیں۔میں ایماناً کہتا ہوں کہ مدعیوں کا الزام جھوٹا ہےاور ذرا بھی سچ نہیں ہے۔اس کی حقیقت بلا مبالغہ یہ ہے کہ گینڈہ جو بدمعاشوں کا سرغنہ ہے اپنے گاؤں کے چند لٹیروں کو ہمراہ لے کر موضع نگلی پر آپڑا جو بدرپور کی حد میں ہے اور بہت سامان لوٹ کر لے گیا۔یہ لوگ لوٹ مار پر تلے ہوئے تھے، چنانچہ پھر مگرولی علاقہ بلب گڈھ میں بھی ڈکیتی کی، اتفاقاً مالگذاری افسران فرید آباد کا دورہ کرتے ہوئے مگردلی کی سرحد میں پہونچے اور جو کچھ ہورہا تھا اسے دیکھا، ان دغابازوں نے اپنی

جان بچانے کی بہت کوشش کی اور چند فرار بھی ہو گئے تاہم مالگذار افسروں نے چند لٹیروں کو گرفتار کرلیا۔ اور ہتھکڑی ڈال کر ریاست کی عدالت فوجداری میں پیش کیا اس مقدمہ کی مسل اور کاغذات عنقریب روانہ کر دیے جائیں گے اگر ارشاد ہو تو مقدمہ مذکورہ کے تمام کاغذات کاروائی اعلیٰ حضرت کی واقفیت و آگاہی کے لیے روانہ کیے جائیں۔ بگھی اور نبی بخش تاجر کے مقدمہ کی روئداد بھی اسی قسم کی ہے۔ خلاصہ یہ ہے کہ برہمن صوبہ دار گیارھویں پیدل نے بگھی خرید کی اور نبی بخش تاجر اس میں بیٹھ کر بلب گڈھ آرہا تھا بگھی میں ایک یا دو انگریزی خطوط پڑے ہوئے ملے۔ اور میں خدا کی قسم کھا کر کہتا ہوں کہ میں یا میرے ملازم بالکل نہیں جانتے کہ کیا معاملہ ہے، کس نے لکھا، کیا لکھا، اور کہاں سے آئے؟ اس سے تو یہ ظاہر ہوتا ہے کہ اس ریاست کے کسی دشمن نے جو انگریزوں سے ملا ہوگا یہ چٹھیاں لکھی ہوں گی اور بگھی میں پوشیدہ کر دی ہونگی۔ اور اس معاملہ کو حضور، مولانا محمد شاہ نظام الدین سے معلوم کر سکتے ہیں۔ امیدوار ہوں کہ جواب سے سرفرازی بخشی جائے ترقی اقبال کی دعائیں۔ عریضہ غلام راجہ ناہر سنگھ بہادر والی بلب گڈھ۔ ''مہر راجہ ناہر سنگھ''

....

(145)

بحضور مورخہ ۵/اگست ۱۸۵۷ء

حضور بادشاہ، جہاں پناہ!

مودبانہ التماس ہے کہ سعادتمندی اور خوش نصیبی ان لوگوں کا حصہ ہے جو اعلیٰ حضرت

کی خدمت میں حاضر رہا کرتے ہیں۔ اگرچہ مجھے یہ خوش نصیبی حاصل نہیں، اور فی الواقع بہت دور پڑا ہوں لیکن صدہا قسموں اور ہزار ہا دلی اقراروں سے میں اظہار کرتا ہوں کہ مجھے ہمیشہ یہی محسوس ہوتا ہے کہ گویا حضور کے تخت شاہی کے روبرو کھڑا ہوں۔ نہایت عاجزی اور ادب سے میں آٹھ مہریں سناہری پیش کرتا ہوں جو عید کا تحفہ ہے اور یقین کرتا ہوں کہ اس تحفہ ناچیز کو قبول فرمایا جائے گا۔ ترقی سلطنت کے لیے دعائیں اور اس کے دشمنوں کے لیے بددیا

حضور کے لیے	۵ سناہریں مہریں
ملکہ کے لیے	۲ سناہری مہریں
شہزادہ مرزا جواں بخت کے لیے	۱ سناہری مہر

عریضہ کمترین راجہ ناہر سنگھ بہادر والی بلب گڈھ

مہر۔ ''راجہ ناہر سنگھ بہادر''

....

(146)

حکم شاہی بغیر مہر و دستخط کے

مورخہ ۸/اگست ۱۸۵۷ء

بنام راجہ ناہر سنگھ

تمہاری درخواست مع آٹھ طلائی مہروں کے وصول ہوئی اور تمہاری خیر خواہی پر مابدولت کو اعتماد رکھنے کا موجب ہوئی۔ چونکہ تم ہمارے خادم خاص ہو، پس ایمانداری اور وفا شعاری سے کبھی غفلت نہ کرنا۔ ہماری مہربانیوں کا یقین رکھو۔

ہمارے لیے۔۔۔۔۵مہریں ملکہ کے لیے۔۔۔۲مہریں

مرزا جواں بخت کے لیے۔۔۔۔۔۔۔۔۔۔۔۔۔۔۔۔امہر

....

(147)

مورخہ ۱۴راگست ۱۸۵۷ء

بحضور بادشاہ ظل اللہ! وغیرہ

مودبانہ گزارش ہے کہ تحفۂ عید کی قبولیت کا مراسلہ پہونچا اور سرفراز فرمایا، میں نے خود کو حضور کی مہربانیوں سے گھرا دیکھ کر بہت صاحب قسمت پایا، لیکن کون سے قلم سے اور کس زبان سے حضور کی توصیف کروں اور شکر ادا کروں؟ مگر یہ دیکھ کر کہ ہنوز بدظنی کا غبار حضور کے دل سے دور نہیں ہوا۔ خداوندا! مجھے عرض کرنے دیجیے کہ میں دیرینہ وفادار اور خیر خواہ ہوں اور میں دل سے اور جان سے حضور کے احکام بجالانا فخر سمجھتا ہوں جیسا حضور پر خود روشن ہے۔ کوئی روز ایسا نہیں جاتا کہ میں حضور کی مہربانیوں کو دل سے بھلا دیتا ہوں، کوئی گھڑی ایسی نہیں گزرتی کہ میں حضور کی شفقتوں کو یاد نہ کرتا ہوں۔ ہر طرح سے مجھے اپنا کمترین غلام سمجھیے اور مجھ پر نظر الطاف ڈالیے کیونکہ میرے اجداد پر بھی حضور کی مربیانہ

شفقتیں مبذول ہوتی رہی ہیں۔ کمترین بھی ان ہی کی اولاد ہے۔ گذشتہ مراحم واحسانات پر نظر کر کے یقین کرتا ہوں کہ ناراضگی کی کدورت آئینہ دل سے دور ہو جائیگی جسے میرے رقیبوں نے حضور کے منور آفتاب نما قلب پر پیوست کر دیا ہے۔ دیگر عرض یہ ہے کہ میں خدمت عالی میں حاضر دربار نہ ہوسکا مگر اب حاضری کا حکم دیا جائے تا کہ میں خدمت عالی میں حاضر ہوں اور ویسا ہی حکم سواروں کے رسالدار کے لیے بھی ملنا چاہیے۔ میں یہ بھی عرض کرتا ہوں کہ مجھے نقارے اور علم عطا کیے جائیں تا کہ حضور کی رفعت وشان چاروں کھونٹوں میں مشتہر کی جائے اور ہفت اقلیم میں حضور کی کشور کشائی کے ساتھ ہی ساتھ جان نثار کا نام بھی سب لوگوں پر روشن ہو جائے۔ حضور کی زیارت کا بہت مشتاق ہوں لیکن بدنصیبی سے دہلی چھوڑنے کے بعد سے اب تک ایسے واقعات پیش آتے رہے کہ جن کے سبب پورا بندوبست نہ ہوسکا۔ حضور کی فتح وفیروزی کے علم سربلند ہوں اور دشمنوں کو ذلت ورسوائی نصیب ہو۔

درخواست فدوی راجہ ناہر سنگھ بہادر والی ریاست بلب گڈھ

مہر۔ ''راجہ ناہر سنگھ''

....

(148)

بنام — مورخہ ۱۶/اگست ۱۸۵۷ء

ملازم خاص نشانِ سعادت راجہ ناہر سنگھ والی بلب گڈھ

خود کو معزز کیا گیا۔ سمجھو بارہا زبانی گفتگو کا موقع پڑ جاتا ہے اور ہمارے وفادار مقربوں میں سے کسی کی ضرورت پڑتی ہے پس یہ بہت ضروری ہے کہ تم اپنا کوئی معتمد ایجنٹ دربار میں متعین کرو تا کہ زبانی گفتگو میں دشواری نہ ہو۔ ہر طرح مطمئن رہو اور ایجنٹ کے قائم کرنے میں دیر نہ کرو۔ اور خود کو سرفراز کیا گیا سمجھو۔

....

(149)

بحضور مورخہ ۲۲/اگست ۱۸۵۷ء

ادب سے عرض ہے کہ حضور پر بخوبی روشن ہے کہ خانہ زاد پشتہا پشت سے وفادار چلا آتا ہے اور میں اور میرے باپ داداؤں نے کبھی حضور کے حکم سے سرتابی نہیں کی، پس میں چاہتا ہوں کہ حضور کے دربار میں باریاب کیا جاؤں۔ میرے دعویٰ کی تائید میں جو ثبوت کیا جاسکتا ہے وہ یہ ہے کہ اگر مجھے حضور سے ارادت خاص نہ ہوتی اور وفاداری کا خیال نہ ہوتا تو دہلی میں انگریزی سلطنت کے زمانہ مین میر فتح علی کی معرفت حضور کی خدمت میں حاضر رہنے کی تمنا ظاہر کرتا۔ اور جب میں نے ایسا کیا تو اعلیٰ حضرت میرے دلی خلوص اور ایمانداری سے بہت خوش ہوئے تھے۔ لیکن سیاسی مصالح کے سبب چونکہ میرا حضور کے پاس رہنا اس زمانہ میں مناسب نہ تھا، آپ نے منع کر دیا، غلام کو ایسی بدنصیبی نے گھیرا ہے کہ اب تک دربار شاہی میں حاضر نہ ہو سکا اور اسکی دو وجوہات ہیں ایک تو یہ کہ جب سے دہلی سے آیا ہوں آئے دن جسمانی بیماریوں کا شکار بنا رہتا ہوں، دوسرے یہ کہ حضور کے لطف وکرم کو

دیکھ کر وہاں حاسد پیدا ہو گئے ہیں اور ڈر ہے کہ انہوں نے میری طرف سے حضور کے مزاج کو مکدر نہ کر دیا ہو اور وہ کوئی ایسی چال نہ چلیں اور ایسی تدبیر نہ کر گزریں جس سے مجھے دہلی آ کر ذلت و رسوائی اٹھانی پڑے۔ یا ان کی دروغگوئی کے تیل سے حضور کی آتش غضب زیادہ نہ بھڑک جائے۔ علاوہ ازیں یہ بھی سنا گیا ہے کہ سلطنت کے ملازمان اور افسران ، روپیہ کے بہت طامع ہو گئے ہیں اور مجھ سے بھی ایک کثیر رقم طلب کرتے ہیں حالانکہ میری آمدنی بالکل قلیل ہے۔ حضور عالی جو اپنے غلاموں کے تمام حالات سے باخبر رہتے ہیں، غلام کے علاقہ کو دیگر ریاستوں سے مقابلہ کر کے دیکھ سکتے ہیں کہ یہ سب سے چھوٹی ریاست ہے اور اسکی آمدنی اتنی بھی نہیں ہے جس سے ریاست ہی کے اخراجات پورے ہو سکیں۔ برخلاف اسکے ہمیشہ سے ہزار ہا روپیہ کی مقروض چلی آتی ہے۔ کمترین کے اجداد نے جو کچھ جمع کیا تھا اسکی بابت عرض ہے کہ میرے سابق افسروں نے فریب و دغا سے وہ سب خرد برد کر لیا اور فرار ہو گئے اور میرے معمور خزانے اور بھرے گھر کو خالی کر کے روپیہ اور مال سے اپنے گھر بھر لیے۔ اور اب دہلی میں بیٹھے میری ریاست کے خلاف منصوبے گانٹھنے اور سازشیں کرتے ہیں۔ ایسی حالت میں تاجدار کیونکر اتنا روپیہ تقسیم کر سکتا ہے اور مصارف فوج کو کس طرح برداشت کر سکتا ہے۔ البتہ اگر حضور کے صلاح کار اور شاہی افسران میرے دغاباز افسروں کو جو تا حال دہلی میں موجود ہیں گرفتار کر کے میرے سپرد کر دیں گے تو میں کچھ وصول کر سکوں گا اس کا نصف خزانۂ شاہی میں داخل کر دوں گا۔ اور اگر ان کا ماخوذ کیا جانا نامناسب خیال کیا جائے تو حضور کے ملازمین بموجب فہرست ذیل خود ہی وصول کر لیں

اور اس میں سے وہ جتنا مناسب سمجھیں خزانہ میں داخل کر دیں، بقیہ مجھے واپس کر دیں۔ نشانِ شرافت و عظمت میر فتح علی نے یہاں آنے کی تکلیف گورا فرمائی اور مجھے نہایت ممنون و مشکور کیا۔ انہوں نے میرے معاملات سے نہایت ہمدردی اور پدرانہ شفقت ظاہر کی۔ تمام زبانی احکام جو میر فتح علی کی معرفت فرما گئے تھے مجھے لفظ بہ لفظ پہونچ گئے اور جوابات قابل تحریر نہیں تھے لہذا میر فتح علی صاحب ہی سے حضور کو معلوم ہو جائیں گے۔ دیگر عرض ہے کہ وہ جو کچھ میرے طرف سے کہیں گے وہ مجھے منظور ہے کیونکہ ان کے مجھ سے دیرینہ تعلقات ہیں۔ بغرض اطلاع واجب تھا عرض کیا۔ حضور کے غلاموں کو فتح و فیروزی نصیب ہو اور اعدا کو ہمیشہ ذلت و رسوائی ملے۔ حسب ذیل لوگوں کے ذمہ میری رقمیں ہیں:۔

حکیم عبدالحق جو وزیر اعظم ریاست ہذا کا تھا	دس لاکھ روپیہ
مکتا پرشاد وکیل	پندرہ ہزار روپیہ
راجہ لال صاحب چیف سکریٹری	دس ہزار روپیہ
نثار علی نائب وزیر اعظم	دس ہزار روپیہ
جوالا ناتھ پنڈت خزانچی	تیس ہزار روپیہ
شیر خاں حکیم مذکور کا ذاتی دوست	پچیس ہزار روپیہ
حصار الدین جمعدار اور میری دہلی کی جائداد اور زمین کا داروغہ جو میرے وکیل کا مددگار بھی رہا تھا	پانچ ہزار روپیہ

امیر علی داروغہ محلات وتوشہ خانہ	دس ہزار روپیہ
سعادت علی خان تھانہ دار	آٹھ ہزار روپیہ
احمد مرزا کاشتکار مواضع بلب گڈھ اور میرے انگوری باغ کا	دس ہزار روپیہ
مبارک علی خان	دو ہزار روپیہ

عریضہ غلام راجہ ناہر سنگھ بہادر

مہر- ''راجہ ناہر سنگھ بہادر''

....

(150)

بحضور　　　　　　　　　　　　مورخہ ۲ر ستمبر ۱۸۵۷ء

بادشاہ ظل اللہ وغیرہ وغیرہ،

نہایت ادب سے عرض پرداز ہوں کہ حضور کے مراسلہ نے شرف بخشا اور اس سے آگاہی ہوئی کہ حضور نے گھوڑا قبول فرمایا اور تسلی دی کہ ریاست بلب گڈھ کے خلاف کوئی فوجی شخص کسی قسم کی کاروائی نہیں کرسکتا۔ زبان وقلم حضور کی تعریف وشکر گزاری سے قاصر ہیں خدا تا قیام قیامت حضور کو زندہ رکھے! ظل اللہ سبحانی! یہ ایک تعجب خیز امر ہے کہ حضور نے تو حکم دیا ہے کہ کوئی شخص بلب گڈھ ریاست کے برخلاف کاروائی یا ظلم وزیادتی نہ کرسکے گا، مگر ۲ر ستمبر ۱۸۵۷ء کو محمد بخت خان کمانڈر انچیف افواج کا ایک خط موصول ہوا ہے جس میں لکھا ہے کہ تمام دیہاتی قیدیوں کو رہا کر دیا گیا ہے، صرف ہردیو بخش، پران سکھ، دھوسر

،اور جماعت خان پاسقل ،ہنوز مقید ہیں ۔اور مجھے ہدایت کی ہے دوسرے قیدیوں کی دستاویزیں اور رسیدیں بخت خاں کو روانہ کر دیں ۔حضور پر بخوبی روشن ہے کہ یہ لوگ اس ریاست کے نمکحرام اور قابل باز پرس ہیں ،کیونکہ لاکھوں روپیہ ہضم کر چکے ہیں ۔اور روپیہ واپس دینے پر رضامند بھی ہو چکے تھے ۔جس کا ان سے حساب طلب کیا گیا تھا پس جو لوگ ایسے ذمہ دار ہوں انہیں کیونکر رہا کیا جا سکتا ہے ۔اگر انہیں رہا کیا گیا تو غلام کو بہت بھاری نقصان برداشت کرنا پڑے گا ۔نیز ان کے چھوڑ دینے سے لاانتہا برائیاں پھیلیں گی اور میرا انتظام درہم برہم ہو جائے گا اور پھر اس کا قائم کرنا سخت مشکل ہو گا ان معاملات کی وجہ سے میں نہایت عاجزی سے عرض کرتا ہوں کہ ایک حکم بنام کمانڈر انچیف جاری کیا جائے کہ جن ملزموں کا تعلق ریاست بلب گڈھ سے ہو ۔انہیں وہاں بھیج دیا جائے بہمہ وجوہ ایسی کاروائیاں بنیاد سلطنت کو کھودنے والی ہیں ۔پس عرض ہے کہ میری درخواست منظور فرما کر احکام جاری کیے جائیں ۔خادم خیر خواہ قدیم ہے اور حضور کی سلطنت کا ادنیٰ غلام ہے ۔زمین و آسمان میں اس کے لیے صرف یہی ایک پناہ گاہ ہے میں یہ بھی عرض کرتا ہوں کہ حکیم عبدالحق و پنڈت جوالا پرشاد وغیرہ کو بھی گرفتار کر کے میرے سپرد کر دیا جائے کیونکہ اس پر تقریباً گیارہ لاکھ پچیس ہزار روپیہ کا میرا دعویٰ ہے تا کہ میں ان سے وصول کر سکوں ۔(ترقی اقبال سلطانی کی دعائیں) کمانڈر انچیف کا اصلی خط بھی ارسال ہے براہ عنایت پڑھ کر جواب کے ہمراہ واپس کر دیا جائے ۔عریضہ خادم راجہ ناہر سنگھ بہادر۔ مہر ۔'' راجہ ناہر سنگھ بہادر''

کاغذات متعلق سرکشی ہندوستان No.22 یونیورسٹی کلکشن، مولانا آزاد لائبریری، علی گڑھ مسلم یونیورسٹی، علی گڑھ کاغذات متعلقہ سرکشان ہندوستان گذرانیدہ ازطرف گورنر جنرل روبرو ہر دو دوانین پارلیمنٹ حسب الحکم قیصرہ ہند ملکہ وکٹوریہ ۱۸۵۷ء۔ ان کی نقول سرسید احمد خاں نے تیار کرائی تھیں۔

دیگر کاغذات متعلقہ سرکشان ہندوستان۔ ان دستاویزات کی نقول سرسید احمد خاں نے اپنی کتاب کی تصنیف کے لیے جمع کی تھیں۔

P-1 ازطرف گورنر جنرل ہندوستان باجلاس کونسل بنام مجلس ہادیان ایسٹ انڈیا کمپنی ازمقام فورٹ ولیم مورخہ ۱۹ جون ۱۸۵۷ء (نمبر ۱۸۲) ہم واسطے تمہاری آگاہی کے احوال جاری ماندہ اون معاملات متعلقہ بدگمانی افتادہ درمیان فوج ہندوستانی کا جو مقامات اس پر لیسیڈنسی یعنی احاطہ میں پیش آئے میں اب ترسیل کرتی ہیں اور جو احوال مذکورہ بذریعہ خط و کتابت اور تاربرقی کے حصول ہوا تھا، اور ہماری علیحدہ چٹھی نمبر ۱۷۶ مورخہ پانچویں بایں حال میں تمکو روانہ کیا گیا تھا وہ حصول شدہ بہت قلیل ہے کس لیے کہ چٹھی باین حالسے ڈاکن الہ آباد سے آگئی بالکل کٹ گئی ہیں۔

الہ آباد:۔ چھٹے پلٹن ہندوستانی پیدل نے چھٹی ماہ حال بوقت شام نو گھنٹہ بجے سرکشی اختیار کی تین رسالہ سواران نے ترتیب متعلقہ فوج اودھ اور باشندہ شہر ہذا اس میں شریک

ہوئے۔ تیرہ افسران ولایتی کے قتل کیے جانے کی رپورٹ کی گئی ہے۔

آگرہ:۔ مقام ہذا میں تاریخ دسویں ماہ حال تک بالکل امن وامان معلوم ہوتا ہے۔

علی گڑھ:۔ سرکشان لکھنو وآب سے گذر کر علی گڑھ میں نمود ہوئی تب فریق والن ٹیر یعنی سپاہیاں بلاقید با نجیب بعد تھوری عرصہ کے تاریخ آٹھویں ماہ حال کو ترک مقام اختیار کرنے کو مجبور ہوئی۔

اعظم گڈھ:۔ وہ صرف افسر جو مقام ہذا میں مارا گیا چن سن کنواز نر ماسٹر رجمنٹ سترہ ہندوستانی پیدل کا ہے جس نے بقصد محفوظ کرنے توپوں مقام ہذا کی جان کھوئی افسران اور میم لوگ داخل غازی پور ہوگئی تھی۔

بریلی:۔ مقام زہذا سے کوئی خبر نہیں پائی ہے۔

بنارس:۔ پلٹن میں تیسویں ہندوستانی پیدل نے بغاوت کی لیکن اسکی چھاونیوں کو پھونک دیا گیا۔ بعض لوگ سکھوں میں سے وفادار رہے۔

بہرام پور:۔ یہاں چین چان ہے

کان پور:۔ چوتھی تاریخ ماہ حال سے مقام ہذا کے بارے میں کوئی خبر نہیں پائی ہے۔

چنار:۔ یہاں سب طرح امن وامان ہے۔

P4

دہلی:۔ اکتیسویں کی ایک جنگ دیگر قریب ہنڈن کے واقع ہوئی برگڈ برونس کی فوج باعانت پلٹن گورکھا اور معہ چند امداد میرٹھ کے قطار ہای فوج انبالہ عین جو باغپت کی کھات

سے دہلی کو اوتری گی بتاریخ پانچویں ماہ حال کو شامل ہونے والی تھی فوج مذکورہ آٹھویں تاریخ کو دہلی پر پہونچی اور باغیوں کو شکست دیکر شہر میں بھگا دیا اور مقامات بلند پر جو دہلی کے سامنے ہیں معہ چھبیس توپوں کے قبضہ حاصل کیا۔

دیناپور:۔ یہاں پندرھویں تاریخ تک سب طرح خیریت رہی۔

ڈاکا:۔ ایک سو ملاح واسطے کشتیاں جنگ کے معہ دو کشتیوں مسلح کے مقام ہذا کو بطور تجویز پیش نہیں کی روانہ کی گئیں ہیں۔ فقط

گیا:۔ ایک فریق ایک سو بیس سپاہیان ولایتی کا برای حفاظت خزانہ کے مقام ہذا کو روانہ کیا گیا۔

ھانسی وحصار:۔ سنتے ہیں کہ پلٹن ہریانہ نے سرکشی اختیار کی۔

جان پور:۔ فریق سکھان مقام ہذا بروقت سرکشان بنارس کے مقام ہذا میں پہونچنے کے اپنی افسر لفٹینینٹ یارا اور دیگر ولایتیوں کو قتل کیا اور خزانہ پر قابض ہوئے اور بہ سمت وہ فیض آباد کو راہی ہوئے ایک مجمدار کو سکھان مذکور میں سے کمان پر مقرر کیا گیا۔ فقط

جھانسی:۔ سپاہ جو رجمینٹ بارھویں ہندوستانی پیدل کا ایک پہلو اور چند سواران رسالہ بے ترتیب بھی باغی ہوئے احوال بغاوت مذکور سے واقفیت نہیں حاصل ہوئی۔

لکھنو:۔ مقام ہذا کے بارے میں چوتھی تاریخ ماہ حال سے کچھ سننے میں نہیں آیا ہے۔

مرزاپور:۔ مقام ہذا میں سب طرح امن سے خزانہ یہاں سے منتقل کر دیا گیا ہے راجہ ریوانی چھ سو سوار یا پانچ سو پیدل اور پانچ سو توپیں نذر گذرانی ہیں اور وہ مقبول ہوئی ہیں۔

نوگونگ :۔ پہلو بارہویں رجمنٹ ہندوستانی پیدل کا اور ہندوستانی توپ خانہ سرکش ہوا احوال مقدمہ مذکور سے آگاہی نہیں پائی ؟

نیمچ :۔ مقام ہذا اور رسالہ سواران حصہ مالوہ کے سرکش ہوجانے کی رپورٹ کی گئی ہے فوج پیادہ متعلقہ حصہ مالوہ وارد مہدی پور کا راست باز رہنا سنا گیا ہے۔

P5

فوج ولایتی جتنا جلد کہ ممکن ہے آگے کو چلنا کی جاتی ہے تمام پلٹن ولاتیاں مدراس کو چاہیے کہ اب الہ آباد میں پہونچ گئی ہو اور پلٹن چوارسی اور تتر ایک حصہ پلٹن چونسٹھ کا بنارس سے آگے پہونچ گیا ہے آخر لوگ اٹھہتر ۷۸ پلٹن ولایتی کی بذریعہ کرانچی کل روانہ ہونگی اور پلٹن بیسوں بعد روانہ ہوئی حصہ پلٹن سنیتیسویں کے روانہ کی جائے گی ایک توپ خانہ ولایتی بذریعہ کشتی دخانی آج صبح کو روانہ ہوا ہے اور دوسرا ابھی اوسی مطلب کے لیے تیار ہو رہی فریق توپ خانہ شاہی کا بھی بذریعہ کراچی روانہ کیا جائے گا۔

الراقم

کرنیل برج

سکریٹری گورنمنٹ ہندوستان

....

P6 راجہ پٹیالہ اور راجہ جھنڈ اور دیگر نے بڑی اعانت دی ہے۔

P8 مقالہ انبالہ میں بھی واردات واقع ہوئی ہے۔

الراقم کرنیل چپسٹر

....

P9 مورخہ دسویں مئی ۱۸۵۷ء (بذریعہ تار برقی)

فوج ہندوستانی نے سرکشی علانیہ اختیار کی ہے چھاونی واقعہ جانب جنوب نالہ جلائی گئی ہے بہت سے افسران ولایتی مارے گئے ہیں فوج ولایتی نے سامرگ کو محفوظ کر رکھا ہے۔

الراقم میجر وانز فیلڈ

پیغام ہذا کو سرداروں اور گورنمنٹ اور تمام مقامات کی اطلاع میں گذرانوں تار برقی کاٹ ڈالا گیا ہے۔

P9 پیغام دوسرا

مرسلہ برگڈیر کمانیر دہلی مورخہ گیارھویں مئی ۱۸۵۷ء بوقت چار گھنٹہ بجے شام کے چھاونی محاصر میں ہے سرکشان میرٹھ متعلقہ تیسر رسالہ نے جن کا شمار نا معلوم ہے اور جن کو ایک سو پچاس مشہور کر رہے ہیں خط و کتابت میرٹھ کو قطع کیا ہے اور کشتیوں کے پل پر قابض ہو گئے ہیں چون ویں پلٹن ہندوستانی پیدل اونکی بر خلاف بھیجی گئی ہے مگر اونکی مقابلہ میں انکار پذیر ہے بہت افسران مقتول اور مجروح ہوئے شہر میں بڑی ترغیب پھیل گئی ہے فوج شہر میں بھیجی گئی ہے مگر ابھی کچھ تحقیق نہیں ہے اطلاع آئندہ بھیجی جائے گی۔

....

پیغام ہذا جو دہلی سے ابھی ورود ہوا ہے بذریعہ افسران تار برقی کے ہمارے پاس بھیجا گیا ہے ہمیں چاہیے کہ دفتر کو ترک کریں تمام بنگلہ سپاہیاں میرٹھ جلا رہے ہیں وہ آج صبح کو داخل ہوئے ہم بھاگ نکلے ہیں میں خیال کرتا ہوں کہ ٹوڈ صاحب مر گئے وہ صبح کو باہر نکلے تھے اور اب تک واپس نہیں آئے ہیں ہم نے سنا ہے کہ نہ ولایتی مارے گئے۔ خدا حافظ

میں نقل پیغام ہذا کی چیف کمشنر پنجاب کو بھی ترسیل کی ہے۔ فقط

الراقم

بارنرد میجر جنرل

تیرھویں تاریخ کو مین نے دہلی ہنگامہ کی خبر سن کر میجر مارس دن سے کہا کہ تم اضلاع سکھان قریب اور جنرل کوٹ لینڈ سے جو پہلی ملازم دربار لاہور تھا اور اب خدمت ملکی پر سے یہ اعانت طلب کرو کہ وی اسقدر پٹھانوں اور سکھوں کو جس قدر کہ تم اونمیں وفادار سمجھو داخل کریں۔

الراقم جیمس برگڈیر

بعد ازآں سرکشان مذکور نے قریباً تمام بنگلوں کو جو نالہ کی جنوب میں تھی معہ بنگلہ گریڈ صاحب کمشنر اور میری بنگلہ اور معہ سرکاری احاطہ مویشیاں اور کمسریٹ والہ صاحب کے مکان اور دفتر کو جلا دیا۔ افعال مذکورہ میں خلقت شہر اور بازار اور دیہات قریب کے اونکی مددگار ہوئی ہر مرد و عورت اور بچہ ولایتی جو اونکی سامنے پڑا سنگ دلی سے مقتول ہوا۔ وہ لوگ جو میرٹھ میں کام آئے حسب ذیل ہیں۔ کرنیل فنس گیارھویں پلٹن ہندوستانی پیدل، کپتان ٹیلر

کپتان میک ڈونلڈ بیسویں پلٹن ہندوستانی پیدل معہ جورو اور تین بچوں اور کارنٹ میک

ناب صاحب ڈاکٹر ان فلپس اور ڈولسن صاحب معہ جورو فقط

مجھے یقین ہے کہ سپاہیان سرکش اوس عرصہ میں دہلی اور علی گڑھ کی سڑکوں کو راہی ہوگئی تھی۔

الراقم ہیوٹ میجر جنرل کمانیر

۱۳ مئی ۱۸۵۷ء بوقت صبح روز پیر۔۔۔ چوون پلٹن پیدل ہندوستانی مسمی حسب ذیل غارنی میں آئی لفٹنٹ کرنیل ریب نے بہت مجروح ہوئے کپتان سمت مارا گیا اور کپتان برولیس مارا گیا اور لفٹنٹ ایڈورڈس مارا گیا اور لفٹنٹ واٹرفیلڈ مارا گیا اور لفٹنٹ بٹ زخمی ہوا۔

اگر اڑتیسویں پلٹن کے آدمی پہرہ کشمیری دروازہ پر نہ ہوتی تو نتیجہ مختلف پید ہوتی اور مرد مان چواٹھرویں رجمنٹ کے ہر آدمی کی سے اوس مقام پر حملہ اور نہ ہوتا مار دیتے۔ ڈاکخانہ اور تار برقی اور بنک اور چھاپہ خانہ دہلی اور ہر ایک مکان چھاونی برباد کردی گئی۔

الراقم میجر ایبٹ کی نیر جو

سترویں رجمنٹ ہندوستانی پیدل

انبالہ۔ کوئی مغل بر ملا سرکشی نہیں سرزد ہوا

لودھیانہ۔ یہاں کوئی بات قابل شہرت واقع نہیں ہوئی

ہوشیار پور۔ مقام ہذا کے باب میں کچھ رپورٹ نہیں کیا گیا۔

جلندر۔ مزاج تمام فوج ہندوستانی کا شکر آمیز ہے۔

گووند گڑھ۔ کوئی فوج بدگمانی فوج کی نہیں پائی۔

لاھور۔ فوج ہندوستانی خاموش پذیر ہے۔

ملتان۔ فوج ہندوستانی کے اہل چلن ہونے کی رپورٹ کی گئی ہے۔

باقی معاملات پنجاب ظاہراً بالکل امن ہے

الراقم کرنیل چیسٹر اجٹسن جنرل فوج

من تھام انبالہ مورخہ ۱۹ر مئی ۱۸۵۷ء

ملفوفہ ہفتہ ہم

از طرف میجر ہوٹ سکریٹری گورنمنٹ ہندوستانی من تھام میرٹھ مورخہ ۲۶ مئی ۱۸۵۷ء

تمام خط و کتابت نے ایک مقامات نیمی کی جانب میں مسدود ہوئی اور باغیان بلند شہر اور علی گڑھ نے تار برقی کاٹ ڈالی۔

اخبار زمانہ حال دہلی یہ ہیں کہ سرکشان دو حصوں یعنی مسلمان اور ہندو میں منقسم ہوئی اور جن کی آپس میں جھڑپ ہوئی اور خون بٹیا گیا۔

نوین رجمنٹ پیدل ہندوستانی معہ خزانہ بلند شہر اور علی گڑہ کے شریک سرکشاں ہوئی۔

الراقم کرنیل برج

....

ملفوفہ بست و ہشتم

ازطرف خواجہ عبدالغنی زمیندار بنام سکریٹری گورنمنٹ ہندوستانی من مقام ڈھاکہ مورخہ پہلی جون ۱۸۵۷ء چونکہ میں مسلمان زمینداروں مقام ہذااور اضلاع قریب میں سے ایک بڑازمیندار ہوں۔۔۔ مجھے یقین ہے کہ کوئی خوف بلحاظ کسی فساد مقام ہذایا کسی اضلاع دیگر میں پیدانہ ہوگا۔

الراقم عبدالغنی

ملفوفہ سی و یکم۔ازطرف میجر جنرل بنام سکریٹری گونمنٹ ہندوستانی من تھام بارکپور مورخہ ۴ جون ۱۸۵۷ء میں اس بات کے باب میں سفارش کامل کرنے کے لیے یہ موقع اختیار کرتا ہوں کہ مدرسہ قواعد بندوقان ڈم ڈم مذکورہ فی الفورتوڑ دیا جائے چنانچہ مقرر یافتہ عرصہ تعلیم عنقریب پوراہوگیا ہے۔

الراقم ترسی میجر جنرل کمانیر
قسمت فوج احاطہ بنگال

....

ملفوفہ سی دسیوم۔ازطرف میجر کلارک بنام اسٹنٹ امٹسٹ جنرل قسمت فوج احاطہ من تھام فورٹ ولیم مورخہ یکم جون ۱۸۵۷ء

مسمی لفٹنٹ باگنال حسینی مدرسہ قواعد بندوقان ہانیہ میں معلّمی حاصل کرنے کے لیے امتحان دیا ہے تھوری عرصہ میں انگلستان سے واپس آکر پلٹن مذکورہ میں شامل ہوگا۔فقط

الراقم میجر کلارک کمانیرہ

ملفوفہ سی ونہم۔

ازطرف سکریٹری گورنمنٹ ہندوستان بنام کمشنر بنارس من مقام فورٹ ولیم مورخہ

دسویں جون ۱۸۵۷ء

راجہ ریوا نے نے اپنی فوج نظر کی ہے اور وہ مقبول نظر ہوئی ہے

الراقم کرنیل برج

ملفوفہ یک صدو چہلم۔ یکم جون ۱۸۵۷ء

ہم لوگ بھی اب عرض گزار ہیں کہ ہمارے نام بھی نیک اور معتبر سپاہیان سلطنت

سرکار میں شمار کیے جائیں۔

اسماء دستخط کنندگان۔

درگا پرشاد　　　　　میر سلطان علی حولدار

کل ۱۶ نام ہیں۔

مورخہ ساتویں فروری ۱۸۵۷ء

ملفوفہ کاغذ نمبر دوئم کا

یادداشت درباب چٹھی محکمہ جن کی از مقام فورٹ ولیم مورخہ ساتویں فروری ۱۸۵۷ء

نمبر ۴۶ چٹھیات سے جو سکریٹری ہی ہیں کپتان بوکسر سپرنڈنٹ شاہی کارخانہ مقام ولوج کو

جہاں کہ میگزین تمام چھوٹے آلات کا واسطے عرض ملکہ معظّمہ کے تیار کیا جاتا ہے میں

دریافت کرتا ہوں کہ چکنای کارخانہ مذکورہ کی جو تیار کرتے ہیں اون کارتوسوں کی مستعمل

ہے جو ہندوستان کو روانہ کی جاتی ہیں ان چیزوں کی بنی ہوئی ہے۔

۵ حصہ چربی پگھلی ہوئی ۵ حصہ سڑابن یعنی وہ سخت عنصر جو چربی کی اوپر ہوتا

ایک حصہ موم۔

مگر چونکہ یہ لوازمات بہت کثرت سے خریدی گئی ہیں اور ولوح میں رکھدی گئی ہیں اس لیے کپتان لوکسٹر اپنی رائے تحقیق درباب قسم خاص اوس جانور کے جس سے کہ وہ چربی حاصل ہوئی ہے بالکل سری سکھائی مگر صرف تحقیق بات یہ ہے کہ سور کی پگھلی ہوئی چربی کی صورت سے نہیں ملی ہوئی ہے۔

۱۸۵۷ء کے غدّار شعراء

۱۔ داروغہ سید واجد علی لکھنوی سحرؔ ۲۔ خلیفہ محمد حسن پٹیالوی حسنؔ

۳۔ نجم الہند سردار محمد حیات خاں راولینڈی حیاتؔ ۴۔ نواب محمد ابراہیم خاں لکھنوی خلیلؔ

۵۔ میر داور علی مارہروی داورؔ ۶۔ مہاراجہ سروگ بجے سنگھ بلرام پوری راجہؔ

۷۔ نواب محمد کاظم علی خاں رامپوری سروریؔ ۸۔ وجیہ الزماں بجنوری رحیقؔ

۹۔ منشی سید امتیاز علی کاکوری صوفیؔ ۱۰۔ منشی شو پرشاد کشمیری دہلوی مہجورؔ

۱۱۔ رائے پردومن کشن مراد آبادی ہوسؔ ۱۲۔ نواب یوسف علی خاں رامپوری ناظمؔ

۱۳۔ نواب کلب علی خاں رامپوری نوابؔ

مندرجہ بالا فہرست امداد صابری نے اپنی کتاب۔ ۱۸۵۷ء کے غدار شعراء، دہلی ۱۹۶۰ء میں دی ہے۔

امداد صابری لکھتے ہیں کہ ''اس کتاب کو کسی انسان سے نہیں بلکہ سبق دینے والے وفادار جانور ''مولا بخش ہاتھی'' کے نام سے معنون کرتا ہوں۔ یہ ہاتھی اپنے آقا بہادر شاہ ظفر کا اس قدر وفادار تھا کہ جنگ آزادی ۱۸۵۷ء کے بعد اس نے دشمن یا کسی دوسرے کے ساتھ رہنا گوارا نہیں کیا اور اس کا حکم ماننا بھی پسند نہ کیا بلکہ بہادر شاہ کی فرقت میں بھوکوں مرا اور جان دیدی'' صفحہ ۵۔

۱۸۵۷ء کے شہید شعراء

۱۔مرزا آغا خاں دہلوی	۲۔مرزا غلام محی الدین دہلوی اشکی
۳۔مرزا احمد بیگ دہلوی	۴۔شاہزادہ مرزا رحیم الدین ایجاد
۵۔عبد الحکیم دہلوی بسمل	۶۔مرزا عاشور بیگ ثنائی
۷۔حافظ داؤد دہلوی داؤد	۸۔نواب ظفر یار خاں ناسخ
۹۔مولوی فیض احمد بدایونی داؤد	۱۰۔منشی اکرام الدین دہلوی رند
۱۱۔نواب غضنفر حسین خاں فرخ آبادی سعید	۱۲۔مرزا عزیز الدین گورگانوی سرور (داماد بہادر شاہ شوہر آغا بیگم)
۱۳۔مولوی عبد الکریم سوز	۱۴۔مرزا بختاور دہلوی شاکی
۱۵۔مرزا غیاث الدین دہلوی شرر	۱۶۔مرزا قمر الدین دہلوی شیدا
۱۷۔مولانا امام بخش صہبائی دہلوی	۱۸۔کرنل امیر خاں عرف کالے ضبط
۱۹۔نواب شیر علی خاں مراد آبادی عاجز	۲۰۔پیر جی شرف الحق دہلوی عاجز
۲۱۔مرزا عالی بخت عالی	۲۲۔مرزا عباس بیگ بریلوی عباس
۲۳۔خلیفہ محمد اسمٰعیل دہلوی برق	۲۴۔میر جیون علی فیض آبادی قربان

یہ فہرست امداد صابری نے اپنی کتاب میں دی ہے۔

63-65

فارسی واردو کتابیات متعلق ۱۸۵۷ء Bibliography Relating on 1857 in Persian and Urdu Language. to book

۱۔سید کمال الدین حیدر حسینی	قیصر التواریخ
۲۔نجم الغنی رامپوری	اخبار الضادید
۳۔منشی دیبی پرشاد بشاش	تذکرہ شعرائے ہنود
۴۔انوار احمد زبیری	خطبات عالیہ
۵۔خلیفہ محمد حسن پٹیالوی	تاریخ الخلفاء
۶۔جلال الدین سیوطی	تاریخ الخلفاء
۷۔نصرت علی دہلوی	ناصر الاخبار
۸۔عبداللہ عاشق	بہارستان اودھ
۹۔کرنل ساندرس الکس ایبٹ	تاریخ نادر العصر
۱۰۔عبدالغفور نساخ	سخن شعراء
۱۱۔لالہ سری رام دہلوی	خم خانہ جاوید
۱۲۔نیاز احمد خاں	تاریخ روہیل کھنڈ

۱۳۔احمد علی خاں شوق	تذکرہ کاملان رامپور
۱۴۔امیر مینائی	انتخاب یادگار
۱۵۔منشی نولکشور	اودھ اخبار ۱۴ر مئی ۱۸۷۶ء
۱۶۔ظہیر دہلوی	داستان غدر
۱۷۔مالک رام	تلامذہ غالب
۱۸۔قادر بخش صابر دہلوی	گلستان سخن
۱۹۔سید محسن علی	سراپا سخن
۲۰۔امداد صابری	تاریخ جرم وسزا
۲۱۔امداد صابری	۱۸۵۷ء کے غدار شعراء
۲۲۔حسن نظامی دہلوی	مقدمہ بہادر شاہ
۲۳۔منشی نولکشور	گلدستہ سخن
۲۴۔منشی قربان علی دہلوی	بہادر شاہ بادشاہ
۲۵۔سید علی حسن بھوپالی	صبح گلشن
۲۶۔محمد عبدالشاہد خاں شیروانی	باغی ہندوستان
۲۷۔خواجہ محمد بشیر	غدر کے حالات وفتوحات انگریزی
۲۸۔راہی معصوم رضا	اٹھارہ سوستاون، الہ آباد ۱۹۶۰ء
۲۹۔سید عاشور کاظمی	۱۸۵۷ء کے غداروں کے خطوط دہلی ۲۰۰۱ء

۳۰۔ غلام رسول مہر — اٹھارہ سو ستاون کے مجاہد

۳۱۔ انیس فاطمہ بریلوی — ۱۸۵۷ء کے ہیرو، کراچی ۱۹۹۳ء

۳۲۔ چندر کرشنا — غدار، دہلی ۱۹۶۷ء

۳۳۔ صادق حسین سردھنوی — غدار، دہلی

۳۴۔ ناصر لاہوری — غدار لیڈر، لاہور ۱۹۳۷ء

۳۵۔ غدر دہلی کے اخبار — دہلی ۱۹۲۰ء

۳۶۔ ضیاء الدین احمد برنی — غدر کی صبح و شام، دہلی ۱۹۳۶ء

۳۷۔ حسن نظامی — غدر دہلی کے افسانے، دہلی ۱۹۱۸ء

۳۸۔ حسن نظامی — غدر کا نتیجہ، دہلی ۱۹۳۰ء

۳۹۔ راشد الخیری — غدر کی ماری شہزادیاں، دہلی

۴۰۔ انتظام اللہ شہابی — غدر کے چند علماء، دہلی

۴۱۔ ظفر تاباں — غدر کے مناظر ۱۹۳۵ء

۴۲۔ کنہیا لال — تاریخ بغاوت ہند

۴۳۔ بہادر لال برہمن جھنوجی — اوضاع سیاسی ہند در ۱۸۵۷ء (فارسی)